hillwalking

The official handbook of the
Mountain Training walking schemes

THIRD ▶ REVISED EDITION

hillwalking

The official handbook of the
Mountain Training walking schemes

Written by **Steve Long**
with contributions from Plas y Brenin staff

hillwalking

The official handbook of the
Mountain Training walking schemes

Copyright © 2014   The Mountain Training Trust

Published by Mountain Training UK
www.mountain-training.org

First printed 2003
2nd Revised Edition printed 2004
Reprinted 2005, 2008, 2011
3rd Revised Edition printed 2014

ISBN 978 0 9541511 9 5

Cover photo: Heading towards Llyn Idwal and Gribin Facet
on a Mountain Skills course in Snowdonia by Bryn Williams

Designed, typeset and illustrated
by Vertebrate Graphics, Sheffield
www.v-graphics.co.uk

This product includes mapping data licensed from Ordnance Survey
with the permission of the Controller of Her Majesty's Stationery Office.
Copyright ©. All rights reserved. Licence reference 100040262

This product contains maps reproduced with the permission of Harvey,
12–16 Main Street, Doune FK16 6BJ.
www.harveymaps.co.uk

MIX
Paper from
responsible sources
FSC® C010256

Printed and bound in China.

Contents

Author's acknowledgements

A project of this scale naturally required the co-operation of numerous individuals and organisations. I am fortunate to have been given free access to the library of reference material at Plas y Brenin, the National Mountain Centre. I am also indebted to the management of Plas y Brenin for their flexibility in making time available at crucial stages in the development of this book, when changing deadlines necessitated late staffing changes from my normal instructional work.

Important contributions were made by several of my colleagues at Plas y Brenin. In particular, Rob Collister wrote the original source material for the section on environmental issues, as well as collaborating with Carl Haberl to write much of Section 10. The section on water hazards was based upon the work of Rob Spencer, and much of the information used in Sections 4 and 5 was researched and drafted by Neil Johnson with valuable assistance from Paul Davies. Useful advice was given by Martin Chester, who also produced the source material for the whole section about weather. I am also grateful to Martin Doyle, Iain Peter, Carlo Forte, Rose Powell, Simon Hale and Sue Savege for their helpful suggestions.

At all stages of writing the manuscript, proofreading assistance was given by each of the national governing bodies for mountain leadership. From Mountain Training both John Cousins and Sue Doyle were constantly inspiring in their enthusiasm for the project. They provided an eye for detail that dramatically improved the quality of the text: I should confess that any remaining minor errors are entirely the responsibility of the author!

I would to like express my gratitude to the many people who have made it possible for me to enjoy walking and climbing for so many years, especially the people who have worked so hard to maintain access to our wild places and who have toiled to limit the continued erosion of the upland environment.

Finally, I would like to take this opportunity to thank the many volunteer leaders who have introduced young people to the magic of wild places; without the encouragement of people like Roy Hill (my scout leader) I might never have ventured beyond the suburbs! I am fortunate to have had parents who encouraged me in my passion for the mountains and who have in recent years provided continued inspiration by taking up hill walking and travelling after their retirement. I only hope that I can provide such a role model for Sion Idwal, my son.

Additional Acknowledgements for the Second Edition

I have been overwhelmed by the enthusiasm with which the first edition of *Hill Walking* was received, and delighted to be contributing these words to a second edition less than a year after the initial publication. This timely revision has enabled me to incorporate the suggestions of several reviewers as well as some of my own observations, and I would like to take this opportunity to thank George Reid, Roger Wild, Pete Stacey and Hugh Westacott in particular for their expert advice. I hope that this edition does justice to the support we have received.

Additional Acknowledgements for the Third Edition

Since the second edition was published the internet and digital media have continued to develop so rapidly that several sections of the book required major updates. I would like to thank Carlo Forte in particular for his assistance with material for the sections on digital mapping and GPS devices. It has also become increasingly apparent that the hills can be enjoyed by people with all sorts of disabilities and medical conditions; some of whom have proven to be excellent leaders and role models for other mountain travellers. Indeed, some of the people who served as an inspiration for the first edition of this book have since lost substantial mobility following various life-changing events, but their passion for the mountains has remained just as strong. I would like to start therefore by thanking John Gladston, Jamie Andrews, Terry Taylor and Paul Pritchard for advice and/or inspiration for this third edition.

Thanks are also due to Ed Jennings for help with improvements to the leadership sections, specifically advice for people with impaired hearing but equally useful for anybody who finds themselves competing with the wind and other elements in order to communicate.

The sections about access to the hills have been updated, and for this I am indebted to help from the Mountaineering Councils and in particular Andrea Partridge, Helen Lawless and Elfyn Jones. Elfyn also provided invaluable insight into developments in mountain rescue for the final sections of the book, which have been further developed with help from Mike Margeson and Dr Bob Sharp, who also helped source some excellent photographs of the current generation of rescue helicopters.

Finally I would like to thank my colleagues in the Association of Mountaineering Instructors, who checked and/or confirmed some of the statistics and measurements through our social media forum.

Steve Long
Plas y Brenin, May 2014

Editor's note

The Mountain Training Trust and its staff at Plas y Brenin have always been keen supporters of Mountain Training and this book is no exception. Based on their knowledge of the leader training schemes, Steve Long and his colleagues have come up with some great ideas in this book and have successfully summed up the tremendous wealth of experience that personifies Plas y Brenin and the Mountain Training Trust.

The publication of the third edition of this book comes at an auspicious time for *Mountain Training* as we celebrate our fiftieth anniversary as well as the launch of a series of updated walking qualifications. Within the volunteers and staff of *Mountain Training* there have been many contributors to the development, editing and production of this book so our thanks to Mal Creasey, Sue Doyle, Carlo Forte, Allen Fyffe, Jon Garside, Brian Griffiths, Nicola Jasieniecka, Mick Johnson, Allister McQuoid, Andy Newton, Anne Salisbury, Bryn Williams, Iain Peter, Paul Platt, and Andy Say for their editorial assistance and wise words.

John Cousins
Plas y Brenin, May 2014

Introduction

The appeal of hill walking

Walking in wild country is amongst the most popular of all leisure activities, and for good reason. The combination of fresh air, open vistas, hearty exercise and adventurous exploration is a heady mix, all the more enjoyable if shared with others. Everybody can enjoy the hills. They offer beauty and challenges that have attracted successive generations, and for many people the adventures provided by days in open country are an essential antidote to the pressures of modern living.

Learning to realise our potential is one of the many benefits and joys brought by travelling through wild places. Walking in the hills demands an honest and realistic appraisal of our personal strengths and limitations – our lifetime's development in diverse situations. For some, the transition from tarmac and concrete even to well-made mountain paths can present enormous challenges. In some places, the fell runner jogging across the high tops may share the mountain with someone who is paraplegic. They each expand an awareness of their individual abilities, which will be both tested and celebrated on a typical day out.

The urge to explore is one of the defining characteristics of mankind. Venturing into the unknown helps us to understand ourselves and re-appraise our place in the natural world. For many societies a formal rite of passage marks the individual's emergence into adulthood. This is something that western society has largely lost. Wild country offers us endless opportunity to explore and to broaden our horizons.

Part of the beauty of the hills is their fickle character; a calm day of sunshine can provide a leisurely picnic but can so easily be followed the next day by a violent storm that lashes the summits with wind and rain. On a misty day magnificent views can appear for fleeting seconds, like an unexpected and momentary glimpse of a precious jewel. Perseverance and resourcefulness are rewarded with very special moments, sooner or later!

Hill walking is an adventurous pastime that offers many opportunities to pit one's skills and experience against challenges, the outcome of which are far from certain. The confidence gained from a successful ascent or journey can help us to tackle other challenges in life, just as the humility gained from a forced retreat or the tenacity required to hone one's skills can provide rich lessons for our everyday lives.

Gaining proficiency

The apparent ease with which an experienced hill walker negotiates a safe route through wild country is misleading. Like any skilful practitioner, the expert has mastered a broad range of techniques and developed the judgement to apply the appropriate solutions for the specific demands of a particular journey. Potential problems are anticipated and measures are taken to nip them in the bud, rather than allowing them to develop into a crisis. Knowing to take a break just before the summit on a windy day means that the experienced walker avoids a chilly stop that would leave others tired before the next leg. However the novice can be forgiven for swinging from naïve over-confidence to a sense of bewilderment as thick cloud descends on a remote hillside.

Hill walking at its best requires a whole collection of skills: navigation, an ability to walk over all kinds of terrain, hazard avoidance and so on. Fortunately despite the holistic nature of skilful hill walking, it is possible to learn the many individual techniques and then select the right ones for a particular job. The company of a more experienced friend can provide an excellent foundation on which to build skills and experience but tales of bravado that are not matched by mature judgement can disguise an unsuitable mentor: *in the kingdom of the blind, the one-eyed man is king*. Gradually extending horizons by completing more ambitious expeditions is the best way to learn – progressively building on personal experience. An epic adventure can sometimes bring accelerated learning, but it is more likely to intimidate and injure if the pre-requisite coping skills have not yet been developed. When it comes to groups of walkers it is critical that a day in the hills should reflect the aspirations and abilities of the least experienced members of the party rather than providing the leader with company for a reckless adventure.

An important aim of this book is to assist walkers in developing their skills and judgement, which will often be in the company of friends some of whom can act as mentors, providing practical examples of good practice. The techniques and skills of hill walking are introduced in a logical progression, from tentative first steps on maintained footpaths through to successful navigation in complex untracked terrain.

About this book

Commissioned by *Mountain Training*, this volume is intended to assist walkers in their development and to provide guidance for all leaders and participants in *Mountain Training's* schemes. The contents have been derived from the collective experience of the staff team at the National Mountain Centre in Snowdonia. Plas y Brenin has been at the forefront of developments in teaching novices and the training of walking leaders since the 1960s: the advice contained within these pages has been tried and tested on thousands of walkers and revised by successive generations.

This book is divided into three sections, reflecting the development of the walker and the leader. Firstly the personal competences required for safe and effective movement through the hills are developed, along with a discussion on the choice of appropriate equipment for personal and group use. Secondly, an understanding of the fragile mountain environment is encouraged, from the laws of the land to the weather, which characterises hills and mountains, particularly in the British Isles. Finally, issues of party management are discussed, from group dynamics to managing risk and dealing with problems. Issues that are particularly pertinent to leaders have been highlighted in boxed inserts.

A practical approach has been used throughout, avoiding the use of jargon wherever possible. We have avoided debating the distinctions between terms such as 'technique' or 'skill' and those of 'coach', 'teacher' and 'instructor'. Instead we have used the everyday language of most hill walkers and leaders.

The material in this book is in no way intended as a substitute for personal experience. We trust that readers will find many practical suggestions to underpin lessons learned in the hills and mountains. However, the wise student can accelerate their education by reflecting carefully upon other people's errors. We hope that the fruits of our collective experiences may help readers to avoid revisiting some of the writers' mistakes. Every day spent in the Great Outdoors teaches all of us something new both about wild country and about ourselves. Enjoy your days in the hills!

ⓘ Learning to lead

Introducing other people to hill walking brings a new dimension to our experiences, but carries a burden of responsibility. Novice walkers rely on the leader's knowledge and skills to guide them safely through potentially hazardous terrain. They may have little idea of the nature of the environment and therefore rely heavily on the judgement of the leader.

Personal proficiency is no guarantee of effective leadership, although it is an essential pre-requisite. A good leader should have awareness of the wishes and sensibilities of every person in their party and be aware of the interactions between individual members.

A successful day will provide challenges without over-extending the party and will build upon previous experiences. Correctly matching everyone's abilities to the conditions is the sign of a good leader, ensuring the day is pleasurable and challenging rather than tedious or terrifying. This process of matching abilities to conditions runs at several levels. The initial route planning should match the group's aims and aspirations. This is continually re-appraised on the journey, according to terrain, prevailing conditions and the group's actual progress. At a more urgent level, the choice between stepping over or around a boulder can make a subtle or significant difference to safety, efficiency, and enjoyment.

The leader should give a focus to the group's aims and direction when necessary, while remaining adaptable in the face of changing circumstances. Sometimes the leader will need to teach skills to the group to increase their immediate safety; sometimes it will be to enable them to become more independent. There is no place for prejudice in a good leader's attitudes; every member of the party should be free to achieve their own potential.

The demands upon the skill and judgement of a leader may appear daunting, but it is very rewarding to witness the joy of discovery sparkling in a novice's eyes or to watch the triumphant return of students from their first unaccompanied expedition. Helping others can often force leaders to reflect on their own skills and this often brings new discoveries, which deepen their own enjoyment and development.

Leadership is a craft that can be developed and this book is intended to serve as a reference for all leaders who take an active interest in this process.

 NB Information that is especially relevant to leaders and leading a group of walkers, is shown in this kind of box.

part1

BRECON BEACONS   PHOTO // BRYN WILLIAMS

Getting around in the hills

Movement skills & route finding

Visualising and then following a safe and efficient route across rough terrain are fundamental skills for hill walkers. It can be surprisingly difficult to set and maintain a sustainable pace, but this is the key to comfortable and steady progress. Awareness of posture and the body's centre of gravity is important on awkward ground, while less experienced members of a walking party can be instructed in the use of skilful foot placements.

1.1 Movement skills

Efficient movement makes the best use of individual physical abilities to cross a specific piece of ground. It is easily recognised, but attempting to define it is difficult because it is the sum of so many parts. Attributes include keeping a steady pace, conserving energy and maintaining the centre of gravity generally over the feet, with the arms free to assist balance.

1.2 Individual factors

People vary in many different ways: physically, mentally, personality, knowledge, cultural background and experience. It is the intention of this book to integrate advice for working with people with disabilities[1] into the main text where possible, accepting that some individuals may need to adapt how they achieve the goal, and their need for any specialist equipment.

As with any adventurous activity it is recommended that hill walkers and ramblers build experience gradually, and gain confidence and awareness in their capabilities within a low-risk and easily escapable environment; ideally in the company of more experienced partners, before progressing to more ambitious expeditions that might test themselves and their equipment.

A detailed examination of the equipment available for people with limited mobility is beyond the scope of this book. It is recommended that readers seek advice from experienced practitioners; much useful information can be found on the internet at websites such as *www.disabledramblers.co.uk*. A brief introduction to the types of specialised equipment that might be carried by group members is also included in *Section 10.1.5* on page 186.

1.2.1 Posture

Posture has an influence over all aspects of movement. Ideally, the head and shoulders are generally kept high when walking, eyes looking several metres ahead. Hands are best kept out of pockets to allow the arms to swing naturally and for recovery in the event of losing balance. The legs are usually swung from the hip rather than the knee, lifting the feet higher than normal when crossing uneven ground, to clear protruding boulders and prevent stubbing the toes or tripping. Rucksacks can make efficient posture more difficult to achieve, so selecting a suitable rucksack to hold light but effective equipment will contribute to the ability to move well in the mountains and moors. On rough ground and on steep ascents, tucking the thumbs under rucksack shoulder straps often eases breathing but then the arms are not available to assist balance, particularly on broken ground.

In descent, the walker's posture is usually more dynamic. The centre of gravity is best kept directly over the feet. An experienced walker in descent tends to have the head centred over the load-bearing leg. This reduces the risk of tumbling forward in the event of the foot becoming stuck. This defensive posture could be described as loose and flexible in

---

1 Disability in this book refers both to the official definition found in The Equality Act 2010, as defined by the Equality and Human Rights Commission, and any short term condition which may affect the activity's risk assessment.

ⓘ 1 Teaching movement skills

Leaders provide a role model for the less experienced members of their party, who may well learn to make progress through the hills and mountains partly by imitation. It should be remembered, however, that group members are just as easily influenced by a bad demonstration. A good teacher can assist the learning process enormously by giving clear examples and setting a focus to observations.

Basic coaching principles work well for teaching movement skills in the mountains. In most cases exercises that fuel the walker's reflection and development are more effective than issuing rules. Thus skills of foot placement can be taught in a variety of ways; ranging from a list of do's and don'ts through to focussing attention on a particular feeling, such as "do you feel better grip with the toe pointing uphill or sideways?" For steeper terrain requiring the use of the hands for support, the concept of maintaining three points of contact can be arrived at by observation and questioning, as group members are invited to traverse a rocky step with their feet less than a metre above a safe landing. This allows learners to discover working principles for themselves rather than trying to mould them into someone else's preconceptions.

Another coaching point that may help learners to understand movement principles is the transfer of balance onto one foot in order to raise the other leg. This apparently simple process is often overlooked and results in strenuous and inefficient pulls with the arms to compensate. One way to demonstrate this is to stand on flat ground with legs apart. Unless the body is tilted so that the head is directly over one foot it is not possible to lift the other foot for more than a split second. However by holding on to an object (or partner) it is possible to lift the foot and thereby overcome an ineffective posture by means of force rather than counter-balance.

Advice to party members should be clear and informative. All too often leaders draw the attention of party members to a difficult step with bland phrases such as "be careful here" or "this bit is slippery so watch out". This information may be helpful to their peers who have the required experience to deal with it (but probably also the observational skills to notice for themselves). For novices, however, this can simply confuse. "Watch out for what...?" Instead, the leader might choose to invite party members to make observations such as the surface water on a polished slab and then manage the group experimenting safely with various solutions. Coaching skills in this fashion takes longer initially but allows novices to develop greater independence in the medium to long-term. On the other hand, overuse of this style of teaching can break the rhythm of the day and sometimes a clear instruction such as "this wet slab is slippery so put your foot onto the flat bit on the left" is more effective.

Movement skills can often be taught enjoyably to both adults and children with simple games whilst on the move. For example, exercises that help develop understanding of efficient movement include a competition to ascend a rock step using the most and the least number of footsteps, followed by questions about which method was more strenuous. Assigning a number to a particular length of stride and calling these numbers in random can be an amusing way to tackle the same teaching objective.

Less experienced hill walkers often require coaching in order to cope with wet turf and muddy slopes. A walker who doesn't have experience of this type of terrain tends to place their feet flat onto a slope, because this has always worked within their range of experience. Unfortunately this is not always very effective on muddy slopes and the feet tend to slip. This is unnerving and potentially dangerous, so timely advice about using the edges of the boots is important.

FIGURE 1.01   STROLL POSTURE

FIGURE 1.02   DEFENSIVE POSTURE
PHOTO // STEVE LONG

nature and is particularly helpful in rough terrain. The knees remain flexed, the hands are held ahead of the centre of gravity, probably slightly out from the body, and the upper body remains upright. The eyes focus more often on the feet but also keep looking ahead to choose the route.

1.2.2 Pace

An appropriate walking pace is linked to the ability to maintain sufficient oxygen supply to the muscles, so if someone walks too fast they'll have to stop and catch their breath. This pace setting depends on a range of factors including fitness, terrain and even the weather. The aims of the day will also contribute to the choice of pace; for example, a group attempting to traverse the Grey Corries of Lochaber in a day will most likely wish to move faster than a family out for a picnic on Hay Tor.

Setting an efficient pace in the hills is very much a 'tortoise and hare' situation. A steady pace allowing ordinary breathing can be kept up almost indefinitely, whereas short bursts of speed are often followed by enforced rests to catch one's breath. The experienced walker can make a

FIGURE 1.03   THE HARE AND THE TORTOISE

A walking leader should develop strategies to cope with different levels of fitness within a group. Many suggestions are included in **Part III: Party management**, starting on page 179.

sensible choice about the pace they set; the less experienced often struggle to appreciate how tiring constantly stopping and starting can be. In the long term, the slowest member of any group should normally set the pace of the walk. Party members who choose to move faster may well experience frustration waiting for the slower members to catch up. (See *Figure 1.03*)

A useful rule of thumb is to move at a pace that would allow conversation without running short of breath. This makes provision for different levels of fitness and environmental factors. For example, it is often harder to breathe in very windy conditions and thus the pace becomes slower.

It is generally less tiring ascending or descending slopes if a diagonal line is taken. This allows a comfortable posture to be maintained and enables more secure footing, particularly in slippery conditions when it may become necessary to kick the serrated side edge of the boot into the turf. This has an erosive effect, however, and should only be used when conditions would otherwise be treacherous underfoot. For a more direct ascent, a series of short zig-zags is effective, with the body turned sideways across the slope.

A direct descent of a steep slope may be made if kicking the heels into the slope gives sufficient grip, but turning the body sideways to the slope allows the side of the boot to kick a larger platform on more

FIGURE 1.04   EDGING

FIGURE 1.05   DIGGING IN HEELS

awkward terrain. It may be possible to step through by bringing the upper leg forward, in front of the other leg, and then kicking a step below and ahead of the other foot, adjusting balance onto the new lower leg and bringing the other (back) leg down alongside, kicking into the turf. Sometimes a shuffle step is more appropriate. Here one foot steps down into a secure platform, and the other foot is brought down into the step vacated by the other foot. This method feels disjointed and does not allow a walking rhythm to be established, but is an excellent defensive technique for particularly slippery ground.

People with limited mobility or who use aids will need to be able to adapt these principles to meet their individual requirements.

1.3 Footwear

Although a skilled walker may be able to get by in dry conditions wearing training shoes, progress can be aided considerably by wearing appropriate walking boots (or for wheelchair users, rugged tyres). The party leader should consider the example they set in choice of footwear; it is common for novices to aspire to using the same type of footwear as their role model.

In wet or slippery conditions, the ability to kick a stiff serrated edge into the slope will increase security and influence posture as the feet are kicked parallel to the slope to create their own platforms. In descent, the walker may again have to turn sideways to the slope if the heels of the boots to do not provide a good biting edge. On closer inspection, clumsy walkers are often discovered to be wearing over-sized footwear. The choice of footwear is covered in more detail on page 106.

1.4 Route finding

Finding safe yet interesting or exciting routes in the hills and mountains requires a combination of many skills and experience. Knowledge of the particular group is also needed since one group's adventure may be another party's nightmare. Many journeys will require some research and planning beforehand. This can help avoid problems on the trip. It also allows a copy of the proposed itinerary to be left with a central contact, which can help in the event of an unforeseen crisis either on the hill or at home.

1.4.1 Planning

Route finding is inextricably linked to *planning*, as is consideration of what is appropriate given the group, the weather and any agreed aims for the trip. Good planning can pre-determine the level of route finding that will be required and how intricate and crucial it will become.

Any detailed route planning has to consider firstly the needs, fitness and aspirations of the group and the reason for the proposed trip. With this information, the party can then plan a journey that should give a safe, enjoyable and rewarding experience. For example, a mature, experienced party may well relish the chance to explore untracked ground, whereas a group of novices would probably aim to stay strictly on footpaths.

When planning a route, much useful information regarding the terrain can be gained from the map. The 1:50,000 scale is excellent for an

2 Efficient movement for the group

A group moving through mountain or moorland can be likened to a living organism. The head tends to navigate; the tail brings up the rear. The significant difference, however, is that for a walking party it is all too possible to get separated; keeping the parts together requires active management. An agreement of common aims is required if the group is to remain intact and morale maintained throughout the party.

A well-managed group moves more efficiently. Rotating tasks amongst the members and appointing a tail marker prevents the group from becoming too spread out and losing stragglers. This will maintain party spirit, increase the individual perception of involvement and allow steady progress. These factors all contribute to party safety.

Some types of terrain are best tackled with the group in a particular configuration. For example, boulder fields and scree slopes present the potential hazard of stones being knocked down on to other party members. This hazard can be minimised by keeping very close together so that rocks cannot build up speed and any rocks that do get dislodged start moving from below head level of those downhill. Zig-zagging up or down the slope is very effective if the party is small enough to allow everybody to be moving on the same diagonal, so that nobody is directly below another walker, in the potential line of fire. In other circumstances, it may be more suitable to tackle the slope in stages with party members crossing the slope one at a time and congregating at safe sites tucked out of the line of any possible stone fall.

FIGURE 1.06 TACKLING A SCREE SLOPE: EASY BUT LOOSE SCREE, PARTY STAYS TOGETHER

FIGURE 1.07 TACKLING A SCREE SLOPE: AWKWARD LOOSE SCREE, PARTY RE-GROUPS UNDER PROTECTIVE BOULDER

overview of an area and for navigating on footpath-based routes. However, 1:25,000 maps give a great deal more detail allowing more intricate route planning. The nature of the ground cover is indicated along with small streams, crag detail, and wall and fence boundaries, allowing a finer level of navigation. The increased level of detail on the map also means that navigating through difficult areas can be minimised or avoided, and boundaries can be crossed at designated points. The walker may have personalised a map to include observed positions of stiles or new fences and then use this acquired local knowledge when planning a route in a familiar area. (See *Figure 1.08*)

Many local authorities and organisation such as the Disabled Ramblers have more detailed maps and use grading systems to help with your planning.

At the moment, disabled people cannot be sure that a walk they have chosen from a map will be free of such impediments. While able-bodied walkers merely grab their Ordnance Survey maps and boots and can expect to get along the paths, disabled people have to forgo this spontaneity as no OS maps or, in my experience, council leaflets show the position of barriers. We have to rely on the kindness of able-bodied supporters checking out the route beforehand, to avoid having to turn around and to ensure there is a way through to our planned destination.[2]

1.4.2 Route finding from the map

Skilful examination of the map allows a picture of the terrain to form in the mind of the planner. This visualisation can be used to great effect and the whole route can be pre-planned in detail, enabling an assessment of the route and an estimation of how the party, route and weather will all interact. It will also allow the planner to work out if the proposed route is achievable in the time available.

Paths normally offer the easiest route in many mountain areas. Part of the skill of planning a route involves avoiding unnecessary ascent or descent and being able to link paths that minimise this, while making the most of natural viewpoints.

When planning an off-path route or using maps with few paths marked, it is useful to be able to pick terrain that is likely to be easy to follow and offer a natural line of travel. This can include spurs and ridges, often providing direct routes that can be drier underfoot and less densely vegetated than valleys. With experience, more subtle features from the map can also be identified and used as navigational pointers. This is described more fully in *3.2 Gathering information* on page 56.

Some planners may wish to use digital mapping to aid this process, allowing additional visualisation tools such as simulated three dimensional 'fly-overs' as well as live updates of distance and timing when the proposed track is modified. This can be very effective on a large screen. Despite the benefits of mapping software and GPS units with screen mapping, printed maps are still unmatched on the hill for visualising details and the wider context simultaneously. Paper maps do not rely on battery power, though it should be remembered that at night a printed map is useless without torchlight: spare battery capacity is therefore desirable for any electric powered tool that might be relied upon for navigation.

2 Rosie Norris – from *Farewell to Kissing Gates* (1 *Open Space* magazine Summer 2008 vol. 29 no.2 p 2–4.)

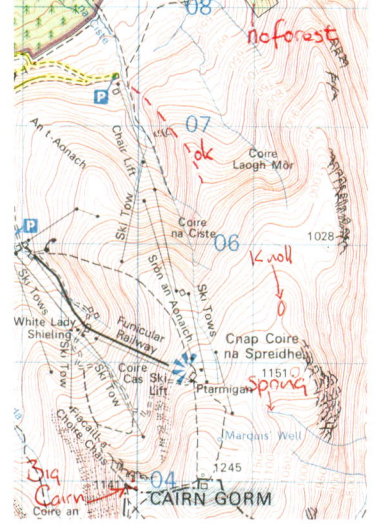

FIGURE 1.08 A MAP THAT HAS BEEN PERSONALISED WITH EXTRA INFORMATION

Further details about digital mapping can be found in *Section 3.12*.

It is crucial that a flexible approach is adopted, as things do not always go according to plan. It is often necessary to change and adapt the itinerary as the day unfolds particularly in spring and autumn, when there are fewer daylight hours. For example, the map may indicate simple moorland that does in fact consist of tortuous heather or waist-deep bracken, causing a party to modify their proposed route. A right of way indicated on the map does not necessarily coincide with the

1.4.3 Route finding in the hills and mountains

Route finding can be as straightforward as following the right path for the day or as complex as negotiating broken ground in poor visibility.

Most terrain in the hills is naturally sloping and covered by a range of different and potentially slippery surfaces. Hill walkers need to develop the ability to pick out a safe route through all types of terrain. Route choice can firstly involve looking at the area and identifying lines that look feasible. Footpaths will often take the easiest line from the valley to the summit. On popular mountains these are often obvious for the entire route, whilst on more remote hills there may be little or no evidence of a path. In these situations, it is useful to be able to see as much as possible of the ground ahead so that walkers can pick a line that is easy to negotiate.

Identifying the line of least resistance is a skill that develops with experience. Reflecting on why paths follow a particular route, often nothing like a straight line, helps to build awareness that becomes especially useful when venturing away from the beaten track.

It is often possible to spot a line of weakness running through mixed or broken terrain on a hillside when still a reasonable distance from it.

A leader must remember that the least able member of the party must be capable of following the chosen route, so this should be the main consideration when selecting an appropriate line to follow, and in considering what, if any, assistance they may require.

This enables the walker to distinguish steep walls and flat areas, features that might otherwise be obscured by the intervening ground. Grassy fault-lines (often known as rakes), terraces, minor gullies or spurs often allow easier progress than the surrounding ground.

FIGURE 1.09 COMPARE SIMPLE TERRAIN (ABOVE) AND COMPLEX TERRAIN (RIGHT)   *PHOTO // NICOLA JASIENIECKA*

When attempting to pick a route up, down, or across a slope, walkers may need to think about avoiding terrain that will be awkward or dangerous to negotiate. This may involve a longer route around the difficulties or hazards but will often result in a faster and safer journey.

Having looked at the ground to negotiate and pick out a line, it can often be useful to break the route down into shorter sections, separated by areas where the team can regroup and assess the next section. This approach is often used in broken rocky terrain and also when poor visibility allows only limited glimpses of what is ahead. An ongoing evaluation of the route is needed to ensure that this approach is combined with the appropriate level of protection. Review the route followed from time to time so that key features can be recognised in the event of a retreat.

Terrain such as scree, boulder fields, steeper vegetated slopes, rocky and broken ground, gullies, wet and boggy areas, and even flat ground covered in tussock grass can all make movement more difficult and in

Rough ground

Scree A ground covering of eroded rock debris, mostly small stones but may be interspersed with boulders of various sizes. Scree slopes are inherently unstable.

Boulder field A jumble of large rocks, mostly more than a cubic metre in size. The gaps between the rocks can vary from ankle diameter through to veritable people traps. Boulder fields are generally more stable than scree but individual boulders may rotate or slide and perhaps take neighbouring rocks with them.

Broken ground Complex terrain that is a mixture of vegetation and rock. Skilful route finding is required to find the most suitable passage, often involving a degree of weaving around obstacles.

FIGURE 1.10 COMPARE SIMPLE TERRAIN (LEFT) AND COMPLEX TERRAIN (ABOVE) *PHOTO // KARLMIDLANE*

some cases more dangerous. It is not always possible to avoid these areas, so experience in negotiating ground that is more challenging can be invaluable – although it may take quite a long time to recognise the value of such experiences!

The possibility of a need to retreat may also influence route choice. An awkward step in ascent that extends the party's abilities to its limits may represent a trap in the event of enforced descent back the same way. Carrying a rope and possessing the ability to use it may extend the possibility of escape – however, an earlier decision to modify the route would normally be the more appropriate solution.

1.4.4 Visibility

Route finding depends on the ability to interpret the landscape and then make informed choices. These choices will therefore be heavily influenced by visibility, which in turn is directly affected by weather, time of day and landscape. In poor visibility route finding and party management generally become more conservative and so the group may need to adopt more defensive strategies.

Cloud and mist often envelop mountain slopes and can bring visibility down to a few metres. At other times, objects may still be visible, but the ability to judge scale and distance is hampered. In these conditions, a flexible approach is necessary, working with an overall plan but weaving around obstacles as they appear. It becomes essential to combine keeping track of distances covered, noting any features that are passed, with effective timing and pacing. (See *3.5 Distance judgement* on page 64).

In some areas an ancient tradition of way marking has resulted in cairns (piles of boulders) being distributed along paths. The use of map and compass has rendered this tradition largely redundant and the creation of new cairns or enlargement of old ones is now regarded as

FIGURE 1.11 PATH POLISH *PHOTO // STEVE LONG*

unnecessary environmental damage. Cairns can give positive feedback about a chosen route but it should be remembered that they also appear on unmapped (sometimes even false) trails and should not therefore be relied upon.

Generally, it is more efficient to stick to established paths where they exist. These have already stood the test of time and evolved into the most economical route in terms of effort and risk management. However, it is important to ensure that the path is going in the desired direction and that it is not followed simply because it exists. Following a path in poor visibility demands observational skills and experience. To inexperienced walkers the evidence that others have been the same way may be difficult to spot and for this reason novices often struggle to keep to a path in misty conditions. To the experienced eye, there are many telltale signs to show where others have trod. Rocks on paths gradually obtain a sheen on edges and bumps, from the polishing effect of countless pairs of boots. They often appear stained a lighter brown colour than surrounding rocks because of mud transported by boots. Scratch marks can sometimes be seen, caused by crampons (or previous generations using nailed boots). In recent years paths and walkways have often been constructed in areas that have experienced erosion problems. They are usually easy to see, mainly due to the lack of lichen in comparison to surrounding rocks or occasionally the use of materials brought in from elsewhere. Parties should be encouraged to keep to these paths, rather than damaging the vegetation on either side and so causing the path erosion to spread.

One of the joys of being able to navigate well is that walkers are not obliged to follow paths, at least where open access is accepted. (see *Section 6* for more details about access) The party leader may choose to follow a route that is more suitable for the interests and abilities of the group than the existing paths in the area, so the choice of route will vary enormously

FIGURE 1.12 VISUAL CLUES – **A**, **B**: WET GROUND VEGETATION **C**: A MINOR PATH THROUGH DRY TERRAIN
PHOTO // STEVE LONG

for different people and conditions. The experienced eye will pick up signs that allow for a more enjoyable journey. For example, the characteristic sheen of red fescue, the distinctive white seed heads of cotton grass or the taller stems of myrtle are clear indicators of wet ground. Changes in vegetation can therefore be used to trace a drier route. The blocky texture of a boulder field usually indicates hard going underfoot even in the dry. When it is wet or damp, the rocks become greasy and difficult to negotiate because of the moss and lichen associated with them. In good visibility, it might be possible to circumnavigate the worst of the boulder field by observing the texture changes that highlight easier ground.

Route finding decisions on slopes that incorporate craggy ground can be seriously hampered by poor visibility. Telltale signs such as horizons where the slope angle changes can be obscured or exaggerated. A cautious approach is thus advisable, particularly when descending towards a steep slope. Even in good visibility, convex slopes like this should be treated with caution. It may not be possible to see the terrain below until perched right on the brink, where a gust of wind or loose scree may surprise the unwary and lead to disaster. Small vertical steps in steep slopes are often not marked on maps, so it is possible for a walker to arrive unexpectedly at an edge. This is especially true at night, when it can be almost impossible to work out the height of a rocky bluff, so route finding decisions are best made erring on the side of caution when working through difficult terrain. A wide berth is usually the best solution at night; areas shown as craggy on a map are usually even craggier in reality and at night the ground will be intimidating at best and progress will be slow.

At night visibility can vary from near perfect at full moon to virtual blindness in fog. In extreme conditions a crag or water feature can be

3 Group abilities

It is important that leaders possess a realistic awareness of the ability of the group and the individual party members – including their own. Leaders who are personally over-extended by terrain will find their decision-making abilities compromised by their anxiety. There is no substitute for personal experience in a variety of conditions and places, including venues more challenging than the proposed itinerary.

Teaching skills to others brings the added bonus of refining a leader's personal ability. By examining the processes that characterise a successful action, greater understanding feeds back into the teacher's own repertoire. Leaders of more experienced parties need to strike a balance between pertinent advice and stating the obvious; observing the group's movements and their reactions to the leader's suggestions will help to indicate the appropriate level of feedback and the right moment to offer it.

almost invisible until you touch it or step in it! Streams and lakes can often be heard if everyone concentrates and listens, for example, for the sound of small waves lapping on the shore. Dead reckoning is a navigational term for combining direction and distance to calculate location and in poor visibility it becomes very important, as it may be impossible to follow poorly defined paths. Navigation will rely more on the combination of following a bearing while making 'dog leg' detours around obstructions or hazards and then back on course. In any case, craggy terrain will become particularly hazardous in these conditions. These navigational strategies are covered in more detail in *Section 3*.

PHOTO // KARL MIDLANE

Navigational tools

Successful navigation is the ability to travel consistently and efficiently from one place to another. On a clear day with distant horizons, this can be deceptively simple. On the other hand complex terrain in mist or darkness can demand total concentration from even the most skilled practitioner and can become impossible without the competent use of a map and compass or their electronic counterpart, a Global Positioning System (GPS).

2.1 Maps

A good quality map is an essential tool for navigation. Some people have successfully made a return trip to the summit of Ben Nevis armed with nothing more than a sketch diagram of the main paths but more through luck than judgement. Straying off the path through poor route finding or lack of visibility could be disastrous for anybody without a map and the ability to use it.

Maps for walkers are an accurate pictorial representation of the land in two dimensions with sufficient detail to allow route finding in all conditions. Choosing the right map is a question of balancing the need for a convenient size against the requirement for a certain level of detail.

In the British Isles the main providers of suitable maps for walkers are the *Ordnance Survey* (OS) and Harvey. In some more technically demanding upland areas (or even some easily accessible areas) it is possible to obtain specialist orienteering maps. The Ordnance Survey produces maps at a range of scales, surveyed using aerial and ground survey and designed to address the needs of a wide range of users. The information provided by their maps therefore varies in its relevance for hill walkers. The OS maps of the UK are now fully digitised and updated (mainly urban areas) on a daily basis. A recent innovation is to develop a number of interactive layers to these maps where members of the public can update certain types of information such as access information and leisure facilities.

Ordnance Survey (OS) is the national mapping agency for the UK, and one of the world's largest producers of maps. The name reflects the original military purpose of the organisation in mapping Britain during the Napoleonic Wars when there was a threat of invasion from France. OS is widely regarded as the most systematic and thorough mapping institution in the world, detailing every corner of the UK long before satellite technology made quality maps of the same standard available elsewhere in the world. Today Ordnance Survey is a self-financing civilian organisation at the forefront of the digital economy, producing digital mapping products and paper maps for a wide range of purposes. For mountain navigators the *Landranger* and *Explorer* series of maps has for many years helped to define when and where we can go in to the hills.

Harvey maps are designed specifically with the needs of walkers in mind and use a sophisticated range of symbols to provide the walker with additional information about the terrain. The base map for a Harvey's map is created by plotting from aerial photos and the consequent map is then field checked on foot to ensure that the significant detail for walkers is included. Only limited areas of the country are available at the time of writing, but the majority of popular walking destinations are covered by waterproof (laminated) British Mountains Maps, which use Harvey mapping.

2.1.1 Choosing the right map

In the UK both OS and Harvey maps provide similar levels of detail although this may be expressed in different ways. Harvey maps are good on complex rocky ground because these areas are shown by grey contours and the major crags are clearly marked. Other rock detail, commonly shown on OS 1:25,000 maps, that is not relevant for navigation or safe passage is not mapped. However in more featureless terrain OS maps show a greater degree of detail due to the difference in contour interval. Harvey maps use a 15 metre contour interval as opposed to OS who use an interval of 10 or 5 metres. This smaller contour interval allows for a more accurate portrayal of the topography.

Scale is often a deciding factor when choosing a suitable map. There are advantages and disadvantages to using any scale of map and some are more suited to certain conditions compared to others. In complex ground a *1:25,000* scale map provides a greater amount of detail whereas in featureless terrain (i.e. moorland or snow covered) all this detail can detract from important contour information. In these situations a *1:50,000* map provides a less cluttered impression of the landscape. When out in the mountains it is always worth carrying a spare map and by taking two different scale maps it will allow you to choose the most appropriate map for the terrain and the task ahead as well as having a spare if one should be blown away!

Maps can be rather unwieldy to use, particularly on windy and wet days. A simple improvement is to remove the map's stiff cover. Protecting the map in a plastic map case is popular but these can then be too bulky to slip into a pocket and if worn around the neck tend to flap about in the wind, sometimes even threatening to garrotte the wearer! A good quality

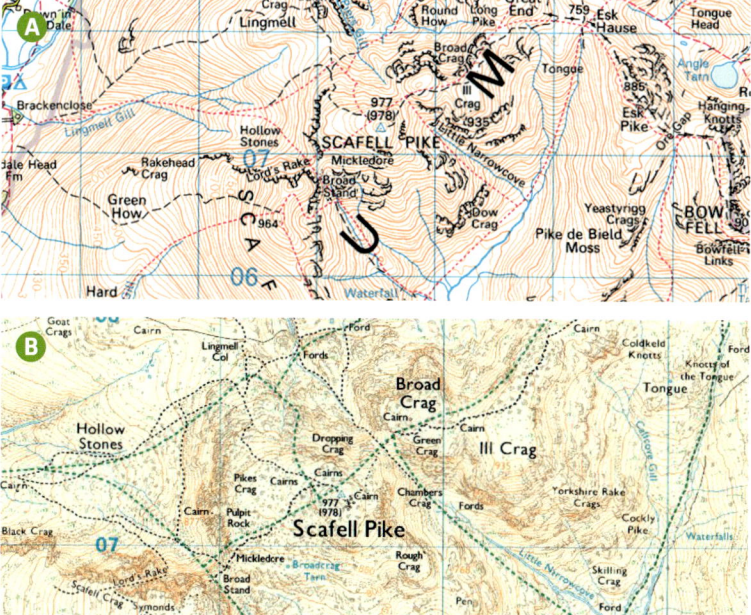

FIGURE 2.01 A DETAIL SHOWN ON OS 1:50 000 SCALE MAPS (SMALL SCALE)   **B** DETAIL SHOWN ON OS 1:25 000 SCALE MAPS (LARGE SCALE)

Map scales

OS 1:50,000 Landranger Maps

1cm = 50, 000cm
1cm = 500m
1mm = 50m
2cm = 1km *(Grid square)*

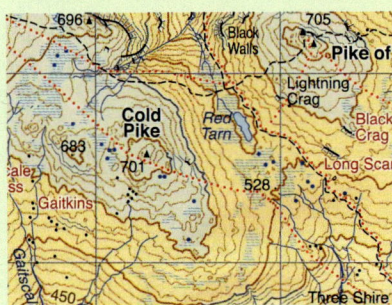

Harvey 1:40,000 Maps

1cm = 40,000cm
1cm = 400m
1mm = 40m
2.5cm = 1km *(Grid square)*

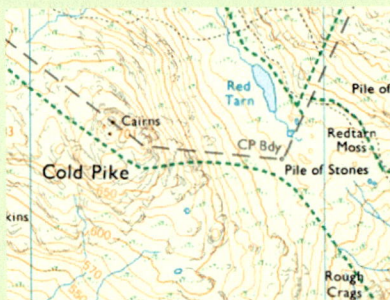

OS 1:25,000 Explorer Maps

1cm = 25, 000cm
1cm = 250m
1mm = 25m
4cm = 1km *(Grid square)*

Orienteering Map 1:10,000

1cm = 10,000cm
1cm = 100m
1mm = 10m
10cm = 1km

Small scale maps = **smaller** amount of detail (cover a large area eg: 1:50,000)
Large scale maps = **larger** amount of detail (cover a small area eg: 1:10,000)

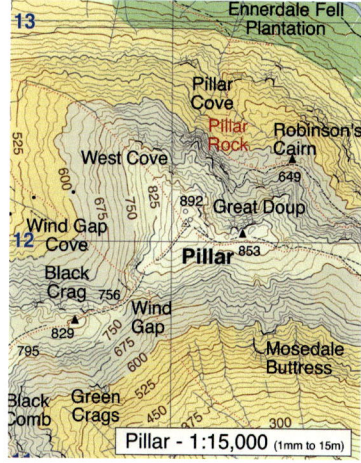

FIGURE 2.02 HARVEY ALSO PRODUCE A RANGE OF ADDITIONAL SCALE MAPS FOR SPECIFIC AREAS. HAVING ACCESS TO THIS LEVEL OF DETAIL FOR COMPLEX AREAS CAN MAKE NAVIGATION MUCH EASIER PARTICULARLY IN POOR WEATHER. (MAP NOT TO SCALE)

FIGURE 2.03 EXAMPLE OF MAP CASE/PROTECTION

rubberised map case will protect the map and allow it to be folded small enough to fit into most map pockets (a strong plastic bag is a cheap and simple alternative).

One recurring problem with constantly re-folding the map is the damage that can occur: more often than not the damaged fold is the exact point on the map where you need every shred of inform-ation. A more sustainable solution is to cut maps into smaller sections. This needs some thought to make sure the sections include as many access and exit points as possible, as well as grid numbers and refer-ence letters, plus a record of mag-netic variation. If this smaller map is laminated, its life expectancy will be dramatically improved, outweighing the preparation costs. This solution is likely to be of more use for the maps to your local area and places you visit on a regular basis. However for the areas you might only visit once a good map case will more than suffice. Some offices have small laminators that can produce adequate results, but check that a flexible plastic is used. Many maps can now be purchased already laminated and some outlets offer the facility to laminate full map sheets.

Digital mapping software is now available and can be readily found via the Internet or through outdoor equipment retailers. Most software is produced under licence and allows an A4 sized map to be printed for personal use only. Use of this technology requires a reliable colour printer with good quality paper, and it is the navigator's responsibility to check that the lines and the scale are not distorted. A poor-quality reproduction is of little use for navigation. The accuracy of a particular scale can be confirmed by measuring the grid squares and comparing them with the appropriate scale, for example 1:50,000 printouts must show the length of each grid square as 2 centimetres. (refer to *Map Scales* opposite for details).

2.1.2 Map scales

The *scale* of a map is defined as the ratio of a distance on the map to the corresponding distance on the ground. In the case of a 1:50,000 map, 1 centimetre (or 1 inch or one 'anything') on the map represents 50,000 centimetres (inches or 'anythings') on the ground. For many activities, such as navigating in a car, a small scale map that covers a relatively large area gives adequate information as the route is physically channelled along roads. For walking, a larger scale map with comprehensive representation of the landscape is required.

On a *1:50,000* map, one centimetre represents fifty thousand centimetres on the ground, (i.e. five hundred metres). One hundred metres is therefore represented by two millimetres.

On a *1:25,000* map, one centimetre represents twenty-five thousand centimetres (i.e. two hundred and fifty metres) on the ground. So one hundred metres is represented by four millimetres.

Since 1:25,000 scale maps are using four times more paper than 1:50,000 maps to represent the same area of land, they are able to show a lot more detail. Of particular significance to the walker is their depiction of field boundaries – often walls and fences, which are omitted from smaller scales such as 1:50,000. On the other hand, the wealth of detail at 1:25,000 can make it harder to get an overall picture of the shape of the land. Lying between these scales, 1:40,000 cover large enough areas for route planning and yet display enough detail when precise navigation is required.

Walkers need to develop the ability to adapt from one scale of map to another. Other scales may well be encountered for specific areas. For example, maps of complex summits such as Ben Nevis are often available in a 1:10,000 scale in order to map the complex ridges and gullies.

2.1.3 Signs and symbols

Features on the ground are represented on maps using *symbols* known as conventional signs. These show the position of a feature but are not always drawn to scale; most houses would be virtually invisible if drawn to the correct scale on a 1:50,000 map. In general, water features and their names are coloured blue, woodland is shaded green and man-made features have a black outline and are named in black ink. Rights of way are also colour-coded but this varies for different scales and publications. Occasionally paths marked on the map may not appear on the ground and vice versa. There may be any number of reasons why this is the case and it highlights the need to check for other features as you travel.

Before departing for the hills and moors and to avoid regularly unfolding the map it is worth spending a little time examining the map's *key* in order to recognise the symbols, which are usually icons that are easy to memorise. There are also subtle aspects to the shorthand that are only revealed by careful examination of the key. For example, there are different symbols for gravel pits, sand pits, chalk pits and disused pits!

2.1.4 Contours

One of the most important representations on a walker's map is *topography* – the shape of the land. Landforms are shown in several ways. At a fundamental level, the form of the land is represented by contour lines. These are generally coloured brown/orange (Harvey maps also use a grey contour line to denote rocky terrain) and connect points that are an equal height above sea level. The interval between contours varies between maps and should always be checked before using a new map.

(i) **4 Symbols**
While the key provides a reference to the map, becoming familiar with the common symbols likely to be encountered can save time. Comparing the key to features on the ground from an early stage will help students to lodge symbols in their memory.

Exercises: Flash cards: use flash cards matching the symbol to the definition (flash cards and games can be downloaded from the Ordnance Survey website).

Symbol search: give people a copy of the key and walk through an area with plenty of features. As they pass a feature they should tick the corresponding symbol on the key. At the end of the leg this information could be transferred to the map to help relocate. By introducing this early it will start to develop the ability to relate the ground to the map: a vital skill required for other aspects of navigation.

In the UK, Ordnance Survey maps generally use a 10 metre interval, although lowland regions have 5 metre contour intervals on 1:25,000 maps, Harvey's UK maps use 15 metre contour intervals and orienteering maps typically use a 5 metre contour interval in upland areas. Maps with the same horizontal scale but with different contour intervals give a very different impression of the terrain. Contours spaced 1mm apart may represent a 20 degree slope on one map but a 40 degree slope on another. French maps use a 10 metre interval, but on the Swiss side of the border, contours are 20 metres apart – this can be very confusing for maps which include both sides of the border, such as when in the Mont Blanc Massif!

Contours give an excellent representation of the three-dimensional shape of land, but successful visualisation requires some practice. At a simple level, the closer the contours, the steeper the slope. Most maps show every fifth (*index*) contour with a thicker line which means that counting index contours is a quick way to calculate the height difference between two points. Often on ground steeper than about thirty degrees only these thicker lines are shown because the contours are too close to show them individually – see *Figure 3.05* on page 57.

In addition to slope angle, contours also allow the slope shape to be visualised. Spurs and ridges are shown as fingers of high ground projecting further than surrounding land, while valleys and basins (often called *re-entrants*) are shown by contours curving into the surrounding higher ground – see *Figure 3.07* on page 59.

2.1.5 Other topographical symbols

Symbols are used to show other topographical features; rocky ground is shown with black lines, differentiating between boulders, loose rocks, outcrops and scree. Different sized symbols will be used to mark scree, with larger symbols at the bottom of the slope, and a varying design to show prominent scree runs, vegetation patches and interspersed boulders respectively.

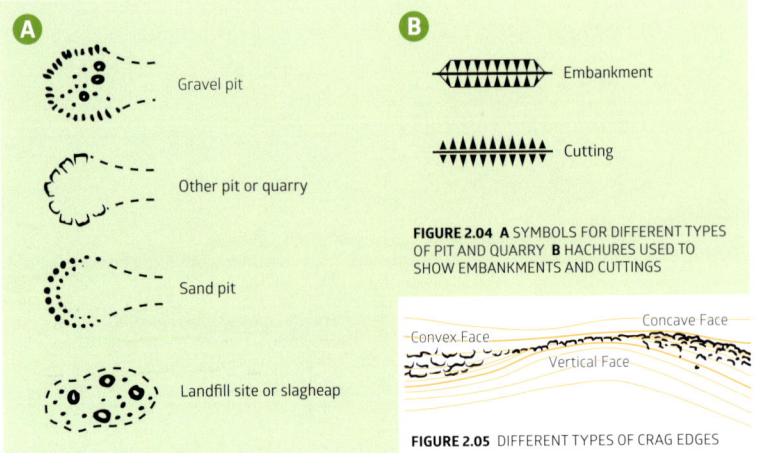

FIGURE 2.04 A SYMBOLS FOR DIFFERENT TYPES OF PIT AND QUARRY **B** HACHURES USED TO SHOW EMBANKMENTS AND CUTTINGS

FIGURE 2.05 DIFFERENT TYPES OF CRAG EDGES

On OS maps crag edges are shown by a representation of the exposed surfaces at the top of the cliff: thus limestone crags are actually depicted in a different way from granite. Concave crags are shown with firm black lines along the top with strata drawn using lighter and more spaced line-work as the angle eases, while convex faces are shown with the thicker black lines at the bottom. It is important to recognise the subtle differences before attempting to negotiate craggy terrain in poor conditions.

For walkers the locations of paths and tracks are particularly important. British maps distinguish between various types of footway, according to whether use is limited to pedestrians or shared with horses or wheeled vehicles. Established footways are symbolised with black dots or dashes according to status, and walled tracks are also specified on 1:25,000 scale maps. These should not be confused with the coloured dashes (red on 1:50,000 and green on 1:25,000) that indicate rights of way. The significance of these is described on page 140 (The legal framework) but it should be noted that unless a right of way is superimposed over a path marked in black, there may be no evidence of the right of way on the ground; indeed some rights of way are marked crossing lakes and precipices!

2.1.6 The grid system

A distinctive feature of British maps is the grid structure of thin lines superimposed over the whole country. These grid lines are the basis of a numerical reference system which allows any position to be pinpointed and communicated. The grid reference is prefixed by two letters that identify each specific 100 x 100km square (e.g. NY for northern Lake District, NG for Skye – see *Figure 2.06*). Grid lines are oriented along the cardinal points of the compass, North, South, East and West and can also be used to set the map and to take bearings using a compass. Grid bearings can then be converted to magnetic bearings or vice versa. All these techniques are covered in detail later (see page 72 *Using a compass*).

The National Grid

A	B	C	D	E
F	G	H	J	K
L	M	N	O	P
Q	R	S	T	U
V	W	X	Y	Z

i. 500 kilometre squares
    of the National Grid

ii. Each 500 kilometres is divided into
    twenty-five 100 kilometre squares

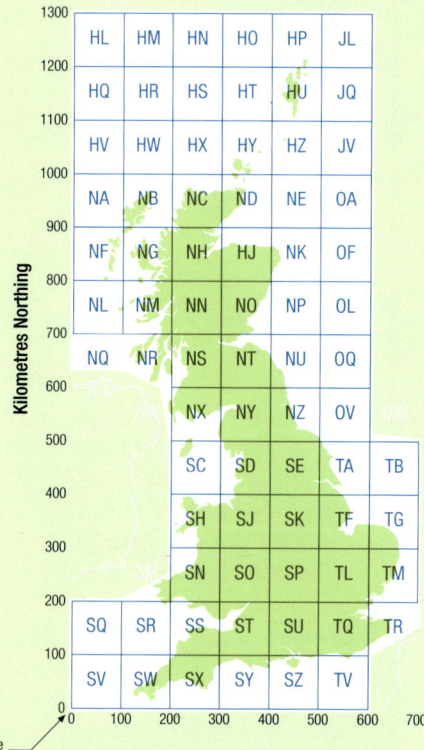

iii. 100 kilometre squares that cover
     Great Britain with their reference letters

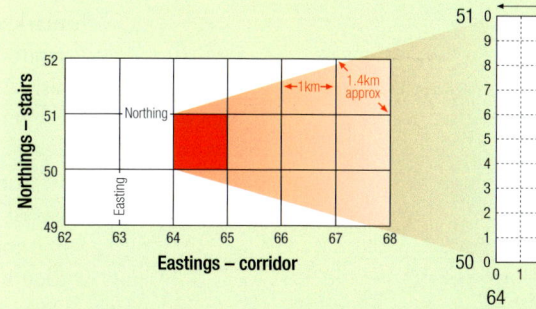

iv. 4-figure grid reference (1km square).
    Grid references must always be read in the
    following order:
    Eastings – "Along the corridor..." (63, 64, 65 etc.)
    Northings– "... and up the stairs" (49, 50, 51 etc.)

v. We can divide each grid square into 10 further
    Eastings and Northings to enable us to mark a
    feature to an accuracy of 100 metres. If we take
    this diagram as grid square 6450 we can plot a
    specific location within the one square kilometre.

FIGURE 2.06 THE NATIONAL GRID

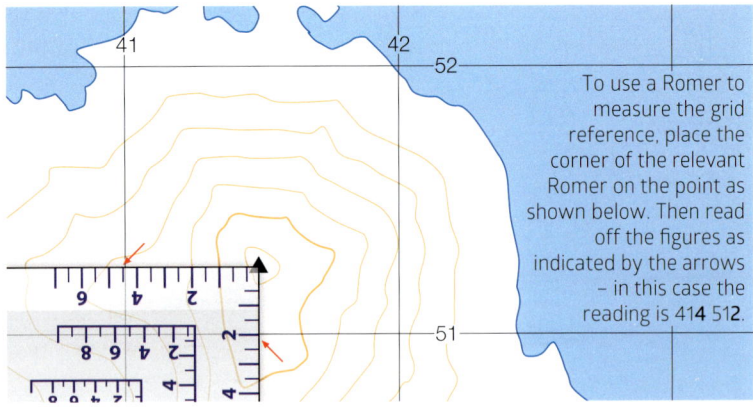

To use a Romer to measure the grid reference, place the corner of the relevant Romer on the point as shown below. Then read off the figures as indicated by the arrows – in this case the reading is 414 512.

FIGURE 2.07 USING A ROMER

2.1.7 Grid references

The main reason for printing a grid system on maps is to create a numerical system for defining a specific location. A grid reference is a descriptive rather than a navigational tool.

The National Grid was developed after the First World War. It consists of a grid across the country that is systematically broken down into progressively smaller squares. The larger squares, which have sides of 100 kilometres, are identified by a two-letter prefix, which starts in the South West on the Scilly Isles. Each area is then subdivided into squares with sides of one kilometre and these are superimposed over the map. Each of these grid squares is assigned a specific four-figure reference.

The convention is to define the sideways location (Eastings) first, followed by the vertical location (Northings). The numbers marked on the map describe the square located diagonally to their right and upwards. While a four-figure grid reference is useful for identifying the location of large features it is too vague for pinpointing smaller ones.

Thus in *Figure 2.08* opposite, Styhead Tarn on Great Gable in the Lake District is situated within square 2209. A four-figure in this example includes several other tarns as well.

For a more precise location, 100m x 100m it is normal to use a six-figure reference. These can be estimated by eye, measured with the compass ruler, or more simply with a romer (a portable co-ordinate measuring device). The latter can either be incorporated into the base plate of a compass or less conveniently as a separate measurer (see *Figure 2.07 Using a romer*).

In both cases the zero point is held against the feature, and the number read against the grid line to the left and then the grid below – fractions should always be rounded downwards. Thus, the source of the outlet stream from Styhead Tarn, that is, Styhead Gill, has a grid reference of 222099 within area NY.

The ability to calculate grid references is a skill that could be crucial in an emergency. It is also an integral aspect of position plotting with a Global Positioning System (GPS). Teaching and learning the use of grid references is ideally suited to an indoor session. The use of a Romer facilitates under-standing of the process as well as being relatively simple and accurate to use.

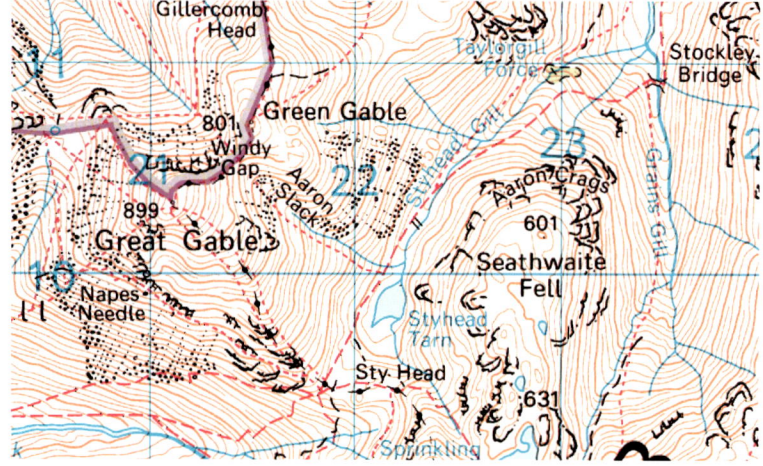

FIGURE 2.08 STYHEAD TARN ON GREAT GABLE

2.1.8 Digital mapping software

Technological advances have led to the production of sophisticated mapping software that has revolutionised navigation. Digital maps provide the navigator with a wealth of information that can be used at every stage, from planning through to reviewing tracks once the route has been completed. When combined with the use of a Global Positioning Systems (GPS) receiver they can provide a powerful tool to assist with navigation. (See *2.3 Global Positioning Systems: GPS*)

Advancing technology means the nature of these tools are constantly changing; it therefore becomes important to research the market before purchasing any products to ensure compatibility with your computer, GPS and the areas of ground you wish to use.

The purpose of any mapping software is to display topographical maps that can then be manipulated in various ways. While there are many products available most perform the following basic functions.

- **Planning routes:** Using colour maps on a screen it is possible to overlay information such as waypoints, tracks, areas or routes. This information can then be printed on paper or uploaded to a GPS for use on the journey. Many packages will display the route properties (distance, height gain, journey length and estimated travel time) all of which can be edited to suit. Many products display the routes in 3D allowing you to gain a greater understanding of the terrain you're hoping to cover. Some packages also interface with online resources such as Google Earth, permitting the display of waypoints and routes on a range of other media such as satellite and aerial images.
- **Printing maps:** It is normally possible to create and print full colour personalised maps at a scale of your choice. Detail and notes about any route can be added before printing and it is usually possible to print a corresponding route card. Long routes can be printed over several pages with automatic paging. Maps can then be laminated or printed on waterproof paper for use outdoors.

- **Programming GPS units:** Mapping software makes the process of creating waypoints, tracks and routes quick and easy and more accurate compared to transferring information from a paper map. Waypoint names can be changed to something more recognisable before sending to the GPS unit allowing them to be easily retrieved from memory when in use.

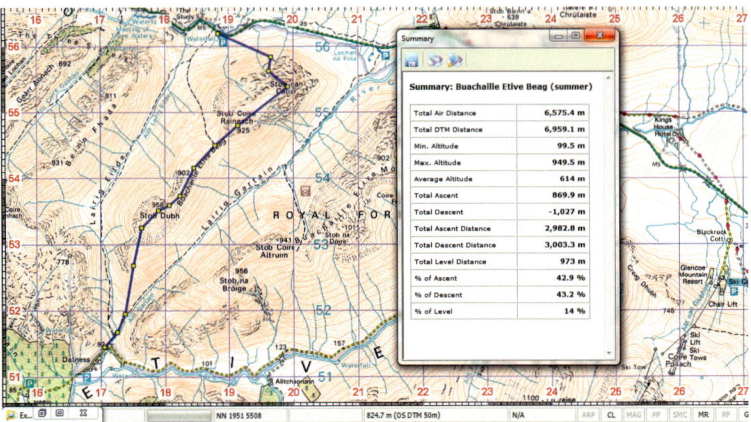

FIGURE 2.09 OVERLAY OF ROUTE SHOWING WAYPOINT LABELS AND ROUTE SUMMARY

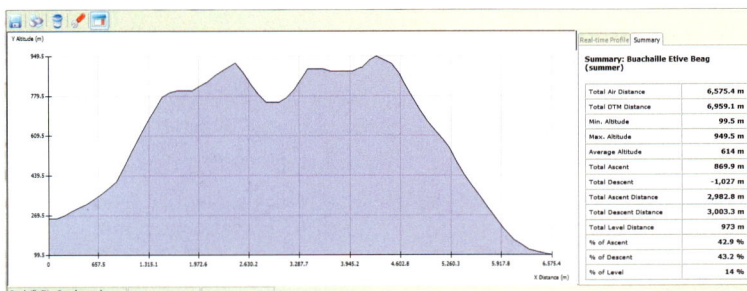

FIGURE 2.10 ELEVATION PROFILE FOR PLANNED ROUTE

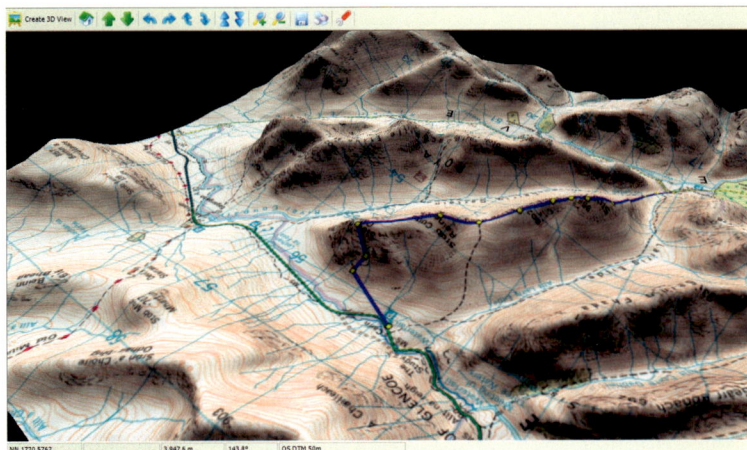

FIGURE 2.11 3D VIEW OF THE TERRAIN AND ROUTE PLANNED IN PREVIOUS FIGURE

- **Plotting positions:** Many systems will connect with a compatible GPS unit and show its position in real time on a moving map display. The development of GPS tracking devices that transmit their position now allows a receiver back at base to track the movements of anyone carrying one of these devices on the hill. This technology is becoming particularly useful for search and rescue operations.
- **Performance review:** Data can also be imported from a GPS unit and used to review your precise track and a range of statistics including speed, distance, height gains etc.

2.1.9 Types of products

There are many manufacturers of mapping software but in most cases their products fall into one of three categories.

- **Standalone software:** This software is designed for use principally on desktop or laptop personal computers. Specific areas of mapping at a particular scale can be purchased, either on disk or by downloading from the Internet, and stored on a PC. The cost will depend on the size and scale of mapping bought, and within the UK, this is predominantly Ordnance Survey maps under licence. Each manufacturer's software provides slightly different functionality but all deliver similar core functionality in a variety of slightly different ways. All can print maps, plan routes, display tracks and interface with a variety of GPS units to transfer routes, waypoints and tracks between the PC and the GPS. Most modern GPS units use the standard 'GPS Exchange Format' (GPX), to transfer data between PC and GPS. However some older units do not and may not be compatible with a particular package. In general, digital mapping cannot be transferred from

FIGURE 2.12 UPLOADING INFORMATION TO GPS UNIT

standalone software to GPS unit and vice-versa although there are units available that permit this function, which can provide significant cost savings. The licensing for this type of software usually only permits its use on two devices e.g.: PC and laptop.

- **Partnered software:** Some manufacturers of GPS devices produce their own software designed only to work with specific GPS units. It is important to stress that such software is only compatible with specific devices, and may only be licensed for a single device and PC; however, often they offer better integration and functionality compared to standalone software.
- **Online software:** There is an increasing range of online software available with maps held on remote computers and accessed via the Internet. Some software is free to use, but will tend to have limited functionality and significant restrictions on the scale, size or detail of mapping. Others are accessed on a subscription basis and, typically, in the UK, these offer Ordnance Survey mapping of the whole country at 1:25K and 1:50K, as well as road maps and detailed aerial photo mapping. These applications offer reduced functionality compared to standalone software currently, but with the added advantage that a vast selection of mapping is available at a variety of scales without having to purchase or store any of it. For the cost of a subscription you have the maps streamed to your cache where they remain even without an internet connection until the subscription runs out or the cache is overwritten. Mapping cannot usually be uploaded to GPS units, but routes, waypoints and tracks can, although this might be a more involved process. Printing is often limited, but nonetheless possible. Subscriptions are usually very good value compared to other options and, most importantly, you can use online software on any computer; however a continuous, reliable, fast internet connection is required for downloading information.

2.1.10 Planning and reviewing

The most useful feature is the ability to overlay these maps with inform-ation when planning routes. Waypoints and routes can simply be added by the click of a button and tracks can be drawn freehand if required. Most software is capable of producing a route card showing a range of information.

Parameters can often be set as to the walking speed and rate of ascent and descent making any calculations more accurate for the intended route. The information can be shown in the form of a traditional tabular route card but it is often possible to produce a printed map displaying the over-laid route details.

Many packages offer extra facilities that allow for a more in-depth appreciation of terrain or routes planned. Hill profiles can be displayed showing the steepness of any ground encountered en route. Using such a function allows you to view the angles of any slopes and highlights the concavities and convexities; this can be particularly useful in the planning of a winter walk when having to consider the snow and avalanche risks.

Buachaille Etive Beag (summer)

Information

Travel Start Date and Time	**08/01/2012 14:53:38**	No. in Party	**4**
Start Place	**Glencoe Car Park NN1883 5620**		
End Place	**Glen Etive (road bend) NN 1705 5145**		
Objective	**Traverse of Buachaille Etive Beag**		
Name (Leader)	**Carlo Forte**	Phone	**0773659000**
Emergency Contact	**01690 720 214**	Phone	
Vehicle Registration	**G818 LYB**		
Parked At	**Glencoe Car Park NN 1883 5620**		

Summary

Travel Start Date and Time	**08/01/2012 14:53:38**	Total Ascent	**869.9 m**
Travel End Date and Time	**08/01/2012 18:53:34**	Total Descent	**-1,027 m**
Total Time	**03:59:56**	Total Ascent Distance	**2,982.8 m**
Total Air Distance	**6,575.4 m**	Total Descent Distance	**3,003.3 m**
Total DTM Distance	**6,959.1 m**	Total Level Distance	**973 m**
Min. Altitude	**99.5 m**	% of Ascent	**42.9 %**
Max. Altitude	**949.5 m**	% of Descent	**43.2 %**
Average Altitude	**614 m**	% of Level	**14 %**

Profile

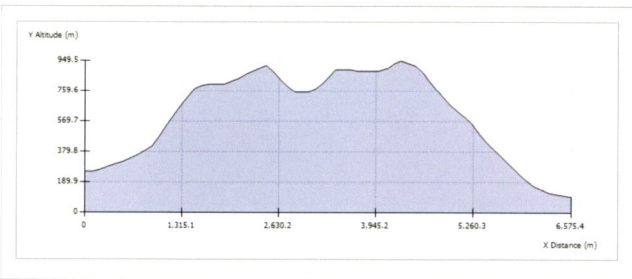

Points

Name	Coordinate	Bearing	Altitude	DTM Distance	Ascent	Date and Time	Note
start, carpark	NN 1883 5620	111.27°	256.6 m	0 m	0 m	08/01/2012 14:53:38	find suitable stream crossing
turn1	NN 1965 5584	-172.93°	414.9 m	909.5 m (909.5 m)	158.3 m	08/01/2012 15:27:03	careful route finding to next point
flat spur	NN 1962 5563	126.16°	553.6 m	1,166.9 m (257.4 m)	297 m	08/01/2012 15:48:15	careful route finding required to next
Stob Nan Cabar spur	NN 1991 5539	-129.97°	775.2 m	1,604.7 m (437.9 m)	518.6 m	08/01/2012 16:22:31	
Stob Coire Raineach 925	NN 1914 5480	132.33°	920.9 m	2,586.7 m (982 m)	664.3 m	08/01/2012 16:55:28	summit, munro
col	NN 1878 5450	-138.38°	753.6 m	3,088.4 m (501.6 m)	664.3 m	08/01/2012 17:07:11	
902 top	NN 1845 5416	155.42°	895.1 m	3,589.5 m (501.1 m)	805.8 m	08/01/2012 17:32:24	ridge narrows to next points
col2	NN 1823 5373	-132.01°	885.5 m	4,072.1 m (482.6 m)	805.8 m	08/01/2012 17:39:14	
spur	NN 1806 5359	-117.73°	900.8 m	4,292.9 m (220.8 m)	821.1 m	08/01/2012 17:44:28	narrow ridge to summit
Stob Dubh 958	NN 1789 5351	137.54°	949.5 m	4,486.9 m (194 m)	869.9 m	08/01/2012 17:53:28	summit, munro
descent spur	NN 1763 5325	169.66°	832.8 m	4,877.3 m (390.4 m)	869.9 m	08/01/2012 18:01:33	careful route finding to next point
spur2	NN 1750 5268	-172.4°	559.5 m	5,523.1 m (645.8 m)	869.9 m	08/01/2012 18:22:37	steep slope to next
spur path junction	NN 1737 5195	159.33°	202.2 m	6,346.6 m (823.5 m)	869.9 m	08/01/2012 18:48:40	follow path to next
path junction	NN 1725 5167	140.27°	123.7 m	6,661.5 m (314.9 m)	869.9 m	08/01/2012 18:50:07	follow path SW to road
end	NN 1705 5145		99.5 m	6,959.1 m (297.6 m)	869.9 m	08/01/2012 18:53:34	road bend

FIGURE 2.13 EXAMPLE OF PRINTED ROUTE CARD GENERATED AUTOMATICALLY FROM A ROUTE PLANNED USING DIGITAL MAPPING SOFTWARE

The 3D function on most software shows a topographical view of the route and the surrounding terrain and when combined with an aerial photography image this can provide a very realistic view of the ground. The 'fly-through' function on some products provides an animated view of the terrain allowing for closer inspection of the route.

Any information created using the software can be saved and stored for future reference. Data collected when using a GPS unit can be downloaded providing the opportunity to review the route and save this information for the future. Some software will allow for access to Internet sites making it possible to share route information created by other people and overlay this onto the map. These routes, waypoints or tracks can then be uploaded to a GPS unit or printed as a route card or map for use. In many cases this information can also be shared with others via email and other social media such as Twitter and Facebook. Depending on how this information is stored it can be used by others to upload to their GPS units. Some software also allows for interfacing with Geocaching websites.

2.1.11 Scanned maps

Some products offer the ability to create your own digital maps that can then be used for planning trips. By using a scanned image of a section of map it is possible to use certain mapping software to calibrate and create an overlaid grid. Once this has been achieved it is possible to then use this map to plan routes and this information can then be printed or uploaded to a GPS unit as before and used for navigation in the field.

2.2 The compass

For centuries, the magnetic compass has remained the most reliable device for finding direction, requiring almost no maintenance and needing no power supply. In good weather the compass may never leave your pocket. However as the route becomes more complex or as the weather worsens the compass becomes an essential tool for finding direction and navigation. While manufacturers have continued to develop compass design over the years, stripped back to the core it is nothing more than a magnetised needle that responds to the earth's magnetic field. As well as showing direction they are very versatile tools, which can provide assistance with other navigational tasks:

- Taking a bearing from the map.
- Walking on a bearing.
- Measuring distances from the map.
- Setting the map in the right direction (see *Section 3.1.1* on page 54).
- Taking an aspect of slope or finding the direction of a linear feature (see *Section 3.9* on page 72).

2.2.1 Choosing a compass
Types of compass
Compasses that can be used in the mountain environment fall into three basic categories.

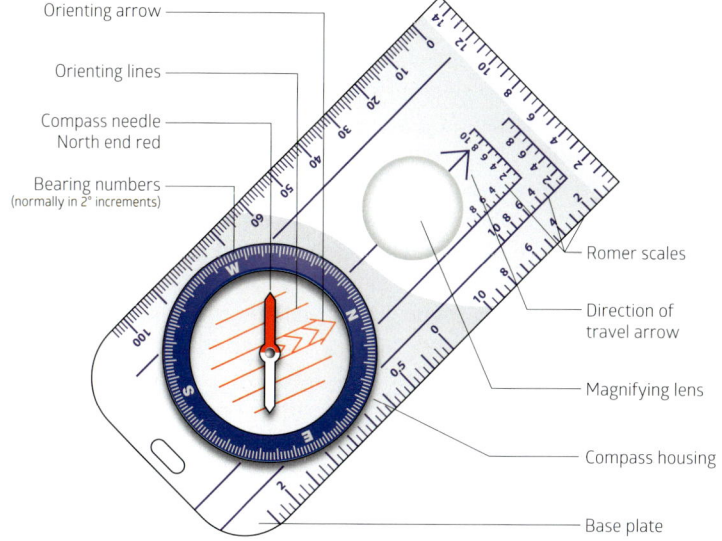

Orienting arrow

Orienting lines

Compass needle
North end red

Bearing numbers
(normally in 2° increments)

Romer scales

Direction of
travel arrow

Magnifying lens

Compass housing

Base plate

FIGURE 2.14 THE BASE-PLATE STYLE COMPASS (EG: TYPE 4 SILVA)

1 Base plate. This is the most commonly used type of compass for mountain and moorland navigation. Lightweight, robust and reasonably priced they are sometimes referred to as protractor compasses. They consist of two parts, a compass housing containing the needle and a base plate made from transparent plastic.

2 Sighting. There are various types of sighting compass; two of the most common being a mirror compass and the prismatic compass. In practice they are good for sighting on objects and walking on bearing accurately. However, they often have small base plates making it difficult to take bearings from the map or measure distances and grid references. While they can still be a useful tool to the mountain navigator they do require familiarity and practice to achieve accuracy. As a result they are not as versatile as the base plate type.

3 Electronic. These are increasingly popular and becoming more reliable with developments in technology. They differ from a GPS compass because they do not require the use of satellites to work out position and direction. However they are often incorporated into watches and GPS units and while they may be good for direction finding the biggest disadvantage is they have no facility for taking a bearing from the map. It also worth remembering that batteries may run down and software might fail so having the backup of a mechanical device such as those highlighted above becomes important.

Compasses are available in a huge variety of shapes and sizes and while they all do the same basic job of indicating direction many are designed for specific applications and are not necessarily suited for use in the mountains. For mountain use a compass will need to be light but tough and consist of all the basic features that would allow it to assist with the tasks outlined previously.

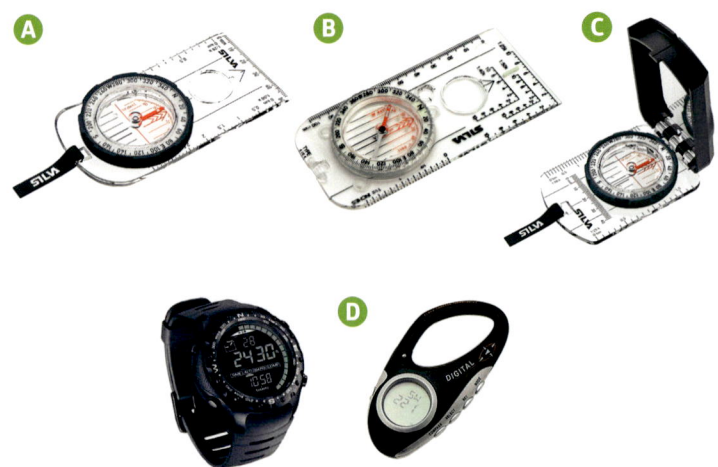

FIGURE 2.15 A VARIETY OF DIFFERENT COMPASSES: **A** A SIMPLE BASE PLATE COMPASS **B** A GENERAL PURPOSE BASE PLATE COMPASS **C** A SIGHTING COMPASS **D** ELECTRONIC COMPASSES

- A freely rotating *magnetic needle* (one end should be a different colour to the other so as to distinguish between north and south).
- A rotating *compass housing* for the needle, filled with fluid to dampen and reduce any vibration, allowing more accurate readings.
- A *graduated scale* around the circumference of the housing – degrees or mils.
- An *orienting arrow* and set of *parallel lines* located below the needle.
- An *index line* marked on the rotating housing, allowing for a grid or magnetic bearing to be read accurately.
- A transparent *base plate* with straight edges and lines for easily measuring bearings from a map.
- A *direction of travel arrow* that can be used to point toward an objective.
- A *romer* scale for measuring grid references or distances.
- A centimetre *ruler* for measuring distances with more accuracy.
- Optional extras that are advantageous when having to use a compass in testing conditions include the following.
- Rubber pads on the base plate – allow for better purchase on map covers when taking bearings or measuring distances.
- Option for attaching a lanyard which can then be clipped to a pocket zipper to prevent loss or damage if dropped.
- Magnifying glass for seeing the detail on the map – good for looking beyond other symbols to see the contour information and other minute details.
- Luminous markings make it easier to use at night.

Good clear markings are essential for measuring distances and bearings. As well as the cardinal points of North, East, South and West, the needle housing should be marked around the edge with the 360 degrees of a full circle, most often in 2-degree intervals.

Other forms of graduation do exist, in particular the 'mils' system used on military compasses. This is more accurate compared to using degrees as there are more mils to a circle than degrees; 360 degrees compared to 6400 mils. For the purposes of recreational mountain walking in all conditions it is universally accepted that a compass graduated in degrees is sufficiently accurate. As some retailers stock both types of compass it is important to check before purchasing; if possible try before you buy. Make sure the needle rotates freely and settles quickly. Good quality compasses use an oily fluid to dampen the needle. This reduces vibration and ensures the compass needle settles to the correct alignment quickly. Moving the compass about will allow you to assess this. Make sure the compass housing rotates freely and can be operated easily with gloves on.

2.2.2 Care and maintenance

Although most products designed for outdoor use are tough and robust there are some steps that can be taken to help increase their lifespan and to ensure they are kept in working order. A protective cover is a worthwhile investment for use on the days when the compass is not needed but carried in your rucksack. In this situation try to ensure it is stored in an accessible pocket and not buried amongst other items of equipment that may cause it damage. Avoid storing a compass next to metallic objects as this can cause reverse polarity leaving the needle pointing South rather than North. Dry compasses carefully when they have been exposed to rain or snow and avoid placing them in direct contact with heat. Periodically clean the compass housing to ensure it is able to rotate freely as this will allow bearings to be taken more easily. When in use try to attach the compass about your person using a lanyard. Attaching to the zipper cord of a pocket allows for easy use and storage.

Occasionally your compass may produce a bubble in the housing around the needle. This should not affect its operation, however it can be annoying. Bubbles develop due to changes in temperature and atmospheric pressure, usually getting larger with increasing elevation and decreasing temperature. Often, when returned to neutral pressure (or temperature), the bubble will disappear. If not, try placing it in a warm environment and if this fails it may have a small leak in the casing allowing air to creep in. A quick check would be to hold it close (but not too close!) to another compass to ensure both needles point in the same direction. If the fluid is missing the needle will be slow to settle and may drag against the compass housing causing it to stick and give an incorrect reading. While it may still be serviceable it may be worth considering a replacement.

2.2.3 Grid North, Magnetic North and True North

Before learning to take and use accurate compass bearings it is essential to understand the relationship between Grid North, Magnetic North, and True North:

• **Grid North** is the direction indicated by the parallel vertical grid-lines on a map and varies very slightly (see below) from True North.

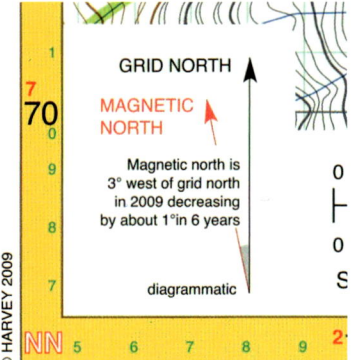

FIGURE 2.16 GLOBE SHOWING THE RELATIONSHIP BETWEEN THE THREE NORTHS

FIGURE 2.17 MAP MARGIN INFORMATION DETAILING THE RELATIONSHIP BETWEEN MAGNETIC AND GRID NORTH

FIGURE 2.18 USING A COMPASS TO SIGHT A BEARING DOWN A LINEAR FEATURE TO DETERMINE ITS DIRECTION

- **Magnetic North/South** is the axis along which a compass needle will align itself in the earth's magnetic field. Magnetic North, which is in a different position to True North, is located to the north of Hudson Bay in Canada and is moving very slowly eastward at a constant rate. In order to use a compass in conjunction with a map, any bearings have to be translated between Magnetic North and Grid North (or True North for continental maps that do not use a grid system). The difference between these two North points is known as **Magnetic Variation** and will vary depending on where you are on the globe. (refer to *Figure 2.17* on declination)
- **True North** (and South) are the geographic poles where the earth's axis meet the surface. For the purposes of land navigation using UK maps True North can be ignored.

2.2.4 Magnetic variation

Magnetic variation, sometimes known as declination, varies both from place to place and with the passage of time. In 2011 as a traveller moves eastwards across Europe towards Russia, for example, the magnetic variation

5 Taking a compass bearing

For many people this can be a difficult skill to master. Initially this could be introduced with a blank grid rather than a map, so that people are not put off by the complex nature of some map detail. Using a blank grid mark two points that can then be used to take a bearing from one to the other. This will help fine-tune the skills of placing the compass base plate on the map and keeping it still while moving the housing.

Exercise: Guess the bearing: it is good practice to guess the bearing before taking it so as to factor in a small 'safety net'. People could spend time guessing bearing between one point and another. An element of competition can be introduced by working in pairs and seeing who is the closest when the actual bearing is taken.

Taking bearings: there is no better practice than actually taking bearings for real; however, opportunities should be created for people to practise in a variety of different environments and conditions in order to develop a more robust skill. One simple way to vary the practice could be to use unfamiliar maps and compasses.

differs from 3 degrees West in Lisbon, Portugal (western seaboard) to 10 degrees East in Moscow meaning if bearings are adjusted with the same variation (3 degrees West) throughout the trip significant error will develop as they move further East.

Complex fluid motion in the outer core of the earth (the molten metallic region that lies from 2800 to 5000km below the earth's surface) causes the magnetic field to change slowly with time. This change is known as secular variation and because this is somewhat unpredictable, corrections given on outdated maps cannot be relied upon. Information regarding magnetic variation can be found on the Internet (*www.magnetic-declination.com*).

Information regarding magnetic variation for a particular region is usually found in the margins of the map or written in the key as in the case of OS and Harvey maps. In the UK in 2013 the variation is about four degrees greater on the west coast of Ireland (-4° 49' west) compared to the east coast of England (-0° 40' west). However this will gradually decrease in significance over the next decade. Despite being relatively small in the UK it should still be taken into account when transferring between bearings on the ground and on the map. There are various popular mnemonics which help the navigator to remember how to make this adjustment, although these will probably become redundant in 2015 when magnetic north is predicted to move east of Grid North.

The simplest reminder is to add when getting bigger (from the map to the ground) and subtract when getting smaller. Another popular reminder is to use the following ditty:

Add for Mag, Get rid for Grid.

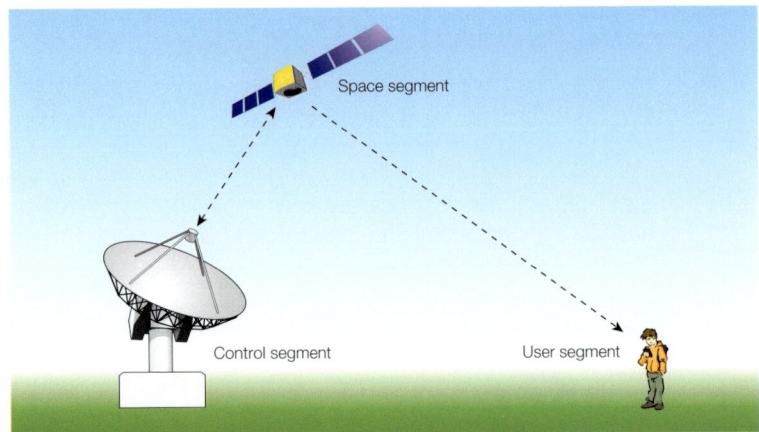

FIGURE 2.19 THE THREE MAIN SEGMENTS OF THE **G**LOBAL **P**OSITIONING **S**YSTEM

At first glance it would appear that the chore of converting between grid and Magnetic North would be eliminated if maps were drawn in relation to Magnetic rather than Grid North. This is not possible because of the variation as we travel from west to east, which would result in grid lines converging and becoming distorted. In addition, maps would become redundant after a year or two because of the movement of Magnetic North.

2.3 Global Positioning Systems: GPS

Devices that make use of Global Positioning System (GPS) technology have become increasingly more sophisticated and affordable year on year, a trend that is most likely to continue. The original GPS concept was conceived by the USA at the start of the cold war as a way of improving the accuracy of ballistic missiles. Despite its development in the early sixties, the GPS did not become fully operational until 1995.

There is now a vast array of receivers to choose from for those venturing into the outdoors, as well as those designed for more general use in cars, boats etc. Apart from providing a position reference, many GPS receivers have extra functions that can provide the operator with a range of useful information to assist with navigation. To gain the best from any GPS device it is important to understand how it works, what the limitations are and most of all how to integrate this tool with map and compass skills.

The GPS is made up of three segments, space, ground control and user. Currently the space segment uses a constellation of at least 24 satellites orbiting 20,000 kilometres above the earth at a speed of 11,000 kilometres per hour. These satellites broadcast radio signals that detail the position of each satellite in the sky and an electronic code. The ground segment is comprised of stations that track, task and monitor the health of these satellites. These stations make the necessary adjustments to keep the system accurate. The GPS unit makes up the user segment; it receives the radio signals from the satellites and calculates its position accordingly. Control and maintenance of the GPS is still managed by the US Defence Department.

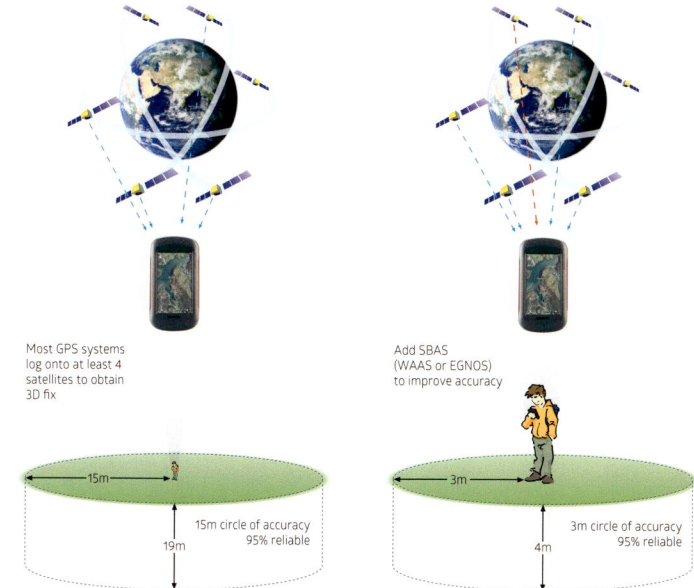

Most GPS systems log onto at least 4 satellites to obtain 3D fix

Add SBAS (WAAS or EGNOS) to improve accuracy

15m

19m

15m circle of accuracy 95% reliable

3m

4m

3m circle of accuracy 95% reliable

FIGURE 2.20 ILLUSTRATING CIRCLES OF ACCURACY FOR SBAS ENABLED AND NON ENABLED UNITS

Further developments in GPS technology have given rise to improvements being developed to enhance the level of accuracy even further. Geostationary satellite systems (satellites that maintain a fixed position overhead) and new ground-based stations are being added to remove actual errors and increase accuracy. Known as satellite based augmentation systems (SBAS) they have patchy coverage across the globe with currently only a few countries having developed their own systems (North America, Europe, Russia and Japan). Most new GPS units come enabled to use these satellite based augmentation systems.

When a GPS unit is turned on, it 'listens' to the radio signals and extracts the satellite location information. Each satellite broadcasts the position information for all the satellites. The GPS unit stores this information so that it is able to determine its own position. Known as the almanac, it takes about 12 minutes to transfer this data to the GPS unit. If the GPS unit has not been used for some time or has been moved a considerable distance (excess of 300 miles) it will need at least this amount of time before it can start to give accurate information.

Each satellite has a highly accurate atomic clock used to send codes containing all this data at exactly the same time from each satellite. Knowing when a signal was sent and when it was received allows the GPS unit to work out its distance from each satellite. Software then triangulates a position in longitude and latitude which can then be converted into a variety of other formats if required, for example the OS grid system. The design of the system ensures there are usually six satellites covering any spot on the globe at any one time. However a GPS unit only needs good signals from four well-placed satellites to provide an accurate 3D fix (location and altitude). If signals from only three satellites are being used the unit may provide a 2D fix; however the location given may be inaccurate and

FIGURE 2.22 THE SATELLITE PAGE GIVES A REPRESEN-
TATION OF SATELLITE GEOMETRY. THE BAR GRAPHS
SHOW SATELLITES BEING LISTENED TO AND THE
STRENGTH OF THE SIGNALS BEING RECEIVED.
AN ESTIMATED POSITION ERROR (EPE) IS GIVEN TO
INDICATE THE ACCCURACY OF THE POSITION SHOWN.
IN THIS EXAMPLE, IT SUGGESTS ± 5 METRES

FIGURE 2.21 USING GPS IN COMBINATION WITH THE MAP

the unit will compensate for the missing satellite by estimating the elevation. Once locked onto satellites the GPS unit will display a continuously
updated position.

2.3.1 Accuracy

Typical accuracy of modern GPS units is to within 15m with 95% reliability. This means that for 5% of the time the information given will be
less accurate than 15m. With SBAS and high sensitivity receivers accuracy improves to 3m, 95% of the time.

GPS units are most accurate when they have good line of sight to the
satellites and receive adequate signals from four well placed satellites.
The stronger the signal they are able to receive the more accurate the
position fix. Reception is not significantly affected by cloud cover and
poor weather but there are a number of other factors that will influence
the accuracy of the positions shown such as deep narrow valleys and
forests (also see *Section 2.3.5 Blocking*).

2.3.2 Using GPS on the mountain

There are three distinct ways of using a GPS unit to assist with navigating.
An additional 'opportunity' also exists that can complement any of these
approaches.

1 Emergency relocation aid. The primary approach to navigation
involves using a map and compass. A GPS unit can be used to
help relocate precisely when either unsure of a location or to help
confirm a location.

2 Primary navigation aid. A map and compass are carried, but stowed
and will only be used if all else fails. The GPS unit is on and always
to hand, it is loaded with a topographical map of the area, and the
route in detail. In addition, it has been pre-programmed with various
escape routes and other possibilities. With proficiency it can be used
throughout the day whatever the conditions. Due to the sophistication
of the information shown it is possible to know exactly where you are,
where you have been and where you are going.

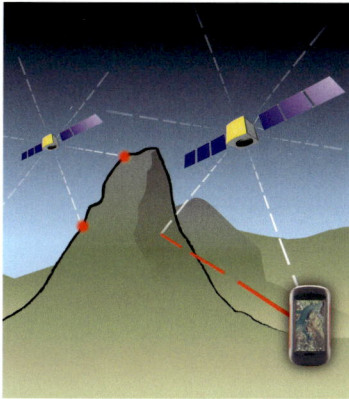

FIGURE 2.23 SIGNALS CAN BE BLOCKED OR REFLECTED BY SURROUNDING TERRAIN

FIGURE 2.24 THERE ARE TWO TYPES OF ANTENNAE: **A** QUADRIFILAR HELIX AND **B** PATCH

FIGURE 2.25 SHOWING THE BEST METHODS OF CARRYING A GPS SO THAT IT MAINTAINS THE ABILITY TO RECEIVE GOOD SIGNALS. **A** SHOULDER STRAP OF RUCKSACK. **B** PLACING GPS UNIT CAREFULLY INSIDE TOP POCKET OF RUCKSACK *PHOTOS // CARLO FORTE*

3 A mixture of the above. The GPS unit is used as an extra navigational tool to complement the map and compass. This will require it to be close to hand so that it may be referred to when necessary. The GPS unit may have the route pre-loaded, however the map and compass are used as the primary tools and the GPS unit for backup.

Whichever approach is required, a GPS unit can also be used in an additional way for data logging. If the GPS unit is on all the time but stowed in the top of your rucksack, or to hand, and provided it can detect satellite signals it can be setup to record all your movements. In other words, it plots exactly where you have gone (and when, what elevation, and possibly other data as well). This information could then be used to assist with relocation. Once saved it may be used to review the journey or to help navigate the route another time. It can also be used to retrace your steps during your journey if required using the *track-back* function. (See *Section 3.12.5 Track-log* on page 93)

2.3.3 Satellite geometry

Satellite geometry refers to the positioning of the satellites being listened to by the GPS unit and is of importance when it comes to the accuracy of the information provided. Modern units will have a display page for this information, along with an Estimated Position Error (EPE).

Using this page it is possible to determine how many satellites the GPS unit is connecting with and where they are in the sky relative to your current location. The ideal configuration for the grouping of satellites for the greatest accuracy is to have one or two satellites overhead with the rest spread out around the sky. In hilly terrain, moving short distances can often improve reception and help to improve accuracy.

If the GPS unit has a 3D fix and the EPE is low, the position fix will be good. Combined with good satellite geometry this becomes even more reliable. It is worth remembering that the displayed Estimated Position Error (EPE) is based only on satellite geometry and does not take into account the various other sources of error.

2.3.4 Reflected signals

Known as multipath, these are signals that have been reflected by some-thing in the surrounding terrain; buildings, cliffs, steep sided gorges. If the signal is reflected, it can have more than one path to the unit's antenna. If the reflected signal is used to calculate the position it will be incorrect. Unfortunately, as an operator it is difficult to determine these errors from the information being shown on the screen. When using a GPS unit, particularly in complex terrain, it is important to be aware of the surroun-dings especially if there is a potential for multipath errors to occur. Always cross-reference any position information with the map and then the surrounding terrain to confirm the location. A modern unit with a high sensitivity GPS receiver is better able to distinguish between true and multipath signals and as a result will cope better in terrain where this could be a problem.

2.3.5 Blocking

Buildings, dense tree cover, cliffs and high ground, and even your body will affect a GPS unit's reception of satellite signals, as they are either weakened or blocked entirely. For best results make sure the signals are able to reach the unit by avoiding objects that may block their path. A common mistake is to carry a GPS unit either in a pocket on your body or buried inside a rucksack. If the intention is to use the device on a regular basis and for it to track your movements it needs to be able to receive satellite signals as you move. Mounting the device on a shoulder strap or inside the top pocket of a rucksack gives the best results. Some models allow for the attachment of an external antenna allowing the unit to be carried in a rucksack and the antenna to have an uninterrupted view of the sky.

2.3.6 Antennae

Handheld GPS units come with one of two types of antenna – quadrifilar helix or patch. The patch antenna is a small, rectangular metal sandwich often mounted within the receiver. Best reception using this type of antenna is achieved when the unit is held or mounted horizontally. The quadrifilar helix antennae are coils of wire beneath a plastic cover and often have to extend beyond the body of the unit.

Quadrifilar helix antennae are more sensitive and tend to outperform patch antennae in situations such as tree cover and in terrain where there is potential blocking due to topography, for example valleys. Best reception using this type of unit is achieved when the aerial is held vertically.

2.3.7 Choosing the right GPS

It is possible to buy a GPS unit to fit almost any budget and the choice on offer from manufacturers can be overwhelming. Not all of these will be suitable for operating in the harsh conditions they may face in the mountains. Many manufacturers produce a range of models to suit all needs from entry level through to advanced. Having said this they will all be able to do the following:

- Display time, location and elevation and while moving will show speed and heading.
- Determine current position, and display this either as co-ordinates or on an electronic map.
- Accept a range of different co-ordinate systems and map datums, particularly important if using with different maps.
- Store the locations of numerous positions called *waypoints* or *points of interest* (*POI*).
- Calculate the distance and direction from your current location to any stored waypoint and navigate you to it.
- Link a series of waypoints together to form a *Route* that can be stored and used later.
- Guide you to a destination you choose from a map (paper or electronic).
- Monitor your movements to create a 'bread crumb' trail or *track-log* that can be stored and used later if required.

Entry-level models often provide more than enough options and functions to assist with navigation. Features on the more advanced units include extra storage capacity for waypoints, routes and tracks, plus it is often easier and quicker to interface with the unit using touch screens or toggle switches to gain access to menus and enter information.

Advanced mapping models now have the option to show on-screen topographical mapping allowing the user to identify their location on a digital map in real time. Currently, manufacturers produce mapping that is usually only compatible with their own products, though this may well change. This comes at a premium, so before purchasing a unit, think about how you intend to use GPS both now and in the future. Some units have topographical mapping built-in, or come bundled with mapping and this is sometimes better value than adding mapping at a later date.

FIGURE 2.26 EXAMPLES OF GPS UNITS FROM ENTRY LEVEL TO ADVANCED: **A**, **B** AND **C** ARE ENTRY LEVEL. **D** AND **E** ARE MORE ADVANCED AND OFFER DETAILED MAPPING FUNCTIONALITY. **F** IS AN EXAMPLE OF A SMART PHONE WITH GPS FUNCTION.

When choosing any GPS unit for use in the mountains make sure it is of a good rugged construction and waterproof, it is always worth considering some form of protective case to help secure and protect the unit when in use. The size of the screen and the brightness are particularly important if it is a mapping unit as viewing the maps will be much clearer with a good quality screen. Think carefully about how the unit will perform in a variety of conditions. Is it possible to operate it with gloves on? Can you see the screen clearly in bright daylight or at night? One essential to consider is a high sensitivity receiver as these perform much better in hilly terrain.

Other options to include for use in the mountains include an electronic compass and a barometric altimeter: it should be noted that these features are also available on non-GPS enabled wrist watches.

2.3.8 The electronic compass

All GPS units will display the direction of travel when they are moving; this is normally shown on a compass page. This screen looks very similar to a compass but is better thought of as a heading indicator (see *Figure 2.27D*). A heading refers to the current direction of travel as opposed to a bearing, which is a straight-line direction from one location to the next. A true heading will only be shown when the unit is moving (usually at a pre-set speed approx. 3kph) as it calculates the direction of movement based on the current location and where it was a few seconds ago. When the unit is being used to navigate to a waypoint, a pointer will appear indicating the direction in which to travel to reach the destination.

A watch or GPS unit with an electronic compass has the advantage in that it behaves in a similar way to a magnetic compass. When stationary (but held level) it will orientate itself and show the actual direction to the chosen destination. Modern units often have a 3-axis compass which does not have to be held level and generally performs better than the standard 2-axis electronic compass. Most GPS units will allow the operator to set the North reference for the compass to one of three options: True, Grid or Magnetic North. If carrying a compass it would make sense to set the GPS unit to display Magnetic North bearings as this can then be cross-referenced or transferred to a compass if required. Along with a barometric altimeter, these features tend to be optional extras and not all GPS units have them as standard.

For the GPS unit to give accurate information these features will need to be calibrated correctly. Most manufactures give on-screen instruction to help with calibration. In the case of the electronic compass this should be calibrated at the start of every trip and when the batteries have been changed. It is important to remember that electronic compasses are sensitive and easily affected by large metal objects like ice axes. If you use your electronic compass close to an avalanche transceiver or have a mobile telephone in a pocket near the GPS, these may affect the reading as well.

2.3.9 Power

Battery life is an important consideration with manufacturers quoting anything from 10 to 25 hours. Depending on conditions and use, this could be dramatically reduced, and is especially true when using GPS units in cold conditions.

Disposable lithium batteries which can be used by some GPS units are largely unaffected by cold conditions and as a result out-perform alkaline and rechargeable batteries in these situations. Rechargeable batteries offer a cheaper and more environmentally friendly option but it is important to use the correct types. Low self-discharge Nickel Metal Hydride (NiMH) batteries with a rating greater than 2000mh perform the best, but it is important with rechargeables that they are stored and conditioned properly for use.

Some GPS functions such as backlights and updating the display place a drain on power so unless being used to navigate it is worth switching off these features until needed. Start each day with fully charged batteries to avoid any changes during the journey, and always carry a spare set. Some GPS units have an input field for the battery-type under settings; it is important to set this correctly in order to obtain an accurate reading from the battery life indicator.

FIGURE 2.27 SIX MAIN PAGES COMMON TO MOST GPS UNITS: **A** MAIN MENU, **B** SATELLITE PAGE, **C** MAP PAGE, **D** COMPASS PAGE, **E** ALTIMETER PAGE AND **F** TRIP COMPUTER.

2.3.10 Setting up GPS

Time spent becoming accustomed with the various button functions, screens and menus will help understand fully how the unit works and make its use in the field much more efficient.

Most GPS units work in a similar way and will display information through a variety of different screens or pages. These screens can often be customised by the operator to display the most useful information.

A simple non-mapping unit may only have a few information pages but more advanced models will allow the user to add more pages from a menu if required. Once familiar with the unit it will need to be set up correctly before use. This is of particular importance if the GPS unit is to be integrated with the map and compass. A *Setup Page* is usually accessed from the *Main Menu Page* allowing the user to configure the unit for the information they require. It is important to configure the GPS unit before it is first used, when it has not been used for a long time, or when moving from one country to another with a different co-ordinate system.

The setup page will often allow the configuration of any personal preferences, however there are some crucial settings required for the unit to function correctly. The following are Essential Settings; information that should be checked or changed before every trip.

- The time zone and country where you are
- The co-ordinate system and map datum to be used. This should correspond with the paper map being used
- All units of measurement. It is best to use the same units as used on the map; for example if the map is metric the GPS unit should

be setup to display any units in metric so that distances shown can easily be cross-referenced

• Calibration of electronic compass and altimeter

Having set the crucial information, many GPS units will allow this to be displayed in more than one way. A range of options will often allow for the change of screen settings, audible alarms and alter the text sizes on various pages. Many pages and in particular the Trip Computer Page have small information boxes known as *Data Fields*. These boxes display a range of navigational statistics and can be changed from an options menu to show the most relevant information.

2.3.11 Before setting off

Prior to setting off on any route make sure the relevant map loaded and any other route details required, and take also a magnetic compass and paper map. Ensure you have enough battery power for the journey and remember that cold conditions and constant use will reduce battery life.

At the start of a walk:

• Switch on the GPS unit, keep it static with a good sky view, and allow it to obtain a 3D position fix; if possible, leave it switched on for a few minutes after it has first obtained its fix as this will significantly improve its accuracy. If the unit has not been used for some time or moved a considerable distance since its last use it will require at least 12 minutes to download a new almanac before giving an accurate position fix
• Check that the **Essential Settings** are correct
• If the GPS unit has an electronic compass or barometric altimeter, calibrate these functions before setting off
• Check the battery life indicator to ascertain if you have sufficient battery life for your journey
• Switch off any functions that may not be required, for example backlights
• Clear the **Track-Log** and alter any settings if the unit is to build a track of its movements
• Reset any **Trip Computer** information if recording data from the journey

Finally, immediately before moving off, check the position given by the GPS unit corresponds exactly with the map to ensure it is working correctly.

2.4 Altimeters

Whether a sophisticated digital type or a classic analogue device, an altimeter is a great lightweight addition to your equipment, and will more than justify its carriage when used properly. Unlike a GPS receiver, an altimeter does not use any external systems for its accuracy. Analogue altimeters need no battery so are almost impervious to cold and incredibly reliable.

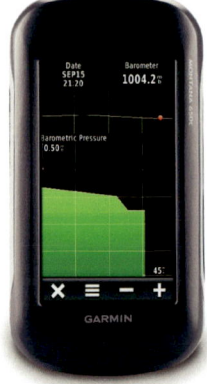

FIGURE 2.29 PRESSURE TREND GRAPH TAKEN FROM A GPS BAROMETER SHOWING A DROP IN PRESSURE OVER THE PAST 3¼ HOURS, WHICH COULD INDICATE A DETERIORATION IN THE WEATHER

FIGURE 2.28 A DIGITAL AND **B** ANALOGUE ALTIMETERS

Digital altimeters are typically very flexible and can support a range of additional features. Some GPS receivers come equipped with an in built barometric altimeter; this can still be used even when the unit is struggling to find its location from satellites.

Altimeters measure altitude by sensing changes in air pressure. The altitude measured can indicate the vertical distance you've covered or your proximity to a particular point on the map. Altimeters measure the air pressure and use formulæ to calculate the height above sea level in comparison to a known point. The altimeter works on the principle that pressure is inversely proportional to altitude, in other words as height increases then pressure decreases.

Most altimeters will offer a reading in two formats: Absolute altitude and relative altitude. Absolute altitude is the height above (or below) sea level. Relative altitude is the height above (or below) a reference point. The absolute reading is particularly useful when locating a position on a map using contour lines or spot heights. It is also useful for determining how much further to go to a given landmark. Relative altitude measurement is most useful for targeting an altitude gain, to avoid climbing too high or on a descent to avoid overshooting and having to climb back up.

In stable atmospheric conditions, this allows altimeters to be accurate to within a few metres, but when the pressure is changing rapidly the altimeter can be wildly inaccurate. Unfortunately, the very weather conditions in which accurate height plotting would be most useful are also usually linked to rapid changes in pressure. This means it is vital to reset the altitude reading regularly to maintain accuracy. This can be done at a location that has a definite altitude shown on the map, for example spot height or summit. On a similar note most altimeters are temperature sensitive and it is important to keep the temperature as constant as possible so as not to greatly affect the altitude reading.

The accuracy of altimeters will depend on three main factors:

1 The **length of time** since the last setting of the reference altitude
2 The **altitude change** since the last calibration
3 The **air pressure changes** due to changing weather and/or location

Practise using your own altimeter will help you anticipate these changes and mean that you can interpret the readings more accurately. The barometric information provided by an altimeter can also be used during an overnight camp to record trends towards higher or lower pressure. If the altitude appears to be steadily rising despite being stationary it is likely that poor weather is on the way. The relationship between pressure and cloud formation is described more fully in *Section 9.4 Creating wind, cloud and rain* on page 167.

Digital altimeters combine various memory functions that allow the operator to record time and altitude measurements. This information can be analysed later in conjunction with a map to work out which route was taken and the total ascent or descent. Ascent rate is especially useful when acclimatising to altitude to help ensure a safe rate of ascent. As well as providing information as to whether you are travelling faster or slower than anticipated it can also be used to help pace an ascent or gauge the likely time to reach the next location.

As with a GPS unit, the altimeter should be considered an additional tool and not relied upon solely or used in isolation of other skills. Upper and lower limit alarms are useful for providing an indication that you have arrived at a predetermined altitude. The generally accepted wisdom of 'aiming-off' with an altimeter is to aim low when ascending and aim high when descending which in both cases avoids overshooting the target and having to backtrack.

The biggest advantage offered by an altimeter is the potential for greater accuracy when navigating in angled terrain. Contouring can be very difficult, for example, particularly in poor visibility; the tendency to walk slightly uphill or downhill in these situations can be removed by simply monitoring the altimeter for any indicated change in altitude. Additional accuracy can be obtained when used in conjunction with a compass to pinpoint a location on a contour line and an aspect of slope.

2.5 Torches

In darkness, the map is useless if it cannot be viewed. A reliable torch should therefore be regarded as indispensable for night navigation and carried as a contingency, whenever there is a possibility of unexpected delay. When navigating with map and compass in the hand, a head torch is particularly useful as it allows one hand to be kept free. For a walking leader a head-torch is really the only practical choice. Selecting a particular model is a compromise between weight and practicality. Tiny lights featuring LED bulbs weigh next to nothing and are perfectly adequate for map reading. In mountain terrain with rocky bluffs, a more powerful torch will allow safer route finding when weaving through obstacles. At the other end of the scale, halogen bulbs emit exceptionally bright

(i) **6 Darkness**

Darkness is often used as a way of training people for navigating in poor visibility. Learning to navigate in darkness is more about developing strategies using existing skills as opposed to learning any new information. Having the confidence to use these skills and strategies is fundamental to successful navigation in these conditions. Consider carefully the environment when planning a night exercise; make sure this is suitable for the aims and objectives of the session. In darkness shape and perspective can play tricks on the eye, making features seem bigger and farther away. Edges and drops can seem like gaping abysses and for many people just being out at night can be a learning experience without having to navigate. Plan short sessions that keep the group engaged and focused.

Ensure group members are suitably equipped and that they have an appropriate torch, preferably a head torch. As well as carrying spare batteries consider a spare torch. If head torches are being used make sure they are worn in such a way that the beam shines straight ahead. If the beam shines to one side people may trend in this direction when trying to follow a bearing. If conditions are particularly poor with darkness and mist, the torch beam may struggle to penetrate the cloud. By holding the torch at waist level in these conditions the beam will tend to penetrate further; similar to the dipped beam on car headlights when driving in fog. Initially the teaching will be done in groups; however once confidence and experience builds students should be given the opportunity to work in pairs or independently. Many of the exercises shown for use in daylight can be adapted to work in darkness.

light but rapidly drain batteries so lots of spares may be needed. It is important that the torch is adequately waterproof to cope with heavy rainfall. A red filter over the torch can help to preserve night vision while navigating in the dark. However in practice, with some maps it can be difficult to pick the contour detail and any other features marked with brown/red lines. Military maps are often produced using ink that can be seen clearly when using red light. On all but the most clear of nights it is advisable to use a torch to find your way over the terrain in the dark so as to avoid any potential hazards.

2.5.1 Eyesight and vision considerations

Having eyesight or vision problems is not a barrier to navigation; however it may require the development of a slightly different strategy and some additional items of equipment. Digital mapping software can allow for maps to be printed at a variety of scales meaning a 1:25,000 map could be printed at a scale of 1:10,000, and may be laminated, making it much easier to see the detail. A large magnifying glass can be useful and there are many products available specifically made for map reading that are light and easy to use; some even have built in lights. Specs can present a problem when the weather is poor, often misting up or requiring constant wiping to remove water. A jacket with a shaped wired hood can help prevent the worst of the conditions effecting vision, as can a peaked cap. Various windscreen products that reduce fogging and increase water repellence can reduce the amount of wiping required. Many manufacturers of goggles now offer the option of fitting prescription lenses to their products. Although they often need wiping in heavy rain a good pair of goggles will have anti fogging properties. Goggles designed for mountain biking that can be fitted with appropriate lenses offer a solution that are not too dissimilar to ordinary glasses, indeed some products are intended to be worn over prescription glasses. Bifocal lenses or wearing a contact lens in just one eye can help with transferring information from the map to the ground and vice-versa however they do take some getting used to at first, particularly if wearing them while walking. An alternative to these are glasses designed for orienteering that have small shaped lenses designed so that it is possible to see over the top of them when looking at the ground.

Marking the map with a pen or pencil will help to avoid losing your place and make it easier to locate the last known point when refocusing on the map. A comparable method used commonly with a folded map is 'thumbing the map' – marking your location using a thumb. It is usual to move your thumb to a new position at a 'check point' such as a path junction or some other obvious feature where you might stop or slow down so as to check your location.

PHOTO // KARL MIDLANE

Navigation techniques

A broad repertoire of navigational skills allows techniques to be varied according to conditions. Observation plays an important part even when clouds of darkness reduce the field of vision. A mental note is kept of any features that are passed, such as slopes crossed or bends in the track. These features can be continually monitored and compared to expectations gained from reading the map.

FIGURE 3.01 THUMBING THE MAP

3.1 Relating the map and the land to each other

One of the fundamental skills in map reading is transferring information gleaned from the map to the ground and vice versa. The most important and reliable information for the walker is provided by the contours, which allow the skilled map-reader to build a mental picture of the three-dimensional shape of the land. Other features can then be superimposed on top of this from the additional signs and symbols on the map. It should be remembered that these other features might change over time; paths or even streams re-route themselves. Field boundaries shown on larger scale maps can be a useful aid to navigation, but are sometimes confusing as they may no longer be visible at ground level, as walls crumble or are plundered for new constructions.

Although maps are remarkably accurate, minor errors occur occasionally – the most common is swapping blue and black inks, in other words showing a stream as a wall or vice versa. In recent years many new fences have been constructed in British moorland and mountains, often after the most recent surveys and latest map editions. Because a map is only a pictorial representation of a section of ground it is open to interpretation and a certain amount of artistic licence when it comes to the positioning of symbols during its production. A good example of this is outcrop markings on mountain slopes. In rocky terrain where there are numerous outcrops it becomes almost impossible to mark each crag accurately. Often the best approach is to litter that particular area with such symbols to give an overall impression of the nature of the terrain. On OS maps at 1:50,000 it can sometimes be difficult to show the subtleties in the contour markings, requiring the user to be even more vigilant in complex ground.

3.1.1 Setting the map

The map is a plan view to scale of an area of ground and as such it should be possible to turn and hold the map so that the features seen around you are in their correct and relative positions on the map. This is known as setting or orientating the map. This is the most fundamental navigation

FIGURE 3.02 SETTING THE MAP USING FEATURES

skill and is often an integral part of any navigational task, in particular those that involve relating ground to map or vice versa. A good habit to adopt is to set the map before commencing any task and, if walking with the map, try to keep it orientated as you move. As the ground is encountered the navigator can observe the features passed and relate them to the map. By constantly comparing features on the map with those on the ground it should be possible to notice and counteract any errors before they become significant.

3.1.2 Setting the map using features
In good visibility the map can be set quite accurately by using the surrounding features. The thumb can be placed beside the present position and the map rotated until the surrounding features line up with their counterparts on the ground. The best features to use for this are linear features such as

7 Teaching group members to set the map
As this is one of the fundamental navigation skills, it is important to introduce the concept of why and how to set a map at an early stage. Learning first to set the map without using a compass helps novices to relate the map to the ground more effectively; the compass can be introduced once the concept has been understood. Good use of exercises and verbal input when introducing these skills will help to establish understanding.

Exercise: Classroom Maps: As a simple start point using a blank sheet of paper draw a bird's eye view (map!) of a room. Place letters on each wall to show North, South, East and West. Group members can then annotate their drawn maps with these points and set the map accordingly. Exercises that involve moving around the room in different directions will allow people to practise a variety of basic skills including setting the map. Encourage them to 'drive their maps' turning them as they move in order to keep them set to the letters on the wall.

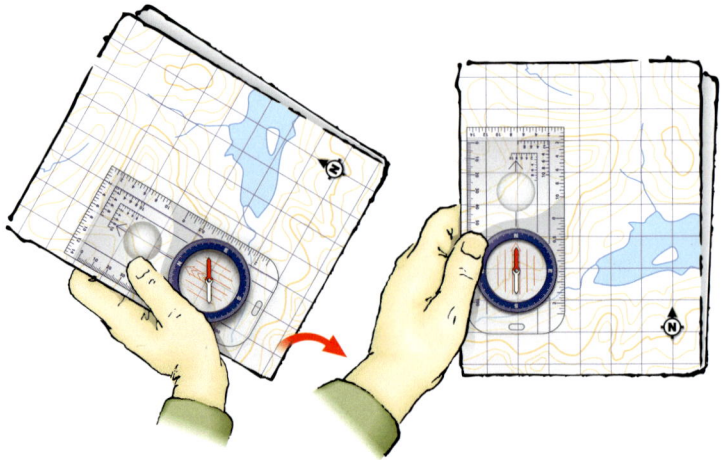

FIGURE 3.03 SETTING THE MAP USING A COMPASS

roads, paths, streams, edges of woodland, boundaries or anything that runs more-or-less in a straight line. By turning the map so that the feature on the ground is parallel with its counterpart on the map it is possible to set the map with a good degree of accuracy. One pitfall to look out for might be that the map is 180° out. Using more than one linear feature or comparing with other features will often highlight and correct this mistake.

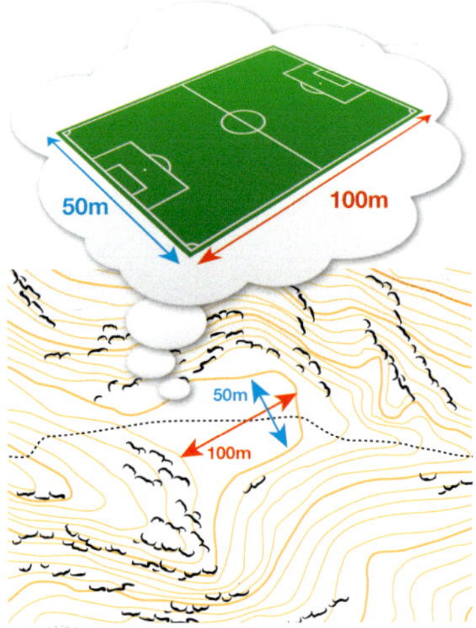

3.1.3 Setting the map using a compass

FIGURE 3.04 COMPARING THE AREA OF A CONTOUR FEATURE TO A KNOWN EXAMPLE OF SOMETHING WITH THE SAME AREA, IN THIS CASE A FOOTBALL PITCH

It is possible to set a map quickly using a compass in any visibility. This is achieved by placing the compass on the map and rotating them together until the needle is parallel to the vertical grid lines. A correctly set map will have its northern edge pointing north. This technique is particularly useful in poor visibility or for relocating, when it can be difficult to identify features. Strictly speaking magnetic variation should be accounted for when using a compass to set the map, however in the UK because the variation is so small at present it can generally be ignored.

3.2 Gathering information

Good observation skills are an important tool for any navigator. The ability to observe your surroundings and sense what the terrain is doing as you walk provides an endless stream of information that can be used to help confirm position and direction. Being able to pick out the detail in the landscape and relate this to the map and vice versa is an essential skill

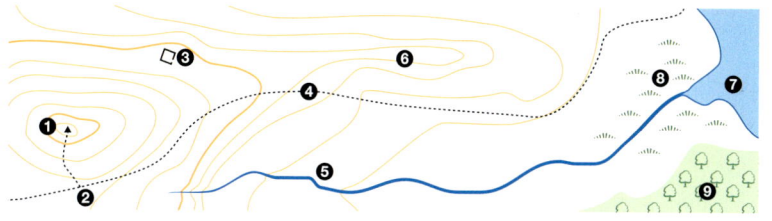

FIGURE 3.05 *SPOT FEATURES:* **1** – SUMMIT, **2** – PATH JUNCTION, **3** – ENCLOSURE
LINEAR FEATURES: **4** – PATH, **5** – STREAM, **6** – NARROW RIDGE
AREA FEATURES: **7** – LAKE, **8** – WOODLAND, **9** – MARSH

to try and fine tune. The same can be said for interpreting the terrain as you move; is it ascending or descending? Is it rising to the right or dropping away to the left? As you move your senses are bombarded with information that could be used to good effect when navigating. Developing an awareness of distance and size can help to relate the ground to the map more accurately. Examples from everyday life can be used to assist with this process:

• An average house is approximately 10 metres high, the equivalent of a 10 metre contour interval
• 25m is a standard length for a tennis court and a common length for a swimming pool
• A football pitch or running track could serve as a good gauge for 100 metres

Using these examples it is possible to judge distances between features or their size more accurately. These skills are particularly useful when having to distinguish between various features in complex terrain.

High vantage points that look down on the landscape are excellent places from which to develop an understanding of the relationship between the map and the ground. Working with a variety of maps and scales also helps to build the ability to visualise the land and the cartographer's attempts to depict it in on a flat sheet.

Features we may observe as we move can be categorised as three types:
1 Spot Single point features, for example house, boulder or cairn. These features pinpoint a particular location
2 Linear Anything elongated but narrow, for example a fence, stream, path, road or narrow ridge
3 Area These are features that do not necessarily have sharp edges, for example woodland, slopes or marsh

When navigating it is all too easy to make the features on the ground match your assumed location on the map, but the competent navigator learns to use every new piece of information to challenge this bias. A useful technique when trying to confirm a particular location is to seek out five features that support the hypothesis that it is a particular place on the map (see *Section 3.11 Relocation* for more details).

3.3 Following linear features

Many features can be used as handrails. These can be very easy to follow, or may require great skill, particularly in poor visibility. Suitable linear features include fences and walls, overhead cables or pipelines, streams, escarpments and sometimes landforms such as ridges or valleys. With good visibility, popular paths are often easy to see, because of the footprints, erosion or even their man-made surface. In these conditions, navigation along handrails consists mainly of keeping track of the direction and distance travelled. Along the way, a variety of features are likely to be passed, allowing navigators to re-affirm their position continually while travelling. These tick-off features can be likened to motorway junctions on a car journey. As long as the car stays on the motorway, junctions will always be passed in the right order. This everyday analogy can be easily applied to navigating in the mountains.

Tick-off features are used almost subconsciously by good navigators, so that ticking off a wall, or a change in slope angle, or vegetation change becomes almost second nature.

Linear features can become indistinct in places or may have even been moved since the map was made, so it is important to continually assess the situation. When following a linear feature it is sometimes possible to overshoot the destination point, particularly in poor weather or if the handrail is indistinct. Having a catching feature in place will allow the navigator to recognise they have overshot the target and prevent them going any further. Catching features are extremely important to prevent the probability of becoming lost when the destination has been missed. Selection of these features should form an inherent part of the planning process for every navigational leg (see *Section 3.10* on *Navigational Strategy*).

The choice of a catching feature needs to be considered carefully. Ideally it will be an obvious linear feature running perpendicular to your line of travel. This way no matter how far you deviate from your intended course you will always stumble across the catching feature. Once on the catching feature you will have a better idea of your location and can then plan how to get to the intended destination. Some quite subtle catching features may have to be considered. Changes in slope angle work very well as these are easy to see but can also be felt as the ground changes under your feet.

3.4 Contour interpretation

Contour lines are the conventional symbols used to indicate height. Being able to visualise the shape of the landscape by looking at the contour lines on a map is a very useful skill that can be developed with practice and experience. In remote and complex terrain where there is an absence of features it is often only contour information that provides clues to our location. Since natural features don't change as quickly or easily as their man-made counterparts, being able to use them to navigate is essential. Creating a mental picture of a 3-dimensional landscape from a 2-dimensional map can be difficult initially; however understanding basic principles and applying simple knowledge will lead to improvement and refinement of these skills.

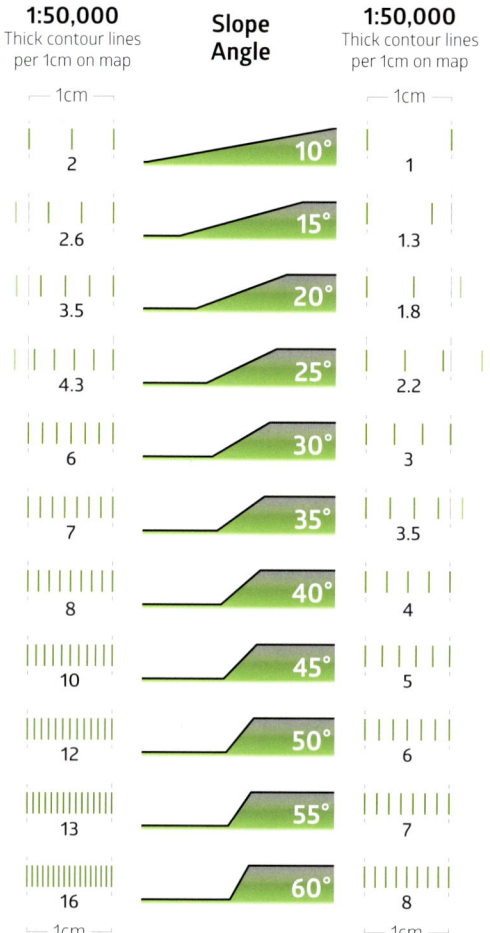

1:50,000
Thick contour lines
per 1cm on map

Slope Angle

1:50,000
Thick contour lines
per 1cm on map

1:50,000	Slope Angle	1:50,000
2	10°	1
2.6	15°	1.3
3.5	20°	1.8
4.3	25°	2.2
6	30°	3
7	35°	3.5
8	40°	4
10	45°	5
12	50°	6
13	55°	7
16	60°	8

FIGURE 3.06 RECOGNISING SLOPE ANGLE FROM CONTOUR SPACING

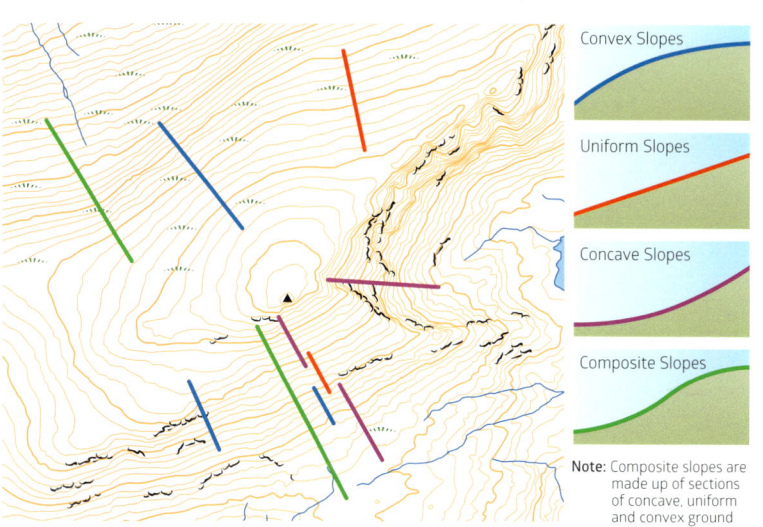

Convex Slopes

Uniform Slopes

Concave Slopes

Composite Slopes

Note: Composite slopes are made up of sections of concave, uniform and convex ground

FIGURE 3.07 CONTOUR SECTION

On distinct slopes, it is often possible to use a contour line as a handrail, by taking care to maintain the same height. Subtle changes in the contour line can be used as a tick-off feature, for example where it intersects with a stream or bulges around a spur.

3.4.1 The basics

Understanding the basic principles provides a good starting point when trying to create a mental picture of the landscape from contour information.

Index contour lines are labelled with a number showing their height above sea level. The top of the figures are orientated pointing uphill, so by finding one of these figures it is possible to work out which is uphill and which is downhill.

Relating the map and the land to each other

Ridge

Ridge

Saddle

Saddle

Knoll

Knoll

Re-entrant 2

Spur

Re-entrant 2   Spur   Re-entrant 1

Re-entrant 1

FIGURE 3.08 RELATING THE MAP AND THE LAND TO EACH OTHER

Practical tips

Practice and experience are essential to becoming more proficient with contour interpretation. The following tips can be used to improve these skills when navigating.

- Always orientate the map before trying to interpret the contour lines. It will make more sense when relating map to ground and vice versa.
- When interpreting the contours for a particular navigation leg, place the line on the compass base-plate on the map linking up your location and destination (as when taking a bearing) and look along the line in the direction of travel. It should then be possible to look at the contour spacing along this line and picture the shape of the ground to be crossed. The more obvious changes in slope angle can be used as tick-off features. Features can also be identified on the right or left side of the line and will appear on the same side on the ground as you travel. However, there is no benefit in interpreting the contours any further than the limit of visibility either side of your line of travel.

The closer together the contour lines are the steeper the slope and the further apart they are the flatter the ground. This is all relative, but knowing this information allows for better understanding of shape and with practice it is possible to determine rough angles of slopes based on contour information alone. The experience gained from walking up and down slopes and comparing them to the contour information on the map will allow for more informed decisions about whether or not slopes confronted in the future are passable. This experience can also provide useful information during the planning stage.

Recognising the basic slope shapes from the map seems straightforward; however in practice the ground is rarely uniform and the majority of slopes will be **composite**; comprising two or three of the basic types.

As well as basic slope shapes, contour lines depict an array of other topographical features that can be seen in the landscape. Learning to recognise such features as **valleys**, **spurs**, **tops**, **ridges** and **knolls** on both the map and the ground will make contour interpretation easier.

Use the magnifying glass on the compass to pick out the contour detail underneath other markings. This is particularly useful when there are a lot of outcrop markings obscuring the contour lines. (Harvey maps remove a lot of these outcrop markings by using a grey contour line to signify rocky ground.)

- If possible try to gain height above your location and look down onto the ground. This will feel like looking at an aerial photograph and can sometimes make it easier to see land shapes and picture contour lines.
- Consider measuring contour features to give an idea of scale and how big they might be on the ground. As an example if you measure a ring contour to be 2mm across on 1:25,000 map you will be looking for a feature that is 50m across on the ground.

- Practise using contours by using 1:10,000 orienteering maps with 5m contours. The features will be more consistently and accurately marked (because they have been systematically surveyed) than on the smaller scale maps.

One of the easiest ways to convert contour lines into a mental picture is to imagine the lines as high tide marks left by the sea. As the water level drops it leaves a 'shoreline' every 5 or 10 metres on the landscape. This analogy can often be used when trying to interpret the ground before consulting the map and is particularly useful when relocating (see *Section 3.11 Relocation*). As an example, if trying to identify the shape of the

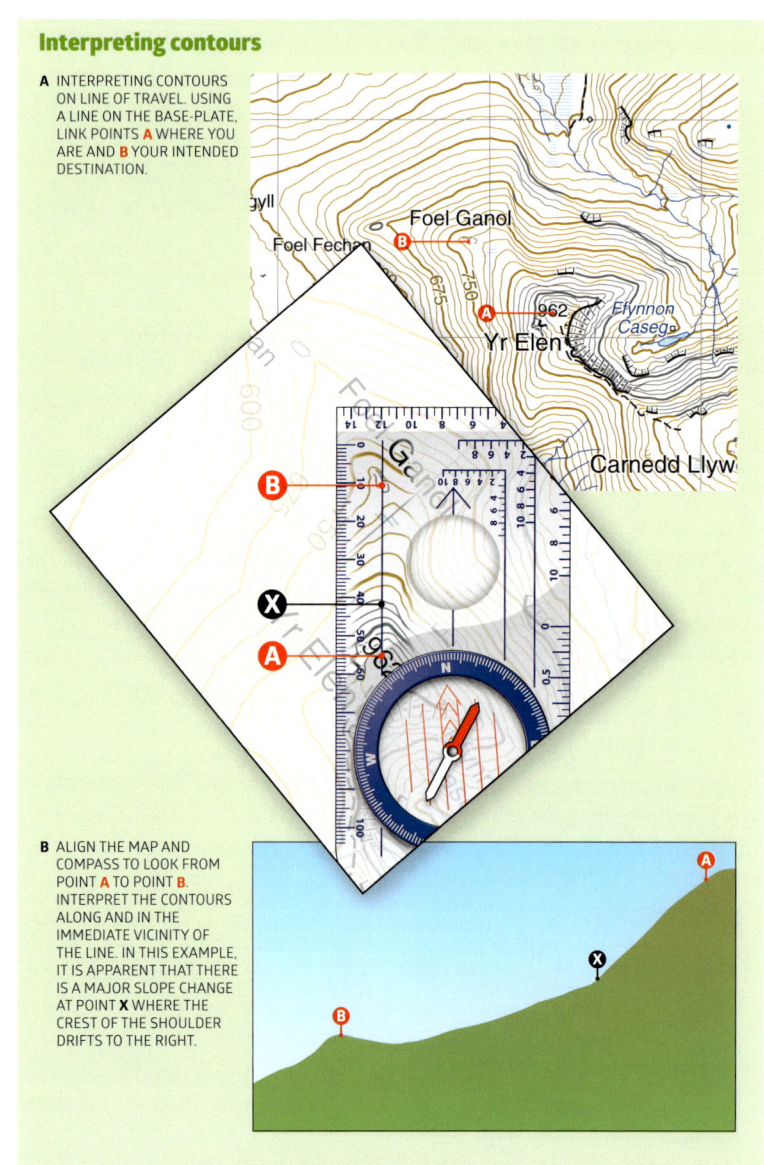

Interpreting contours

A INTERPRETING CONTOURS ON LINE OF TRAVEL. USING A LINE ON THE BASE-PLATE, LINK POINTS **A** WHERE YOU ARE AND **B** YOUR INTENDED DESTINATION.

B ALIGN THE MAP AND COMPASS TO LOOK FROM POINT **A** TO POINT **B**. INTERPRET THE CONTOURS ALONG AND IN THE IMMEDIATE VICINITY OF THE LINE. IN THIS EXAMPLE, IT IS APPARENT THAT THERE IS A MAJOR SLOPE CHANGE AT POINT **X** WHERE THE CREST OF THE SHOULDER DRIFTS TO THE RIGHT.

ground around a particular location, imagine standing on the shore with water lapping at your feet. Remember that water fills to a level. It should now be possible to trace out the shoreline left and right of your position.

3.4.2 Reading between the lines

It's worth bearing in mind that a contour line will only show the shape of the ground at that particular height. Smaller features may be missed by

---

ⓘ **8 Teaching contour interpretation**

Introducing and developing contour interpretation skills can be a challenging aspect of teaching navigation. A carefully planned progressive approach is required for people to understand how to use all forms of contour information. A good starting point is to define what contour lines signify and the nature of contour interval. The basic principles of uphill, downhill and steepness need to be mastered before progressing onto considering relief and general landforms. As people develop their understanding and ability to use contour information the terrain can be changed to offer more subtle landforms. Using contours and in particular more subtle contour information is a conceptual process that may prove difficult for some people. Giving people simple analogies that link to existing knowledge can break down some of the barriers to learning. Classroom sessions can help to introduce and reinforce these skills. Use of modelling exercises using sand or play dough can be a good fun way to introduce various concepts. The 3D and 'fly-through' facility on most digital mapping software products provides a very powerful resource to help teach these skills. A more realistic approach is to compare a map with photographs or slides of various locations.

Practice is the key to improvement and various exercises focused on these skills will help to enhance the learning.

Exercises: *Contour walk:* simply use a contour line as an imaginary footpath: students should consider whether the path moves to the left or right as they move along. *Draw the contour:* give group members a blank sheet of paper (laminated works well) and ask them to draw the contour line they are standing on. They can then repeat the process for the contour line below and the one above. This will construct a simple contour map of an area that can then be used to navigate with. People can mark points on these maps for other individuals.

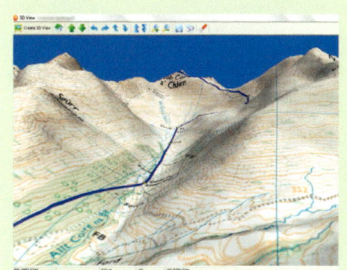

USING KNUCKLES AND A PEN TO HELP ILLUSTRATE THE BASIC CONTOUR PRINCIPLES

falling within the contour interval. If a feature is 9 metres higher than the previous contour line it may not appear on a map with contour lines at 10 metre intervals. This can be surprising when viewing the actual landscape as it may contain features you were not expecting to see. In some situations the terrain may undulate dramatically although this may not be shown on the map. With experience of the terrain you are walking through it is sometimes possible to 'read between the lines.' Indications on the ground around a current location may provide clues that the ground ahead might be more complex than indicated by the map. Often the problem arises when the horizontal spacing between contour lines is large. Generally when the ground is steep there is less likelihood of there being features that do not appear on the map. Plateau areas, gentle slopes and undulating ridges provide more scope for the land to rise and fall within a contour interval. This problem can be exacerbated when using a map with a greater contour interval. Harvey maps use a 15 metre contour interval; although they use a dotted interim contour called a form line to mark significant features that fall between contour lines. (see *Map scales* on page 20 – refer to the Harvey's Orienteering (i.e. close-up) map).

3.5 Distance judgement

In difficult conditions or in featureless terrain, observing features is often not enough to confirm a particular location. Keeping track of distance covered becomes increasingly important, whether following a path or a bearing. Techniques for estimating distance are useful at all times, but become crucial in poor visibility when otherwise identifiable features are obscured.

There are various methods of estimating distance, enabling an experienced navigator to achieve a high degree of accuracy (plus or minus ten per cent of the actual figure on most terrain). As with all navigational techniques, this information should be used in conjunction with other observed information.

3.5.1 Measuring distance

Being able to measure distance from the map allows for the calculation of how long a navigational leg or series of legs may take. It is an integral part of the planning process if timings are to be calculated to ascertain whether or not a journey is feasible in the allotted time. Conventionally measured distances are stated in the metric system rather than in yards and miles. Various tools can be used to measure distances ranging from a piece of string (see *Figure 10.03* on page 191) through to a specific map measurer. For planning purposes simply counting up the grid squares will give a quick rough estimate of the distance and help you decide whether the route is an appropriate length for the group you are walking with.

On the hill the most convenient method to measure map distance is to use the romer scale found on the base plate of some compasses. This is particularly useful when the distance is less than 1km, although separate romers can be purchased which can measure greater distances. When using a romer it is possible to measure distances down to 50m on a 1:25,000. However, for greater accuracy on any scale of map it is preferable

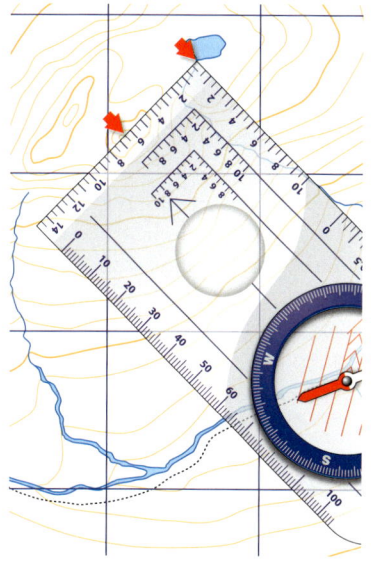

Distance travelled metres	Speed kilometres per hour			
	5	4	3	2
1,000m	12 min	15 min	20 min	30 min
900m	11 min	13½ min	18 min	27 min
800m	9½ min	12 min	16 min	24 min
700m	18½ min	10½ min	14 min	21 min
600m	7 min	9 min	12 min	18 min
500m	6 min	7½ min	10 min	15 min
400m	5 min	6 min	8 min	12 min
300m	3½ min	4½ min	6 min	9 min
200m	2½ min	3 min	4 min	6 min
100m	1 min	1½ min	2 min	3 min
50m	½ min	¾ min	1 min	1½ min

The timings have been rounded to the nearest ½ minute

FIGURE 3.09 USING THE ROMER SCALE TO MEASURE BETWEEN TWO POINTS. IN THIS EXAMPLE THE DISTANCE MEASURED IS 650 METERS

FIGURE 3.10 SPEED/DISTANCE TRAVELLED CHART

to measure using the millimetre scale. This achieves an accuracy of 25m when using a 1:25,000 scale map.

Estimating distance on the ground is covered in the next two sections; however accuracy can only be achieved if attention is paid to measuring distances from the map. In certain circumstances a lack of concentration while measuring could give a 50m error which could mean the difference between hitting the target or missing it. Before measuring a distance try to estimate by eye as this will give some idea of what the distance should be. If a radically different distance is measured then it will force you to re-evaluate and probably measure again. A similar system is used before taking a bearing from the map to avoid any early errors (see *Taking a bearing* on page 73).

3.6 Timing

Timing is a useful way of measuring distances travelled over the ground. By estimating your speed it is possible to use a distance measured from the map and calculate how long it will take to arrive at a chosen destination. Using modern variations of the formula published by W.H. Naismith in 1892 it is possible to calculate the time required for a journey and with skilful application the distance travelled can be estimated reasonably accurately.

Naismith's formula suggests:
Average party will walk at 4kph and ascend at a rate of 10m/min

Naismith's formula takes a basic horizontal travelling speed and adapts it to undulating ground by adding time for travelling uphill. Quite simply, walkers travelling at 4 kilometres per hour on flat ground would cover 1km in fifteen minutes, or 100m in one and a half minutes. However, there are many factors that affect speed: weather, terrain, fitness and loads. In practice the situation is usually more complicated, as walking speeds vary considerably and will fluctuate throughout the day. Most parties walk at between 3 and 5 kilometres per hour; some groups and families achieve an overall average of only 2 kilometres per hour.

Heavy vegetation, boulder fields, wet rock or snow will slow even a fit party travelling with light rucksacks. Steeper ground, perhaps requiring the occasional use of the hands for support can slow a party dramatically. From this it is possible to see that it becomes difficult to apply a rigid formula to every situation. While Naismith's formula works as a planning tool for gauging the overall timing of a mountain day, it becomes less accurate when applied to shorter navigational legs. Therefore when calculating time for a single navigation task it is important to adopt a flexible approach, taking into consideration all the variables that may affect speed. Only by doing this will it be possible to achieve a high degree of accuracy. With experience, a kinaesthetic awareness of speed evolves – heart rate, leg rhythm and ease of breathing all relate to speed of travel and angle of slope. Comparing the time taken to walk set distances at different levels of effort can assist developing this 'feeling' of speed. *Figure 3.10* is an example of a crib card showing timings for various distances at different speeds. Used by many navigators, these help to reduce the need for mental arithmetic on the hill.

Timing is only effective for estimating distance if the party moves at a reasonably steady pace and any time spent stationary should be excluded from the total. A stopwatch becomes a useful item of equipment when using timing. Used carefully it will allow the navigator to constantly compare estimates with the actual time taken for each section of a journey. By doing this it is then possible to make adjustments while travelling. This is particularly important if for any reason the speed changes due to unforeseen circumstances.

When timing, try to adopt the habit of starting your stop watch as you begin to walk and pausing it when you stop moving. In doing so you only record the time taken while you are moving (which is the calculated time) and not the time that you stopped. GPS receivers can often be setup to show a range of timing displays. See *Section 2.3.10 Setting up GPS* for more details.

3.6.1 Timing ascent
Ascent of any angle of slope will influence speed to a greater or lesser extent. Generally, a minute is added for every 10 metres of ascent. When using maps with contours at 10 metre intervals it is a simple matter of adding one minute for every contour crossed in an upward direction (refer to *Figure 3.11* for *Calculation of timing on an undulating ridge*).

Adding one minute per 10 metres of height gain is not always appropriate and once again requires a flexible approach depending on the nature of the terrain. On a very steep slope it may be more accurate to use more than one minute per 10 metres and on less steep terrain it may be that 0.5 or 0.75 of a minute per 10 metres height gain is more effective.

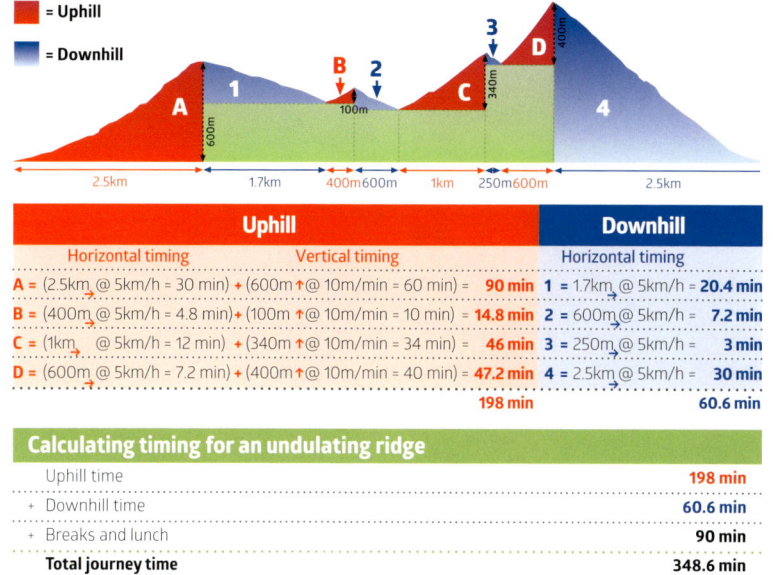

Uphill		Downhill
Horizontal timing	Vertical timing	Horizontal timing
A = (2.5km @ 5km/h = 30 min) + (600m↑@ 10m/min = 60 min) = **90 min**		1 = 1.7km @ 5km/h = **20.4 min**
B = (400m @ 5km/h = 4.8 min) + (100m↑@ 10m/min = 10 min) = **14.8 min**		2 = 600m @ 5km/h = **7.2 min**
C = (1km @ 5km/h = 12 min) + (340m↑@ 10m/min = 34 min) = **46 min**		3 = 250m @ 5km/h = **3 min**
D = (600m @ 5km/h = 7.2 min) + (400m↑@ 10m/min = 40 min) = **47.2 min**		4 = 2.5km @ 5km/h = **30 min**
	198 min	**60.6 min**

Calculating timing for an undulating ridge	
Uphill time	**198 min**
+ Downhill time	**60.6 min**
+ Breaks and lunch	**90 min**
Total journey time	**348.6 min**

FIGURE 3.11 CALCULATING TIMING FOR AN UNDULATING RIDGE

As an alternative method, when ascending it is often possible to employ a simplified formula using only the vertical distance covered, that is the number of contours. For many walkers one and a half minutes per 10 metres of ascent with no addition for distance covered is quite effective. For a lightly laden fit group this may well be reduced to one minute per 10 metres. This system works best when calculating time for steep slopes where there is little horizontal distance being covered. Once the contour lines become more spaced and the horizontal distance increases it is more accurate to adopt the previous method.

3.6.2 Timing descent

Many people assume that downhill sections can be ignored as gravity takes over, meaning it is possible to walk at a faster speed. On gentle slopes and easy paths this may well be the case. As a rule of thumb on easy ground, one minute for every 30 metres of descent can be subtracted from any timing calculations. However, speed over a downhill section can be influenced by the same set of factors that reduce speed over an uphill section meaning it can often take longer than planned to descend a section. Steep descents may require a similar amount to be added to the total time, and rocky sections can take even longer.

3.7 Pacing

Counting steps is a well-established method of estimating distance and is known as 'pacing'. Imagine walking with the feet joined by a half metre of rope: every time the left foot touches the ground, a distance of one metre will have been covered. This is the basic principle behind counting paces. Although the length of a natural stride varies, mainly according to leg length, everybody develops a stride over the course of their lives that is

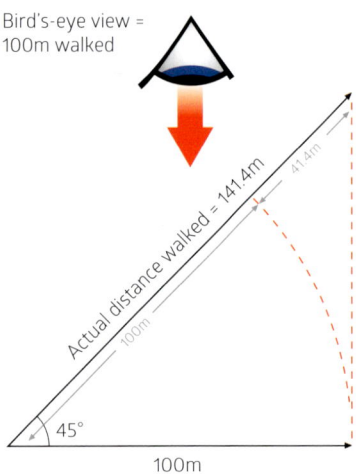

FIGURE 3.12 USING COUNTING TOGGLES WHEN PACING TO HELP KEEP TRACK OF DISTANCE COVERED

FIGURE 3.13 DISTANCE TRAVELLED UPHILL VERSUS HORIZONTAL

remarkably consistent for any given individual on level terrain as long as there are no obstacles and it is firm underfoot.

Normal practice is to measure 'double' paces, counting only when one designated foot touches the ground. To establish the counting rhythm, pacing should start by stepping forward with the other foot. Counting double paces simply keeps the numbers more manageable; the average for adults is about 64 double paces for 100 metres. Normally, pacing is used to count off 100 metre sections. This is a convenient unit of measurement; the same unit is used in 6-figure grid references. One hundred metres is long enough to allow a natural walking rhythm to be established, but short enough to sort out any errors without resorting to lengthy back-tracking.

There are various reminders available for keeping count of multiples of 100 metres travelled. One simple method is to pick up some pebbles and transfer them one at a time to another pocket or hand.

A useful customisation is to fix five plastic draw-cord toggles on the compass lanyard or even a separate cord attached to a rucksack shoulder strap. From a central starting point these can be slid individually to one end of the lanyard every 100 metres for the first half kilometre, and back to the other end for the next. An extra refinement is to use alternating colours to aid visual identification. If the compass lanyard is used, check that any springs in the draw-clips do not cause the compass needle to deviate from north!

Alternatively, there are various electronic pedometers available that record the number of steps taken and the distance covered. These vary in reliability and accuracy, with some prone to freezing in cold conditions.

....

Pacing, as with timing, can be taught and practised anywhere, but initially a track with clear tick-off features conveniently spaced allows the technique to be matched to the map. Alternatively, 100 metres can be measured out in various types of terrain to compare variations; a 50-metre rope makes an effective tape measure.

....

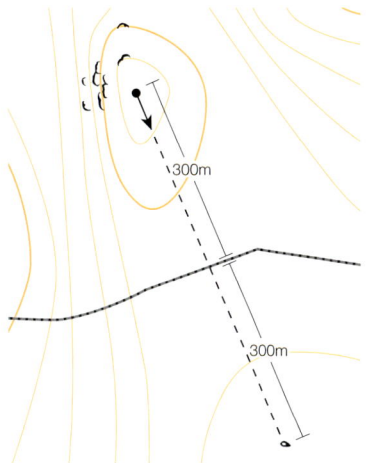

Double paces per 100m	Conditions underfoot		
	Good	**Moderate**	**Poor**
Flat	60	70	90
Uphill	80	100	120
Downhill	85	70	90

FIGURE 3.15 AS EVERYONE WALKS DIFFERENTLY AND HAS A DIFFERENT STRIDE LENGTH THESE FIGURES CAN ONLY EVER BE AN EXAMPLE. WITH A LITTLE PRACTICE ON A VARIETY OF TERRAIN IT WILL BE POSSIBLE TO CONSTRUCT A SIMILAR TABLE TO HELP WHEN USING PACING

FIGURE 3.14 AN OBVIOUS HALFWAY FEATURE PROVIDES A USEFUL CHECK WHEN MEASURING DISTANCE

FIGURE 3.16 STEEP COMPLEX TERRAIN MORE SUITED TO TIMING THAN PACING WHEN COVERING LONG DISTANCES

Pacing is not an exact science since the length of stride varies with many factors. Wearing a heavy rucksack will result in shorter strides, as will terrain demanding more care in foot placement. Wet conditions, rocky ground, coarse vegetation and snow are factors that will significantly increase the amount of paces needed to cover a set distance.

Pacing is dramatically affected by slope angle. When measuring ascending slopes from the map it is worth remembering that any distance measured is only a two dimensional representation of the slope and on the ground this distance will be greater. The third dimension of height results in greater distances being covered than the simple measurement on the map. For example, take a distance marked as 100 metres on the map; on a 45° slope you would have to walk 140 metres to cover the distance measured. It is also important to consider that it may not be possible to walk straight up a slope.

Pacing uphill is further complicated by the need to take smaller steps and can also be exaggerated by rocky or eroded ground. Detours may have to be used to avoid hazards or zigzagging may be required to reduce the angle of the slope to make walking easier. Either way it will increase the amount of distance covered and therefore the amount of paces. It is quite common to double the number of paces required to cover the 100 metres marked on the map. The ability to make suitable allowances comes with practice and requires a flexible approach to modify the number of paces totalled as the terrain changes. On long slopes it may be more appropriate and accurate to consider using timing over pacing, especially if the ground is complex requiring deviations from a straight course.

In practice it is often possible to customise your pacing to a particular situation and therefore easily make it more accurate. In *Figure 3.14* the distance from the top to the ruined fence is almost identical to the distance from the ruined fence to the boulder and as it covers similar terrain you can just count your paces to the fence and then repeat the same number of paces to find the boulder.

In descent, gentle slopes may allow striding out with bigger steps, thus reducing the number of double paces required to cover 100 metres. However, complex ground will require more careful foot placements and thus extra paces. It is worth stressing that the greater the distance paced between two points, the greater the potential error. Greater accuracy can be achieved over shorter distances. As a general rule 500 metres is an optimum distance although this will be dependent on terrain and conditions.

3.8 Choosing the right techniques

Experience allows the navigator to adjust distance estimation constantly by monitoring the ease or difficulty of progress. In good visibility, it is often possible to gain sufficient information by spotting the tick-off features and estimating the distances between them. Conditions and the composition of the party will influence the selection of the most appropriate technique for estimating distance.

Accurate judgement of distance travelled becomes particularly important when navigating through featureless terrain, where direction and distance become essential elements in navigating by dead reckoning, that is calculating location by estimating the distance travelled from a known point on a bearing.

....

Counting paces is particularly effective as a navigational tool in poor visibility but destroys the navigator's ability to converse. A leader may well choose to delegate this task to other members of the party and perhaps get somebody else to keep a running total of multiples of 100 metres. This requires considerable skill from these individuals and may require further coaching in how to make suitable adjustments when crossing varied terrain. In certain situations it may be easier to let someone else manage the group and for you to take responsibility for the navigation. Practise before you really need it.

....

Timing is often used for 'rough' navigation in easier conditions. For example, if a party has walked for ten minutes along a linear feature on flat ground, it is simple to estimate their position as within 600–900 metres of the starting point. Experienced walkers maintaining an even pace can estimate distance using timing alone and achieve much greater accuracy. A reasonable target for a walker travelling at a known speed is to be within 10% of the actual figure. Timing can be of limited use when an individual or group is constantly stopping for rests or crossing obstacles, although attentive use of a stopwatch can counteract this problem.

In very difficult conditions, a combination of all the methods listed above allows the maximum information to assist navigation. If the timing

(i) **9** Pacing and timing

Becoming competent with these skills takes time and practice. People need to be given the opportunity to use these tools in a variety of settings to build a good understanding of how best to apply them. Being able to measure a distance from the map is the first skill required. While it is important to be realistic about the 'accuracy' of a measurement, people should understand that if they cannot measure distances from the map they can never hope to be accurate when measuring on the ground.

Exercises:

Guess the distance: pick a variety of points on the map and get students to guess the distances between them. This is good practice in any case to reduce the risk of error due to mistaken use of the wrong scale (surprisingly common!)

Track calibration: pacing of 100 metres can be calibrated using a set distance on a good flat surface such as a track or road.

Vary the surface: once the person has set their paces to 100 metres, they should be given the opportunity to discover how this may vary in different terrain.

GPS: a GPS unit can be used to check both pacing and timing plus give an indication of walking speed at a particular time. This feedback can help people to build a kinaesthetic awareness of their speed.

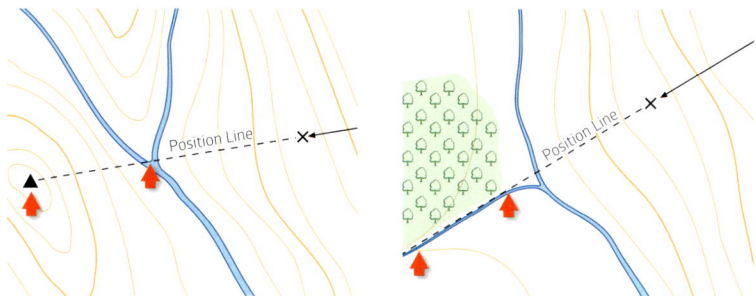

FIGURE 3.17 USING SPOT AND LINE FEATURES TO PROVIDE TRANSIT POINTS

suggests that pacing is leading to over-estimating distance then unless the party has sped up dramatically, the number of double paces representing 100 metres should be increased for similar conditions. If the pacing and timing are in agreement, then the unexpected appearance of a feature will not faze the navigator.

Leaders can easily get a feel for the walking speed of their group by timing some simple legs at the start of the day. Speeds can be calculated over a measured distance and used as a reference when using timing at a later stage in the journey. Being able to judge how long a group will take to complete a particular route is a basic mountain leadership skill. These judgements should be used to plan the day but more importantly to adapt the route during the day so that the route covered matches the group's ability.

3.9 Judging direction

A navigational bearing is the measured angle of the line between two objects; usually from where we are now to where we want to go. Following the bearing means tracing a line on the ground that follows this angle. It can be regarded as a 'virtual' linear feature.

3.9.1 Transit points

In good visibility it is often possible to identify two features that are in line with each other, for example a building or a boulder or perhaps a distant wall running towards the observer. Only moving directly towards or away from these two features will keep them in line; otherwise, they will begin to drift apart visually. This is a simple and effective method of walking accurately in a straight line when following a bearing.

3.9.2 Using a compass

A compass can be used to measure bearings and transfer them between

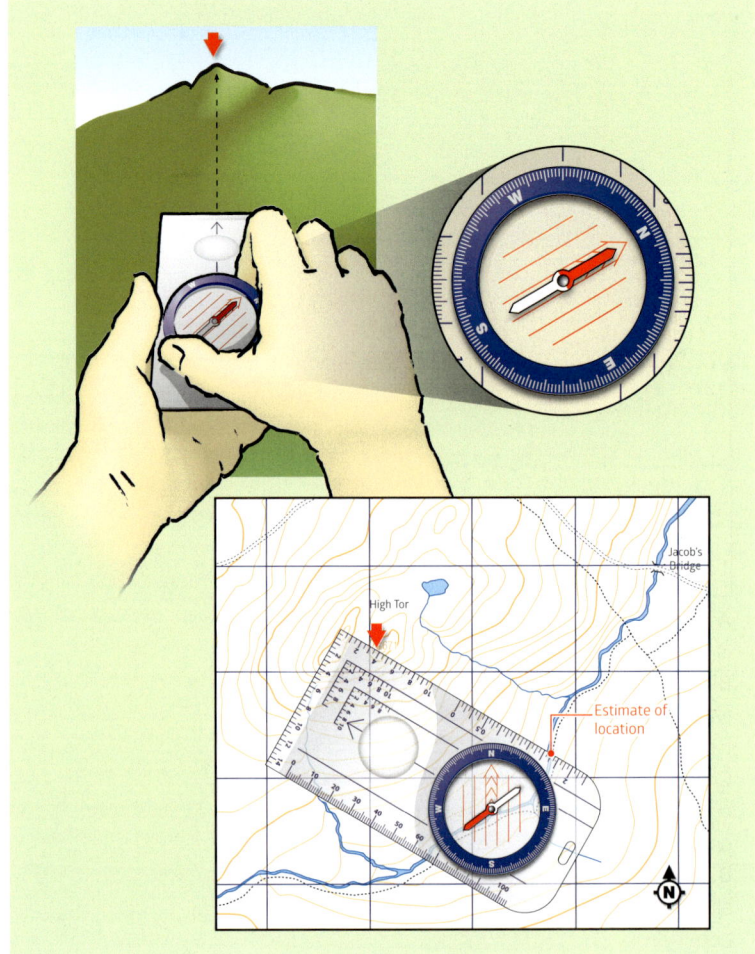

FIGURE 3.18 SIGHTING A BEARING AND USING THE INFORMATION TO ESTIMATE LOCATION

the map and the ground. It can also be used to follow a bearing and is particularly useful when poor visibility obscures natural transit points.

Taking a bearing from the ground

Taking a bearing from the ground has many applications and is particularly good for gaining information about the direction and aspect of features. It is possible to use sighted bearings to work out the direction of a path, the flow of a stream and the direction a slope faces. It is often possible to transfer the bearing back to the map to help confirm a position or hypothesis.

Taking a bearing from the map

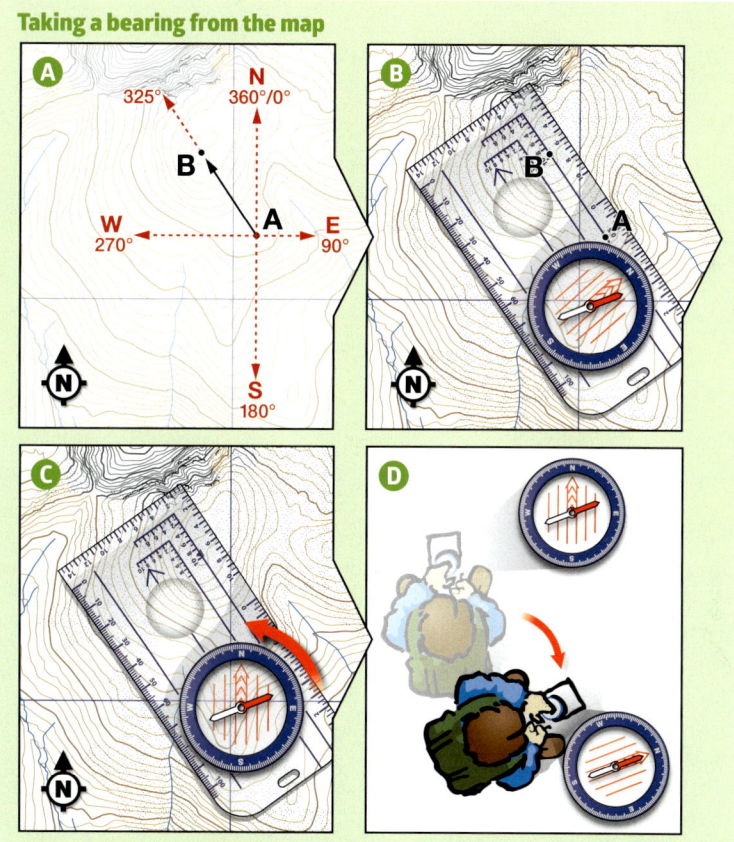

A Estimate the angle (grid bearing). Travelling from **A** to **B**, the angle is just over half way between 270° and 360° – roughly 320° to 330°.

B Using a line on the baseplate, link points **A** (where you are) and **B** (your intended destination) with the direction of travel arrow pointing from **A** to **B**.

C Rotate the compass housing to align the orienting lines with the north—South grid lines on the map, with the orienting arrow pointing north. Rotate the compass housing to compensate for magnetic variation.

D Remove the compass from the map and rotate the entire compass to align the north (red) end of the needle and the orienting arrow. Keeping both needle and arrow aligned, follow the direction of travel arrow.

FIGURE 3.19 USING A COMPASS TO SIGHT A BEARING   *PHOTO // STEVE LONG*

To take a sighting bearing simply hold the compass horizontal and point the direction of travel arrow toward the subject; either along it in the case of a linear feature, or straight at it in the case of a spot feature. Once fixed on a subject, without moving the base plate, rotate the compass housing until the orienting arrow is directly underneath the needle (see *Figure 3.18*). A bearing can then be read from the index line. This inform-ation can then be compared to the map, or if greater accuracy is required it can be converted to a grid bearing by making allowance for the magnetic variation before transferring onto the map.

Sighted bearings can also be of use when the visibility is constantly changing. You may catch a glimpse of the way ahead or a sight of some feature which you can identify on the map. By taking a quick bearing it could provide information to help confirm position or line of travel.

3.9.3 Following a bearing

Featureless terrain and poor visibility are common aspects of hill walking in the British Isles. The ability to follow a compass bearing accurately is therefore essential when landmarks are not visible. Once a magnetic bearing has been obtained the compass is then held with both hands immediately in front of the navigator's navel[1] with the *direction of travel* arrow pointing straight ahead. By locking elbows into the sides of the body it ensures the compass is maintained in a horizontal plane so that the needle can rotate freely. The navigator then rotates on the spot with the compass until the north (usually red) end of the magnetic needle

1 Some *sighting* compasses are designed to allow the needle to be kept orientated accurately while sighting at eye rather than waist level. These can allow very accurate bearings to be taken, but this method should only be used with these specialised compasses.

FIGURE 3.20 FOLLOWING A BEARING IN MISTY CONDITIONS   *PHOTO // STEVE LONG*

floats over the *orienting arrow* on the compass housing. At this stage, the compass has been 'set' and the direction of travel arrow points along the bearing. Make sure the compass housing is not moved accidentally when holding or moving the compass as this will change the bearing.

To walk along a bearing, the navigator sights along the direction of travel arrow towards a fixed object that is located on the bearing line. This is why the compass should be pointing straight ahead from the body, minimising any tendency to make an inaccurate sighting. Ideally the object should lie somewhere in the middle distance as objects on the far horizon may disappear in the mist or become hidden by intervening undulations. Having fixed on an object it may now be possible to put the compass away and walk to it via the most appropriate route. This will avoid having to walk in a straight line with the compass set although for certain situations (fog, darkness, white out) this is an essential skill to develop.

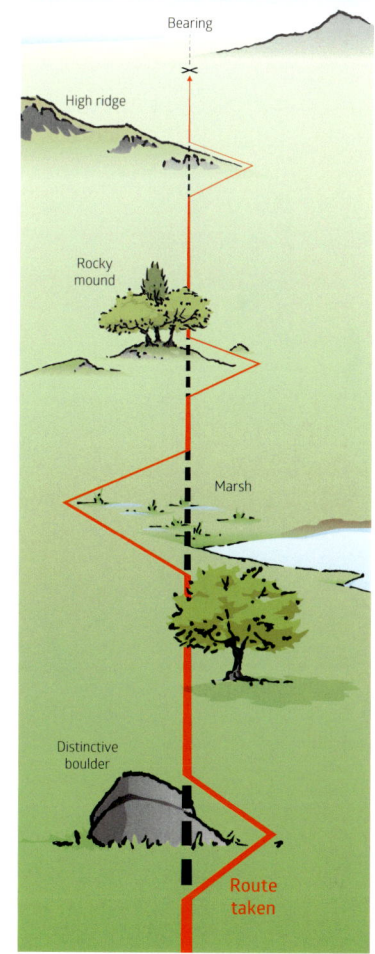

Bearing

High ridge

Rocky mound

Marsh

Distinctive boulder

Route taken

FIGURE 3.21 'DOG LEG DETOURS'

10 Walking on a bearing

Being able to walk on a bearing and hold a straight line across a variety of terrain can be challenging for the novice navigator. Initially these skills can be introduced in easy terrain, even a park or playing field will suffice. However if people are to become truly proficient at this skill, then proper contextual practice is necessary. As well as using bearings to help navigate to points these skills can also be practised in isolation. The following exercises require a safe area of terrain to operate on.

Exercise: *Star burst:* from a central point group members are sent out on a bearing for a set distance to leave a marker, for example their rucksack. On return to the central point they then swap the information with another person to then go and retrieve that person's marker. Extended star burst: as for above; however the person sent out to retrieve the marker now moves it to a new location using a different bearing and distance. On return to the central point the information is swapped and the marker is then retrieved by having to navigate a 'dog-leg'. This can be extended further to include more legs, provided all the information can be remembered. *Searches:* if markers are lost from the above exercises, search techniques could be introduced to find them. In the case of a spiral search using compass bearings and distances, this will help to reinforce these skills.

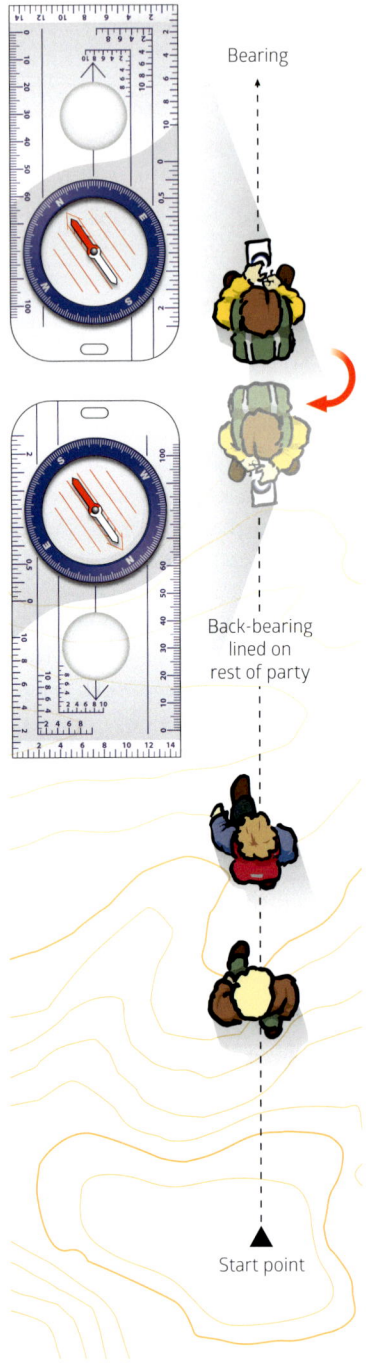

Bearing

Back-bearing lined on rest of party

Start point

FIGURE 3.22 TAKING A BACK-BEARING

Having identified an object that lies on the bearing, the navigator heads towards it. Shortly before reaching it, the object can be used to sight through to another target and continue the process. With practice it is possible to re-sight the bearing on a new object by merely slowing down, reducing the need for prolonged stops or compromising any distance estimation (timing or pacing). Heading towards an identifiable object while en route also allows detours to be made, avoiding obstructions or hazards such as boggy or craggy ground. This can be done without losing track of the bearing or having to make complicated adjustments. (see *Figure 3.21*)

In very misty conditions, it can be difficult to find suitable objects for sighting ahead. A technique used by some navigators is to send members of their party out in front to act as sighting points. This usually requires signalling for communication and is very time consuming. In addition, the stop-start nature of this technique invariably leads to inaccuracies and furthermore, splitting up in this way may well compromise safety. However, it is very rare for no identifiable natural objects to be visible; even snow tends to have identifiable bumps and marks. Following a bearing in exceptionally poor visibility requires great concentration but it is possible to achieve without splitting the party. Careful attention must be paid to subtle variations of the ground within the field of vision, lining them up with the direction of travel arrow. A navigator should develop this skill to a high standard.

3.9.4 Back-bearings
Taking a bearing back along the route already travelled can often allow the direction of travel to be checked. This is a simple matter if the starting point can still be seen, but even in poor visibility, a back bearing can often be taken by aiming back along the other members of the party. The simplest way of obtaining a back-bearing is to rotate the compass so that the south end of the magnetic needle floats over the north end of the orienting arrow on the compass housing. It is also possible to add or subtract 180 degrees from the bearing and alter the housing, but this is usually unnecessary work and more likely to lead to error. If drifting from the correct line has occurred, it may be possible to solve by turning at right angles and walking until the back-bearing has returned to the correct line. (see *Section 3.9.7 Boxing*)

3.9.5 Slope aspect and shape
Observing changes in the angle and direction of the slope as a route is travelled is a useful skill to acquire, particularly when walking in featureless terrain. Often in these situations it is the shape of the ground and the direction it faces that provides the most useful information to help pinpoint a location. The direction a slope faces is referred to as its aspect and can often provide a vital clue when trying to relocate.

Slope aspect can be measured accurately by taking a bearing straight down the fall line – in other words the line down which a rolling stone would travel. In poor visibility, care should be taken to check that this

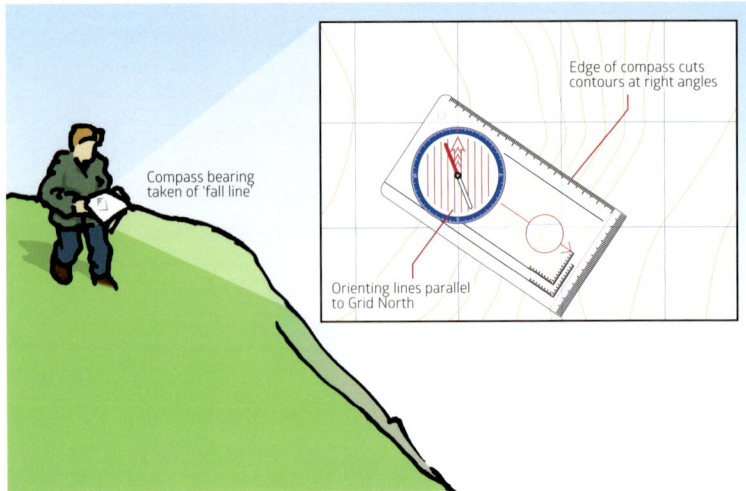

Compass bearing
taken of 'fall line'

Edge of compass cuts
contours at right angles

Orienting lines parallel
to Grid North

FIGURE 3.23 COMPASS AND MAP: SLOPE ASPECT

is the main slope and not a small basin confusing the overall picture. The magnetic bearing shown will instantly give an idea of which way the slope is facing. For example, a bearing of 315° will mean it is a North West facing slope. This may be all that is required to confirm a location, however greater accuracy can be achieved by transferring this bearing to the map. After making the appropriate adjustment to the bearing from magnetic to Grid North, the compass is placed on the map and rotated until the orienting lines on the compass housing are parallel to the vertical grid lines. The compass can now be moved over the map, maintaining the same orientation. The edge of the compass will cross through the contours at right angles on any slopes with the same aspect – all other slopes are eliminated. If there is already a rough idea of location this information might provide a more accurate fix.

3.9.6 Aiming off

Drifting off from a bearing by as little as 5 degrees will lead to an error of nearly 50 metres after walking only half a kilometre. This is a good reason for keeping navigational 'legs' relatively short, but also means that trying to walk on a bearing straight to a point feature such as a bothy is quite optimistic in thick mist.

Imagine trying to journey through featureless terrain in dense mist with the hope of finding a bridge over a stream. As long as the bearing cuts across the stream, it will not be very hard to find this line feature: but if the bridge is not visible, should the party turn upstream or downstream? Aiming off is a classic navigational technique, which will eliminate this quandary. The party deliberately sets a bearing a few degrees to the side of the bridge – usually uphill if descending, then turns downhill upon reaching the stream, using it as a 'handrail' to reach the bridge. The uphill deviation is used to prevent dropping down too low and then having to regain height to find the destination. This technique is particularly useful for finding junctions or other points located on linear features.

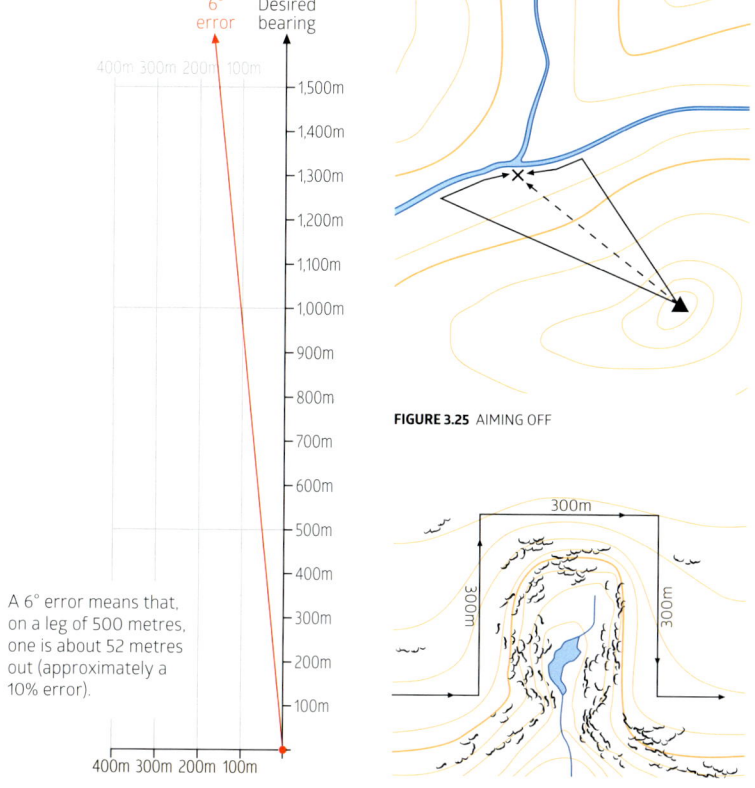

6°
error

Desired
bearing

400m 300m 200m 100m

1,500m
1,400m
1,300m
1,200m
1,100m
1,000m
900m
800m
700m
600m
500m
400m
300m
200m
100m

A 6° error means that,
on a leg of 500 metres,
one is about 52 metres
out (approximately a
10% error).

400m 300m 200m 100m

FIGURE 3.24 EFFECT OF A 6° ERROR

FIGURE 3.25 AIMING OFF

300m

300m

300m

FIGURE 3.26 BOXING AROUND AN OBSTACLE

3.9.7 Boxing

Sometimes when following a bearing it is necessary to make a detour around an unexpected obstruction that you cannot see the far side of, for example an unmarked enclosure, boggy ground or escarpment. It may be possible to make a series of turns around the object in order to get back in line with the bearing. This technique, known as boxing, is simplest when 90° turns are made.

The first step is to turn at right angles from the bearing, until the magnetic needle aligns with the East/West markings on the compass (according to the direction turned). The direction of travel arrow now shows a bearing at right angles, without having to make any calculations. This bearing is followed, while measuring distance until beyond the obstacle. The original bearing is then followed until it is possible to turn back beyond the other side of the obstacle. The navigator turns to move back towards the original line of travel, until the magnetic needle points to West or East (the opposite of the previous detour). This is followed for the same distance as the detour and thus the original line is reached, having followed three sides of a square – only the side that is parallel to the original bearing should be included in the total reckoning of distance travelled.

Whenever possible, a box with sides that are parallel or at right angles to the slope will make it easier to keep on course.

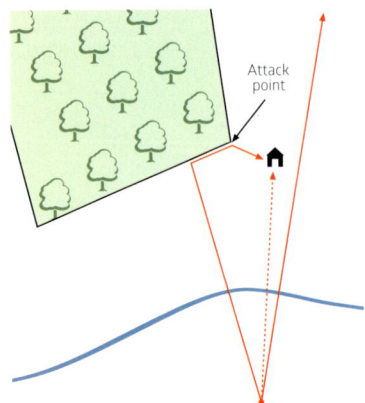

Attack
point

FIGURE 3.27 USING AN ATTACK POINT

3.9.8 Attack points

A useful technique in any conditions for seeking a poorly defined feature is to identify something clearly distinguishable within a few hundred metres of it. Having located this *attack point*, a more cautious systematic approach can be used to pinpoint the required feature. This is often described as using two different styles; 'rough navigation' to locate the attack point, and 'fine navigation' to find the actual feature.

For example, in poor visibility it might be necessary to locate a sheep-fold for shelter. In open moorland this would be a difficult task but with a clear feature 200 metres away, such as a large lake, it might be possible to use rough navigation to find the lake and then fine detail navigation for the final 200 metres. It is important to choose an attack point that can be found using rough navigation otherwise no benefit is achieved. In the same way 'reverse' attack points can be useful; when you are leaving a known point and want to head off in a particular direction you can use an attack point to check that you are walking on the right bearing.

3.10 Navigational strategy

An effective navigator will make many strategic decisions in the course of a journey. Navigating in good visibility will usually be very different to navigation through difficult terrain in poor visibility. When conditions are challenging navigation can be stressful with a real possibility of missing vital pieces of information. In these situations it is easy to become focused on one particular technique to the detriment of others. For example in poor visibility concentration may be so focused on taking a bearing that hazards, distance, tick-off and catching features are overlooked. A good strategy in any situation will bring together the most appropriate set of skills and techniques to solve any particular navigation problem and help to avoid any oversights. A check list can help ensure nothing is overlooked and the following two examples can be employed in any situation. By answering these questions the risk of forgetting vital pieces of information are reduced.

3.10.1 The 5 Ds
1 Distance How far to the intended destination?
2 Direction Which direction will you need to head in?
3 Description What are the tick-off features and catching features en route, and what does the destination look like?
4 Duration How long will this leg take?
5 Dangers Are there any potential hazards en route?

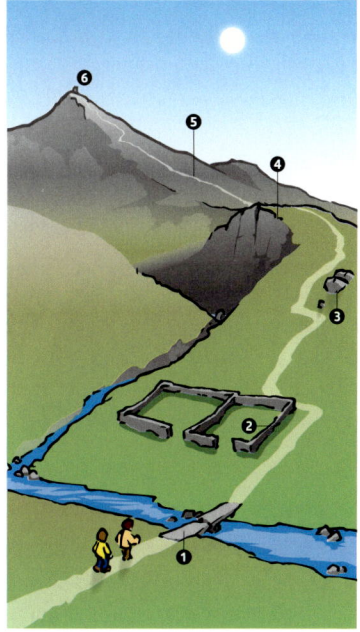

The enclosure wall (**1**) and the river (**2**); the copse (**3**) and the escarpment (**4**) and finally the valley itself (**5**) all guide the walker onto the path, making them useful funnel features.

FIGURE 3.28 HANDRAILS AND TICKS *(LEFT)*

FIGURE 3.29 FUNNEL FEATURES *(ABOVE)*

Handrails and tick features cross the bridge (**1** Tick), then follow the edge of the enclosure (**2** Handrail), strike out for the boulders (**3** Tick), and follow the top of the escarpment (**4** Handrail). Ascend the ridge (**5** Handrail) to reach the trig point on the summit (**6** Tick).

The benefits of using a checklist or aide memoir are particularly important to less experienced navigators and anyone operating in challenging conditions.

3.10.2 Breaking a route into sections

Dividing a long navigational leg into more manageable sections is a common technique for navigators to employ. Often in poor visibility, this will necessitate 'micro-navigation', that is moving from one small feature to another, relying on detail that would probably not be needed if conditions were clear. This is an important skill for navigators to develop to a high standard of accuracy if all-weather route finding is to be achieved.

Navigational requirements in difficult conditions often affect the choice of route. Sometimes a direct line to a destination takes the party through vague, indistinct terrain, whereas a circuitous route can link several identifiable features, allowing regular confirmation. Choosing a route that crosses or passes several features allows more than one opportunity to confirm that things are on course. Regular checks allow warning signals to be picked up rapidly if a mistake is made, helping to minimise the distance covered in the wrong direction. It may be also possible to link two sections together using funnel or corridor features, such as valleys, converging crags or walls. These form a natural boundary which leads the navigator naturally to a chosen point.

3.11 Relocation

Even the best navigators will experience moments of uncertainty in difficult conditions, possibly forgetting the number of paces or losing concentration at the wrong time. But many are able to relocate quickly enough so that their mistakes cost them seconds rather than minutes or hours! Continuing 'blindly' can easily compound the problem, so it is always best to stop and evaluate the situation and have a positive strategy for finding yourself.

3.11.1 Calm down!

Getting lost can be an unpleasant feeling and so the first job is to calm yourself down and make sure you are capable of rational decision making! Quite often people are not completely lost, they might not know exactly where they are or how to get back to their original route but often they can find a safe way off the hill or even retrace their steps. A good way to calm down and regain control is to simply describe out loud what can be seen, "I can see a stone wall, it is in a North South direction, etc".

3.11.2 Gather information

The first stage in relocation is to collect all the available information. Initially this should be done with a thorough inspection of the surrounding area. It is common for people to over examine the map and to neglect the wealth of information that can be gained from their surroundings. A creative mind can make any point on the map fit with their current location! However it is only the information gained from your surroundings that will help to confirm where you are; so look around before consulting the map.

- How much time has elapsed since leaving the last known point? How certain was that location? Answering these questions allows the present location to be narrowed down to an area based on your travel speed.
- Were there distinctive features, slope angles and aspects passed on route? This information can be plotted on the map to further narrow down the likely location.
- If walking along or close to a linear feature such as a wall or stream, a bearing can be taken along it and compared with the map. A sharp bend is particularly useful, as the shape of the bend and bearings on either side give additional information.
- What is the current slope aspect and angle? This information effectively rules out most of the map, as long as a local hollow is not mistaken for the main slope.
- If any identifiable features are visible, a bearing can be taken and plotted on the map (remembering to make any adjustments for magnetic

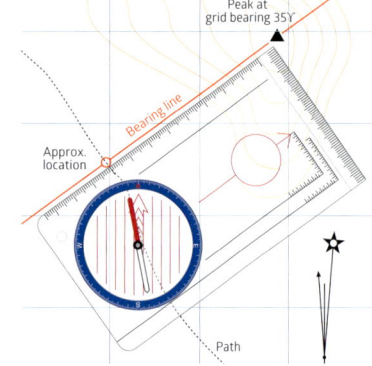

FIGURE 3.30 PINPOINTING POSITION ALONG A LINEAR FEATURE

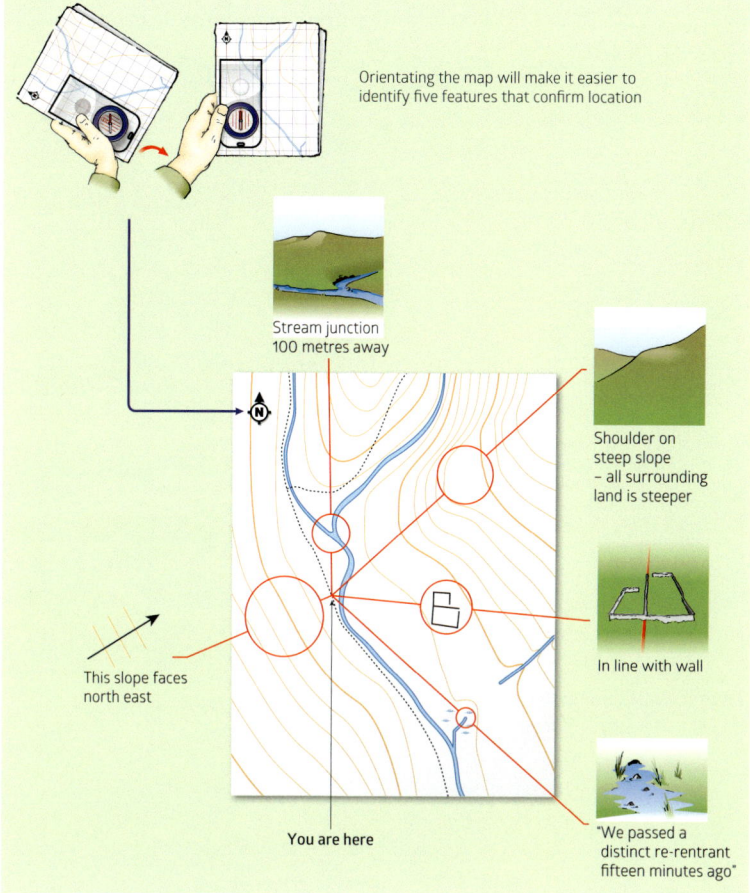

Orientating the map will make it easier to identify five features that confirm location

Stream junction 100 metres away

Shoulder on steep slope – all surrounding land is steeper

In line with wall

This slope faces north east

You are here

"We passed a distinct re-rentrant fifteen minutes ago"

FIGURE 3.31 FIVE FEATURES CONFIRMING LOCATION

variation). Two or more features, preferably on bearings at about right angles to each other, allow the location to be narrowed down to an area around the intersecting lines in a technique known as resection. However, competent navigators rarely need to relocate when several landmarks are so clearly visible. Sometimes location along a linear feature such as a wall, ridge or even contour line can be pinpointed by taking a bearing on a spot feature and noting where the bearing crosses the line feature on the map.

- Seek out five features around you that confirm your position on the map.
- Using a GPS device or altimeter can provide very accurate information (see *Sections 2.3 and 2.4 GPS and Altimeters*).

Once all possible information has been gathered it is important to place more emphasis on that which you believe to be most accurate and reliable. If visibility is poor due to weather conditions or undulating terrain then it may be necessary to move location or use the technique of *mapping* to gather sufficient information.

The process of relocation

Trying to locate your position in unfamiliar terrain can be a difficult business. It is often small pieces of information that can be easily overlooked that will confirm the correct position. Using a simple checklist in these situations will mean information is gathered in a systematic way.

1 What did I see on the way?
Consider the following:
- **Distance** from last known point
- **Direction** from last known point
- **Terrain** covered since last known point
- Major tick off features encountered

2 What can I see around me?
Gather information from surroundings. Try to work from ground to map first. Seek out at least **five features** around you. (*Section 3.11.2* and *Figure 3.31*)

3 What can I see if I walk further?
Walk around the location as this can often provide more information. In poor visibility you will need to use a structured approach such as **Mapping** or **Searches** (*Section 3.11.3* and *3.11.6*) Beware of potential hazards in this situation, they are easy to overlook when attention is elsewhere.

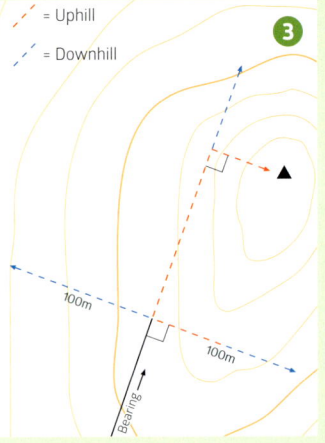

= Uphill

= Downhill

100m

100m

Bearing

4 What other techniques can be used to give more information?
Consider using the following techniques if conditions allow
- **Aspect of slope** (*Section 3.9.5*)
- **Back bearings** (*Section 3.9.4*)
- **Resection** (*Section 3.11.4*)

5 What if I cannot relocate?
It may be possible to head to an obvious feature seen from your location that can be identified on the map. Your **catching feature** could be used in this situation. (*Section 3.3 Following linear features*) If all else fails you should retrace your steps to the last confirmed location.

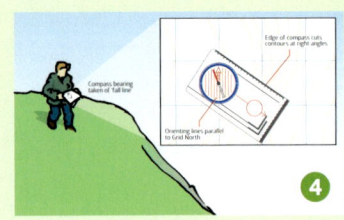

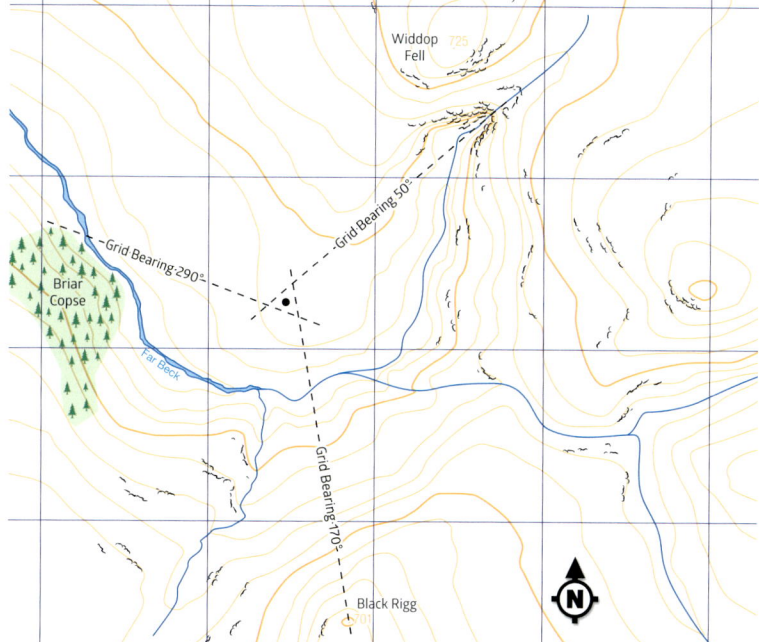

FIGURE 3.32 DIAGRAM SHOWING A RESECTION

3.11.3 Mapping

Sometimes it can be very difficult to form a mental picture of the surrounding land in poor visibility. In these circumstances, it is possible to map the area by walking a measured distance at 90° to the direction of travel, then returning to the starting point. On the way slope, aspect and shape are noted, along with any features passed. This allows information to be collected quickly and systematically, without needing to split up the party. An excursion in the opposite direction can also be made if necessary. As information is gathered it can be transferred to the map to help establish the location.

3.11.4 Resection

Resection is a fairly time consuming procedure, and many would argue that if you can see clearly identifiable features then you are unlikely to have to use such a method to pin point your location. This is true to some extent; however it does have its place in certain circumstances. When navigating in featureless terrain such as open moorland or snow covered plateaus pin pointing a location can be tricky even on a clear day. In these situations you will roughly know where you are and in the absence of any other information resection may provide a more detailed idea of your location. The procedure relies on being able to definitely identify at least two or preferably three features. These features should be identifiable within the landscape and also appear on the map. The greater the angle between these points respective to your position the greater the level of accuracy that can be achieved in determining your location. By taking a compass bearing to each feature and converting them to grid bearings it is possible to plot them onto the map (see *Figure 3.18* and refer to page *74* on *Sighting a bearing*). Depending on the accuracy of the bearings there will be a small triangle created where the lines intersect. Your position will be somewhere in this region and by using other information it may now be possible to pin point the location.

3.11.5 Plan of action
Having collated all the available information, it is now possible to formulate a plan of action.

* It may now be possible to continue along a route, checking that the landform continues to match the map. If it does not, the party should stop immediately and relocate, using the techniques described above
* It may be possible to continue towards a clear bounding feature such as a road or ridge that will allow simpler relocation, assuming there are no serious obstacles in the way
* It may be necessary to retrace the party's steps to the last identifiable point and recommence from there

If none of these options is possible it may be necessary to extend 'mapping' operations until sufficient information is found to allow the probable location to be determined. A series of excursions based on right angles from a particular bearing allows information to be gathered without straying even further from known ground.

3.11.6 Searches
Isolated features such as cairns on flat summits are notoriously difficult to find in poor visibility. Strategic use of party members can reduce the likelihood of passing the feature without spotting it. Party organisation is an essential pre-requisite for systematic searches both in terms of effectiveness and safety. The co-ordinator must ensure that all members understand their role and remain within communication range throughout the exercise. These methods are not suitable for crossing areas with craggy ground or similar hazards.

3.11.7 Sweep search
This classic search technique adapts very well to seeking point features, for example a cairn or bothy. The party spreads out at right angles across the direction of travel and for the sake of effective communication the co-ordinator is probably best placed in the centre. The spacing between each group member can be varied according to the visibility but for safety, it is best for each to remain within the range of vision of the next person.

A sweep search requires careful leadership to retain party cohesiveness. All members should maintain a similar speed, so broken or craggy ground makes supervision particularly difficult. A communication system is best discussed before commencing the search; ensuring that any message is

FIGURE 3.33 A SWEEP SEARCH *PHOTO // CARLO FORTE*

passed all the way along the line. If the line begins to break up, the leader should reorganise the party before communication is compromised. The party reconvenes when the feature is found or the leader calls a halt (when it is felt that the party has overshot its objective). In the latter case, the group can be moved sideways and a new search started on the back bearing.

3.11.8 Outriggers

A variation of the sweep search can be used to ascertain slope angle and aspect in poor visibility, when it is possible to distinguish

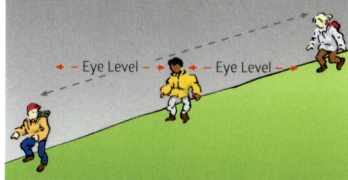

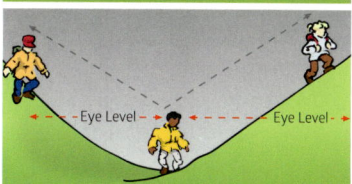

FIGURE 3.34 USING OUTRIGGERS

shapes but not see any horizons. The search method is unchanged but by watching the relative height of party members on either side it is possible to observe the landform around the searchers. This technique works best with party members of similar height and can be particularly effective at night using head-torches. With practice, this method can assist in finding quite subtle variations in slope.

Putting it together

Having looked at all the skills and techniques it is important to see how they might fit together so as to navigate safely between two points. The example below shows how you might navigate from point **A** to **B** in good visibility.

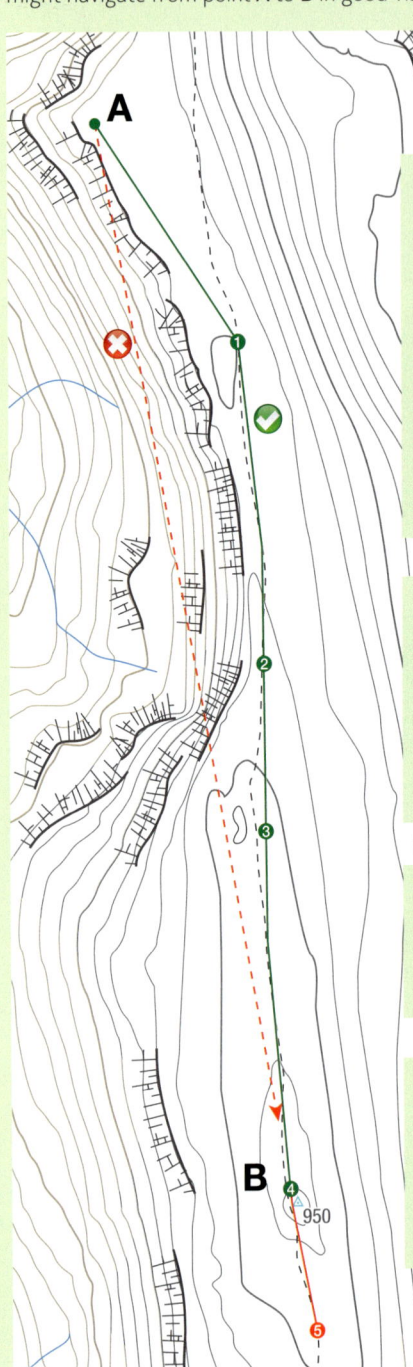

Set the map and confirm your current location. Select a suitable navigation target; Trig point 950m. Can you see this from your current location? If so you may be able to walk there by just using the ground in front of you to route find to the destination. Assess the weather/visibility and terrain. Work through '5 Ds' to gain information about the route. With good visibility it is now possible to walk the route keeping track of the ground and features identified between the two points.

From the start walk 500m across flat ground rising slightly (10m max) to first feature. **1** **Ring contour.** To continue note the slight change in direction and descend no more than 10m (one contour) following ridge with steep ground to the West and broad convex slope to the East.

2 After a further 400m ground rises gently, the ridge also broadens to the West as the crag line turns away. **3** Continue to climb gently passing a **small ring contour**.

4 Reach trig point, set map and confirm destination by mentally working back through strategy and indentifying the features surrounding location; ground descending on all sides. **5** The **catching feature** of descending ground can also be used to confirm destination.

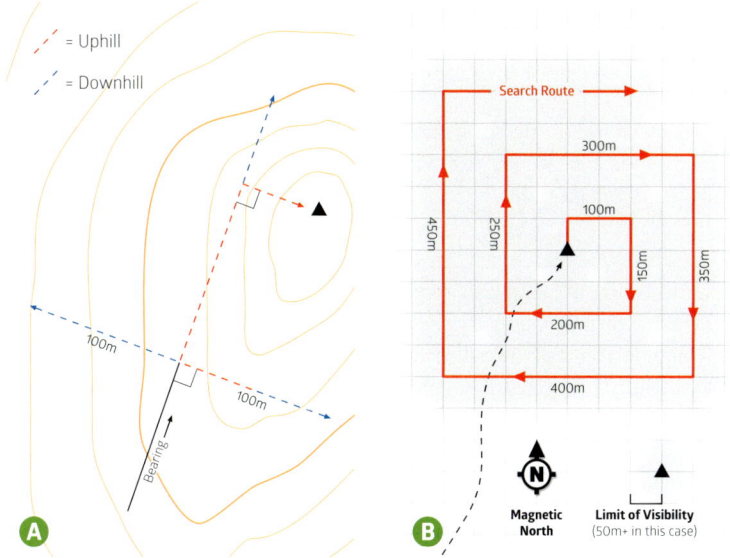

FIGURE 3.35 'MAPPING' THE LAND **A** AND A SPIRAL SEARCH **B** TO FIND A FEATURE

3.11.9 Other searches

Some navigators advocate a spiral of expanding right-angled turns walking multiples of the limit of visibility. This allows an exhaustive search but it is time consuming and it can make it difficult to return to the starting point. The technique involves walking two sides of a square with sides of 100 metres (if the visibility is 50 metres), followed by the next two sides at 150 metres, and the next two at 200 metres. This allows any objects within 50 metres of the line of travel (i.e. the limit of visibility) to be spotted.

3.12 Navigating with GPS in the mountains

For mountain navigation, GPS unit technology came of age when the displays began to include full-colour mapping. These models behave like a (tiny) map with a marker showing the unit's current location and the track it has taken. The main limiting factors are screen size and battery life, and it is likely that these will continue to develop, although price remains another factor. Smartphones and tablets can also be used as digital maps with a 'live' location marker, but are less reliable, much less rugged and only available with touchscreen controls. GPS becomes an even more powerful tool when used in conjunction with other navigation skills, map, compass and observation, and in any case should not be regarded as a substitute for them.

The mapping style of GPS unit can be used in many ways, the simplest being as a 'live' map giving reasonably accurate feedback of location. A good navigator will continue to monitor the landscape and double-check the accuracy, but the location marker is remarkably comforting. However, as with any location data gathered from satellites rather than environment, over-reliance can lead the unwary walker into a navigational cul-de-sac that might only be escaped by using the classic relocation techniques described above. The tiny screen makes it much harder to retain awareness of the wider surroundings than with a printed map although judicious use of the zoom controls can help.

Contrasting a map display with a numerical read-out is rather like comparing a '*Windows*'-type graphical interface[2] with the ori-

FIGURE 3.36 SETUP OF TRIP COMPUTER PAGE DEFINING WAYPOINTS, TRACKS AND ROUTES

ginal generation of computers. Both use the same data, but the visual output is much more easily assimilated by most users.

A full examination of the wide range of GPS units and their functions is beyond the scope of this book but they all share some basic functions that should be mastered by anybody wishing to add GPS navigation to their toolkit; time spent familiarising oneself with the various pages available, and customising the data-fields will pay significant dividends on the hill.

The 'live' map function may well prove sufficient for some users, however for mountain navigation there are a handful of basic skills required to make the most of a GPS unit's functions. These basics are:

• Setting up the GPS (*Section 2.3.10 Setting up GPS*)
• Programming and storing waypoints using co-ordinates, either using the unit's internal mapping or taken from a map or your current location
• Navigating to a stored waypoint
• Creating and navigating a *route* consisting of waypoints linked in succession between a start point and final destination
• Creating a *track* either to review the journey or to use *track-back* to a known location
• Cross-referencing information from the GPS unit to the map and vice versa, especially useful when relocating

3.12.1 Using waypoints

Waypoints are one of the most basic GPS concepts. They are simply the GPS equivalent of an address that are stored in the GPS unit for use when required.

There are four ways to create and store waypoints:
1 By saving the current location, where you are right now
2 By reading the co-ordinates of a location from a paper map and enter these into the unit manually
3 By using digital mapping software to create a waypoint at a desired location and then uploading this to a GPS unit
4 If using a mapping GPS unit, waypoints can be created from the digital maps shown on the screen

2 Graphical User interface (GUI): e.g. Windows and the Apple OS vs. programming language and DOS.

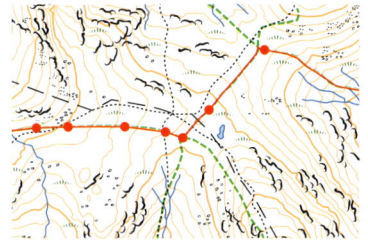

FIGURE 3.37 WAYPOINTS POSITIONED CAREFULLY BEFORE AND AFTER DECISION POINTS ENSURE THE CORRECT DIRECTION IS MAINTAINED

(RIGHT) **FIGURE 3.38** COMPASS PAGE

Every GPS unit will have a slightly different method of creating way-points using various keys and screens. Being familiar with how a unit marks or edits a waypoint will ensure points are saved correctly and retrieved easily when required. Their uses are either plotting a route in advance, or storing the current location as a point of interest.

When a waypoint is created, the GPS unit will assign it a default name, usually a number 001, 002 and so on. As the database of waypoints increases in size this can make it difficult to find specific waypoints for specific locations, so when convenient it is a good idea to edit with a memorable name.

3.12.2 Choosing waypoints

Waypoints are essential to GPS 'GOTO/FIND' navigation and therefore choosing the correct locations requires some careful consideration. The number of waypoints and where they are placed will depend on a number of factors, for example the terrain, the weather, the hazards and personal requirements. Use the map to identify appropriate locations to use as waypoints. Review the route carefully, deciding on key navigational features or decision points that may be encountered. Make sure they are clearly labelled with an easily identifiable name that corresponds with the location (e.g. CAR PARK 1). Try to position any waypoints in such a way that even with some error taken into account they are safe places to try and locate.

With a waypoint stored the GPS unit will always be able to show how far away and in what direction that particular point is from its current location. Returning back to that waypoint at any time is a simple matter of setting the GPS unit to navigate to that location.

3.12.3 Navigating to waypoints

All GPS units will have some form of GOTO function (sometimes called Find). This is one of the most important functions, allowing the operator to choose a waypoint and use the GPS unit to navigate to that particular location. The most useful pages for waypoint navigation are the compass page or the Trip computer, which can be customised to show specific information (including the unit's own calculation of its degree of

FIGURE 3.39 WAYPOINTS POSITIONED CAREFULLY BEFORE AND AFTER DECISION POINTS ENSURE THE CORRECT DIRECTION IS MAINTAINED   *PHOTO // WWW.PYB.CO.UK*

accuracy, based on comparing anomalies within the information it is receiving). The map page (if available) is less useful for this style of navigation as the GPS superimposes a line between current location and the waypoint, which tends to obscure the map symbols. Remember that in hiking mode the GPS unit[3] makes all its calculations based on a straight line between the current location and the destination, making no allowance for terrain, conditions or hazards. It is therefore important to use the map and the ground ahead to identify the most appropriate and safest route, especially if the terrain is complex.

The advantage of using a GPS device in these situations is there is no need to stick religiously to the straight-line bearing. By choosing the most appropriate route, even if deviating from the original bearing, the GPS unit will be recalculating the distance and direction to the destination every second. In complex terrain it is worth considering the use of intermediate waypoints in order to avoid any hazards or route finding problems en-route to the ultimate destination.

The data fields often provide some useful navigational information including estimated time of arrival based on your recent average speed and distance to destination. Because the GPS unit provides so much information it is very easy to ignore the printed map and magnetic compass, particularly when confronted with difficult ground. However, it is at times such as this when it is important to use all three tools. Cross-reference the information from the GPS unit with the map and vice versa on a regular basis. Use the map to look for the safest and most appropriate route to the destination.

Most GPS units will sound an alarm or show a message to indicate arrival at a destination. Audible alarms and flashing messages can often be missed if conditions are poor or you are carrying the unit in a pocket. Therefore it is important when using a GPS unit to navigate to a waypoint to periodically check the information to monitor progress. Once a destination has been reached and you have confirmed the correct position then it is possible to move onto the next point.

3 Some GPS units have a dedicated driving mode, which assumes that the vehicle will have to follow roads in order to reach the waypoint.

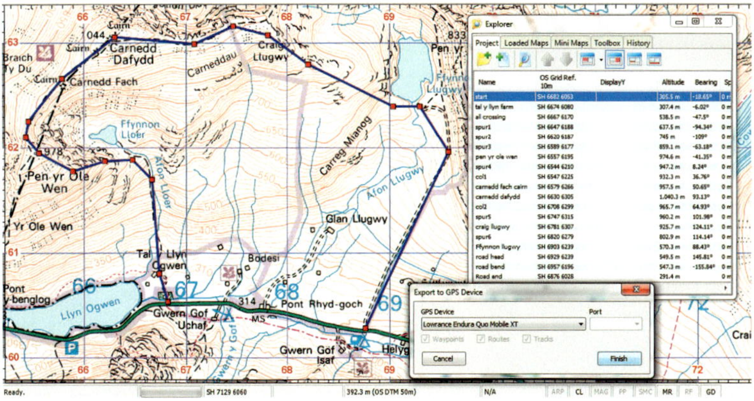

FIGURE 3.40 DIGITAL MAP WITH A ROUTE MARKED ON USING WAYPOINTS AND LINK LINES

3.12.4 Using the route function

A route consists of a list of sequentially linked waypoints. Creating a route can be done in two ways, either by using waypoints currently saved within the unit's database or more conveniently by using digital mapping software and uploading the information to a GPS unit when complete. A third method involves using a mapping GPS unit with the relevant map to create a route on the screen that can then be followed or saved for future use.

When using a route, the GPS unit is conducting a series of GOTOs by automatically navigating from one waypoint to the next. Using this method, it automates the navigation process and reduces the time that would be required to navigate to each individual waypoint using the GOTO function. However the point at which the GPS unit switches from one waypoint to the next can vary between units and could be before or after the location of the waypoint. If the route consists of many twists and turns the unit may skip a waypoint in favour of another it feels is closer – here switching temporarily to the GOTO function may well be the best option.

It is easy to become ruled by the convenience offered using the GPS and ignore the map. Ensure the map is to hand and check at regular intervals to confirm the location. Use the map to identify the best route between one waypoint and the next taking account of any potential hazards. The big advantage of a mapping GPS unit in these situations is that it offers the map to hand on screen.

If the route has been created using mapping software it will be possible to print a copy showing the route with the waypoint labels marked on. It is also possible to annotate a standard map with the route and waypoints; this can be used to help keep track of progress and show the next waypoint in the sequence.

3.12.5 Using track-log function

Most GPS units have the capacity to record and store their movements in a *track-log*. As the GPS unit moves it creates a 'breadcrumb' trail of the path taken known as a *track*. Once a track has been created it is possible

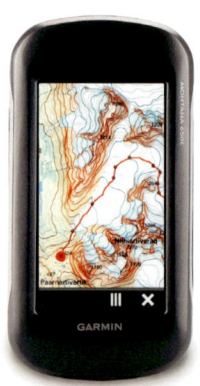

FIGURE 3.41 MAP PAGE SHOWING A TRACK THROUGH COMPLEX TERRAIN WHERE WAYPOINTS HAVE ALSO BEEN INCLUDED AT TURNS AND HAZARDS

to navigate back along it using *track-back*. This function allows you to follow the twists and turns of the track back to the start point. It can also be used to navigate the track in either direction. This is useful if saving the track for a future repeat. If the terrain is complex, waypoints can be added at important locations, or at a safe distance from identified hazards.

With digital mapping, it is possible to upload the track-log to a PC and review the journey. If required, the track can be edited and even changed into a route before returning it to the GPS unit or saving for future use.

The track-log should be cleared at the start of every journey if you wish to record your movements during the day for use at a later stage.

3.12.6 Dealing with problems

There may well be occasions when the GPS unit might display inaccurate information or cease to function. If its use has been integrated well with map and compass skills, dealing with any problems can be handled in a straightforward manner, by reverting back to using these traditional tools. If time can be spared, there are steps that can be taken to troubleshoot some of these problems.

- Start by cross-referencing any information displayed with the map and the surroundings
- Make sure the GPS unit has a good 3D fix and is still functioning properly
- If you have an electronic compass and you believe the heading shown to be wrong, re-calibrate this feature
- Check that the batteries are still good. If not, replace them, switch back on, let the unit warm up and get a 3D fix of its position
- GPS units, like computers, crash from time-to-time. Check that the GPS unit has a good 3D fix, that it still responds to key presses, and the displays update. If any of these are not the case, switch the unit off, and then wait 5 seconds before turning it back on. If the unit will not switch off, take the batteries out and wait for the display to go completely blank before reinserting them

If you are unsure of your location and the route ahead, it is important to relocate using a map and compass before venturing any further (refer to *Section 3.11* on *Relocation*).

INSIDE A GROUP SHELTER *PHOTO // BRYN WILLIAMS*

Clothing &
equipment

Travelling in the hills will always involve a compromise
in equipment if the walker is to avoid moving like a snail –
admirably well-equipped but too slow to go anywhere.
The choice can be quite bewildering and with an
increasingly large fashion element it can be very
difficult for hill walkers to make an informed decision.

When choosing suitable clothing and equipment the best policy is to consider value for weight, within the constraints of a budget. A waterproof that is described as 'top of the range' may be ideal for a winter storm in Patagonia, but needlessly bulky and heavy for a summer rain shower on Kinder Scout.

Walking leaders will not only have to consider the clothing and equipment they choose for themselves, but also give advice to others on suitable clothing at realistic prices, based on current knowledge of market trends.

4.1 Physiology

Man is a tropical animal with a reasonable ability to adapt to small variations in temperature. In warm conditions the body uses processes for cooling including *vasodilation* (dilation of blood vessels) and perspiration to increase heat exchange with the environment. In cold conditions *vasoconstriction* reduces heat exchange thereby maintaining warmth, while *shivering* increases heat production through exertion. These processes help to maintain the body core at its optimum working temperature of around *37.4°C*. Maintaining this balanced temperature state is known as *homeostasis*.

The body has also retained in varying degrees its ability to hold a layer of warmed air in contact with the skin as an insulating buffer. In cold conditions the body is able to increase the layer of warm trapped air in contact with the skin. Involuntary erector muscles cause body hairs to stand up, trapping more air and producing the characteristic goose pimples. Obviously, hairy animals are much better at this than humans, hence our need at times to wear insulating clothing in anything cooler than tropical climates.

In order to choose the best personal equipment for the job it is useful to have a basic understanding of how the human body works in a mountaineering environment. Throughout the duration of a mountain day or expedition, the body has to work efficiently so that it can meet the wide variety of demands placed on it. Indeed walking on rough ground can expose an individual to a unique environment that places greater demands on the body than normal life. The equipment used in this environment essentially aims to help the body to maintain a state of homeostasis.

The body responds to exercise in a number of ways:

4.1.1 Increased respiration rate

In order to meet the demands placed on the muscles the body requires an increased supply of oxygen. Therefore both the rate and depth of breathing are increased, to increase the availability of oxygen being transported in the blood from the lungs to the working muscles. Typically, the breathing rate at rest is *12–18 breaths per minute* – during strenuous exercise this rate can increase to *45–50 breaths per minute*.

4.1.2 Increased heart rate

In order to transport more oxygen to the working muscles the heart starts to beat at a faster rate. The heart rate at rest is usually in the region of *50–70 beats per minute*. At the onset of exercise the heart rate will increase as it tries to meet the oxygen demands of the working muscles. However, heart rate cannot increase indefinitely, and maximum heart rate will be reached if the work being completed is hard enough and of sufficient duration.

> Maximum heart rate can be estimated to within plus or minus 15 beats by using the following formula:
>
> **Maximum Heart Rate = 220 – age of walker**

4.1.3 Increased body temperature

At rest, a significant proportion of the energy that the body utilises simply keeps the body core temperature stable. The amount of heat generated in this way is approximately equal to the heat produced by a 100-watt light bulb. Any surplus heat is lost through the processes of conduction, convection, radiation and evaporation. During rest, at a room temperature of 21°C, the majority of this heat loss occurs though radiation (60%). Approximately a quarter (25%) is lost through evaporation from the lungs and skin, one tenth (10%) is lost through convection air currents and a minimal amount is lost through direct contact with the floor (approximately 3%). When exercising other mechanisms are therefore needed to maintain homeostasis.

4.1.4 Increased perspiration

The body normally loses fluid in perspiration ('sweat'), urine, faeces, and the water vapour in expelled air from the lungs. Strenuous exercise can cause up to a twenty-fold increase in heat production, meaning that the body now has to deal with the same amount of heat as that given off by 20 x 100-watt light bulbs. In order to maintain the core temperature, the body increases its perspiration rate, dramatically increasing the body's ability to lose heat. The body cools by secreting tiny water droplets on the skin's surface, which quickly evaporate, drawing heat energy for the process and thus cooling the body.

During exercise, approximately 80% of the heat loss is achieved through evaporation, with conduction and convection contributing to approximately 15% and the remaining 5% being lost through radiation

The rate of sweating depends on many factors including body mass, environmental conditions, intensity of exercise and fitness of the individual. While it is difficult to give a general value to the amount of liquid lost through sweat during a hill day it would be realistic to anticipate a loss in the region of *300–800ml per hour*. If the loss were 500ml per hour for an eight-hour day, this would be 4,000ml – or 2 x 2 litre drink bottles!

During exercise or activity in a cool environment, the body can deal with this heat load relatively easily. In hot conditions, where heat may also be gained from the environment, the body faces major challenges in trying to keep the core temperature stable. The amount of insulation worn on a mountain day will also dramatically affect the rate of heat loss: the ideal clothing design would complement the body's efforts to shed heat yet switch automatically into heat conservation when necessary.

The layering system

Base layer
Wicking underwear to transport moisture away from the skin.

Can include:
- Thermal top
- Thermal trousers
- Socks

Mid layer
Insulating layer which may have wind-proofing properties.

Can include:
- Hat
- Top/jacket
- Trousers
- Thin gloves

Outer layer
Waterproof and windproof layer.

Can include:
- Waterproof jacket
- Waterproof trousers
- Gaiters
- Thick gloves/mittens

FIGURE 4.01 THE LAYERING SYSTEM

4.2 What to wear

4.2.1 The layering system

When a range of temperatures is likely to be encountered, either through external conditions or varying energy requirements, the normal solution is to use layers of clothing, which can be added or removed in order to cope with the weather. Technological advances make it possible for a single layer to cope with a widening range of conditions by combining insulation, wind proofing and water resistance in various proportions.

Staying comfortable: clothes next to the skin

The body can maintain homeostasis more easily if it can keep a dry layer of air around the body and allow sweat to escape. The layer of clothing in contact with the skin (often referred to as the *base layer)* can therefore make an enormous difference to the effectiveness of everything else carried. Underwear should feel comfortable and assist the body in maintaining its optimum working temperature. Strenuous exercise leads to the body heating up and unless a perfect balance of ventilation and insulation is achieved, perspiration begins automatically, designed to cool the body by producing the droplets of liquid for evaporation. Despite valiant attempts by some manufacturers to create a single layer that combines fleece and a thin windproof material with plenty of ventilation zips, the perfect balance has yet to be achieved.

Coping with perspiration is the main design problem that outdoor clothing manufacturers have to tackle. Clothing retards the cooling process, allowing moisture to collect and saturate the material. Not only does it hamper the intended cooling process, but it also continues to cool the body when exercising is reduced or ceases.

The once ubiquitous string vest had an oily texture that prevented the strings soaking up moisture. Perspiration therefore migrated easily to the outer layers. The holes encouraged the insulating air layer to remain stationary and thus heat exchange was minimised. In contrast, the cotton T-shirt is a seriously unsuitable garment for underwear when walking in cool climates. Cotton soaks up moisture and retains water next to the skin, cooling the body as it evaporates. To make matters worse, cotton is an inefficient insulator even when dry.

Clothing designers have examined the requirements for successful base layer materials and confirmed the following ideal criteria:

- Good insulation, to feel warm in cold conditions and cool in the heat
- Comfortable
- The ability to wick perspiration away in order to keep the skin dry
- Remain odour-free
- Easy to wash and dry

Leaders should be aware that despite recommendations to wear thermal underwear, this clothing is too specialised for many young people, as their parents may be unwilling or unable to purchase it. Loaning out underwear is impractical, so sufficient warm clothing should be carried in order to replace or compensate for damp under layers, since in an emergency this could be a significant factor in party members succumbing to cold exhaustion.

Synthetic materials have replaced cotton by out-performing it in every criterion except perhaps its comfort when dry (and with mixed success on the issue of odours). One traditional material for under-garments that has survived the synthetic revolution is silk, due to its comfort and strength. However, silk is only used nowadays by the outdoor enthusiast as a base layer where perspiration is not an important issue, for example balaclavas and gloves. A recent return towards traditional materials has been spurred by the fine-fibred Merino wool, which has good thermal properties and is less prone to bacterial odour than synthetics.

Synthetic materials dry rapidly because the fibres do not absorb moisture: these fabrics generally rely on their *hydrophobic* (water-hating) qualities to transfer moisture away from the body and retain a dry micro-climate next to the skin: this quality is commonly known as *wicking*. Some manufacturers have gone a step further by giving their base-layer clothing an outer coating with *hydrophilic* (water-loving) properties to physically siphon moisture outwards.

For outdoor activities in a cool climate, *thermal underwear* is far more effective for minimising cooling through evaporating sweat than absorbent fabrics such as cotton. Most thermal underwear is made from synthetic materials such as polyester, which gradually transport moisture away from the body through a wicking process. When the moisture eventually evaporates far less heat is drawn from the wearer's body to provide the required energy. In a hot climate, absorbent fabrics such as cotton are of course ideal for maximising the cooling effect of the evaporation of perspiration.

Underwear that becomes soaked with perspiration causes problems when the amount of energy required in order to dry it by evaporation is no longer available. Whilst continuing to walk at a steady pace, sufficient heat is usually generated to warm this moisture for evaporation. However, when the individual is stationary, or becomes exhausted, this continued leaching of heat can be disastrous. In windy conditions, this process is accelerated. Wet clothing is much less effective at insulating than when it is dry.

Any clothing worn next to the skin has to cope with moisture transportation. Items such as a hat or gloves are usually simply taken off if perspiration becomes a problem, but cotton underwear prevents moisture effectively reaching the outer layers and can even render breathable outer fabrics somewhat pointless.

Base layer fabrics have a jersey knitted construction (sometimes referred to as interlock) and are fairly similar in appearance to cotton, albeit somewhat more shiny in texture. Some materials are knitted into a ribbed pattern for extra warmth. Most fabrics are also treated to retard the

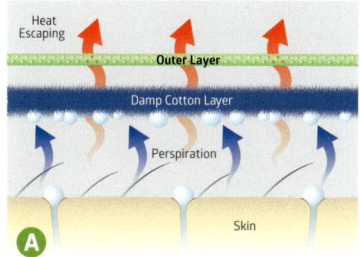 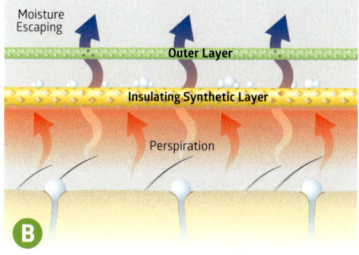

FIGURE 4.02 A PERSPIRATION COOLING WITH COTTON BASE LAYER AND **B** SYNTHETIC BASE LAYER WICKING MOISTURE AWAY FROM THE SKIN

development of odour-producing bacteria, which is a characteristic drawback of polypropylenes.

Apart from moisture transportation, there are other design criteria influencing the effectiveness of the base layer. Thermal shirts are available with many neck designs; ranging from a high neck with or without a zip, through to v-necks. All of these styles have their advocates, but a high neck with a zip extending down to about the sternum is the most versatile, as long as the zip is soft enough against the skin. The choice between short and long sleeves comes down to personal decision; long sleeves are of course warmer. Shirts that are too short can result in chilling around the kidneys, as the shirt tends to ride-up, particularly when wearing a rucksack. For colder conditions, base layers with an elastic content fit snugly and therefore retain more warmth.

Retailers are often unwilling to let people try on underwear due to potential hygiene problems. Nonetheless, it is worth bearing in mind that ill-fitting thermal underwear can be very uncomfortable, particularly if too tight around the shoulder, armpit and crotch.

Staying warm: insulation

The walker is faced with a bewildering range of *mid-layer* clothing. While the ideal is a small wardrobe of different garments, which could be collected for different conditions, a few items that do several jobs can suffice. Thus, for mild, wet conditions a close fitting thin garment with a zip neck is a good choice, whilst for cool, dry and windy conditions a wind-resistant fleece would be very effective, especially if fitted with additional ventilation zips – however for cold conditions it should be noted that soft-shell fleeces currently focus on comfort and wind resistance more than insulation.

For many years wool was the material of choice for mountain travellers due to its woven structure and rough surface, which trap insulating layers of air. However, synthetic materials have gradually evolved into a more effective basis for outdoor clothing, as they do not share the inherent drawbacks of wool. Wool traps water in wet conditions and becomes very heavy. It is slow to dry and is quite difficult to tailor for specialised requirements. Fleece garments are now available in high street stores at lower prices than most woollen products. Nonetheless, wool still performs reasonably well and can provide a refreshing change from ubiquitous synthetics. Merino wool has steadily gained popularity since its introduction and has already become fairly popular for underwear, including socks.

The original synthetic material, known as fibre-pile, has excellent thermal properties but is bulky, rather shapeless and lacking in wind resistance. However, it is relatively cheap and is therefore a cost-effective choice for group issue. Fibre-pile trousers are generally too warm for walking, and tend to sag when wet.

Developments in polyester-based woven materials in recent years have produced a range of fabrics generally known as fleece. These materials have long woven fibres which trap air very effectively whilst having strong water-repellent properties. Many different weights of fleece are available with a wide range of styles. Additionally, some fleeces have been developed with particularly high wind resistance. Fleece products continue to develop rapidly because of the high demand from high street fashion outlets. For pure warmth to weight ratio, feather down remains the best material. On the other hand, down is not a practical choice of active wear, apart from in exceptionally cold dry conditions. It is too warm for walking and it becomes virtually useless when saturated with water. Synthetic duvet type garments are also too hot for active wear in summer – though are sometimes carried as spare clothing for emergencies.

Keeping wind and water out: outer layer

The cooling effect of cold water on warm skin is a good thing if the body is in a state of overheating – however, when insulation from heat loss is required, cold water next to the skin can have fatal consequences. The aim of wearing an *outer layer* of waterproof clothing is therefore to keep water out and simultaneously release the moisture created by the body. The primary function of a waterproof shell is therefore to assist thermo-regulation.

Clothing choice should be adequate to cope with whatever pace the walker sets and the consequent response from the body. Alternatively, walking parties should travel at a comfortable pace, avoiding excessive heat production.

For windy but dry conditions, a popular compromise is to wear a breathable windproof top made from a tightly woven material such as Pertex®, with a lightweight waterproof tucked in the sack for unpredicted cloudbursts. Cold, windy and wet days, on the other hand, can test the mettle of even the most expensive waterproofs.

Waterproof materials offer a high degree of wind and rain resistance, but have to contend with perspiration. Heavy-duty (16oz) PU[1] or Neoprene-coated nylon was the traditional favourite for basic waterproofs and remains the most cost effective choice for group issue. Unfortunately, perspiration from exercise can result in clothes becoming very damp. This is not a serious problem for the occasional or less active user and the perspiration is at least to an extent prevented from cooling the body through evaporation.

Breathable waterproof fabrics are now readily available from a range of manufacturers. These use either a membrane or a coating to transport

---

1 Polyurethane.

perspiration to the outside of the garment. *Beading* water droplets enhances the waterproof properties, so that the water pours off, rather than soaking into the fabric.

Gore-Tex® membranes revolutionised waterproof garments, allowing water vapour to escape

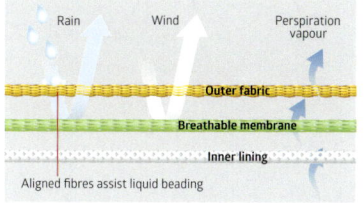

FIGURE 4.03 OUTER FABRICS AND HOW THEY WORK

from within the coat, while shedding water droplets on the outside; these materials were not the first breathable fabrics but were the earliest to find widespread appeal and to resolve many of the earlier teething problems. These membranes are bonded to various fabrics and designs to give a balance between performance, durability and weight.

Fabrics laminated with a membrane offer the most effective breathability. The membrane is micro-porous, allowing only water vapour to pass through the tiny pores. It is protected by either a three-layer construction that sandwiches the membrane or by a more supple two-layer construction that has an additional fabric or mesh lining on the inside. Several clothing manufacturers have produced their own brand of breathable membrane fabric, all of which guarantee a minimum life expectancy for the product. However, membrane fabrics are expensive and do have a limited life span, as the sandwiched materials de-laminate over time. With regular weekend use and reasonable care, this type of garment should give reasonable service for about three years. The performance of these fabrics can be improved by washing from time to time and tumble-drying to help re-align outer fibres to shed droplets more efficiently. These waterproofs should be tape seamed at every joint, and baffles should be fixed at any zip or *Velcro*[2] adjustment point, to prevent leakage and to avoid wind cooling the body.

Coated or impregnated fabrics are less expensive to produce than membranes but as yet are not able to transmit moisture quite as rapidly as micro-porous membranes when new. However, they do not de-laminate and can be re-impregnated to give a longer and more consistent life span. Some of these materials do not require tape seaming as the waterproofing effectively seals the stitch holes. Modern coated or impregnated garments can provide a very cost-effective alternative to traditional waterproofs.

In continuous wind-driven rain, water will eventually enter even the best shell layer. The key is to postpone this for as long as possible. The most obvious leakage points are the neck and cuffs, so using the hood and adjusting the cuffs and neck will help. Pockets should be closed in prolonged rain. Shell garments should be washed regularly in order to keep membrane pores open and reduce the build up of dirt and organic deposits that attract bacteria and can lead to de-lamination. After cleaning, ideally using proprietary cleaning agents designed for waterproofs, shell clothing should be tumble-dried to align fabric hairs and

2 *Velcro*: tape with plastic barbs or felt, allowing a quick fixing that is easily ripped open when required.

assist beading of surface water. Cautious ironing on a very low setting is also said to help prolong the beading effect.

Close inspection of a shell garment will give some indication of how long and effectively it will perform.

Useful checks are:
• Quality and finishing of stitching
• Zip quality
• Seam seals
• Cuff and neck construction
• Quality of draw cord materials and toggles

4.2.2 Jackets

A vast range of jackets is available from specialist retailers and on the high street. Cost will naturally be a factor when making a choice. Generally, heavy-duty impermeable waterproofs are standard outfits for schools, youth groups and outdoor centres because breathable membrane fabrics are too expensive and fragile for group issue. Ventilation is important, and a full zip is beneficial if the jacket is likely to be worn as a windproof in dry conditions. Optional features such as underarm zips are similarly useful when rushing uphill, but all zips and seams are potential leakage points.

In recent years, the technology for waterproofing zips has received much attention and this is certainly a developing area. Underarm zips need to be flexible and unobtrusive to avoid sore armpits. The main zip needs to be rugged enough to withstand heavy use and should open from both ends, a significant aid to ventilation. Most zips are protected with a flap fastened with *Velcro*, which should be easy to open. It is a good idea to check the tailoring to see if any leakage through the Velcro is funnelled away from the zip.

Outer chest pocket for map

Inner map pocket (can cause leakage in wet conditions)

Optional pocket for compass or whistle

Pockets above belt height

Flap to protect zip

Rucksack belt

Drainage holes at lowest point of pocket

FIGURE 4.04 POCKET DESIGN AND LOCATION

Pockets are very useful for a map, compass, hat, gloves and any snacks. Beyond that, however, too many pockets are superfluous. They tend to fill with water (some do have drainage holes at the bottom) and it is easy to lose items if there is a plethora of storage locations. Pockets should be located on the chest to allow access when wearing a fastened waist belt and should be large enough to hold a map but not so large as to sag around the chest. An internal map-pocket is not always a good idea, as during heavy rain gaining access to the map can result in a soaking.

Other factors to look for when choosing a jacket are hood and cuffs. The hood should sit comfortably on the head and allow unhampered vision even when turning the head sideways; something well worth checking in the store before purchase. In poor conditions it is essential to have a hood that can be drawn tight, while still allowing the wearer to see and to breathe. A small visor helps protect the eyes from wind-lashed rain and hail; it should be noted that an inserted wire has a limited life span while thicker fabrics last as long as the garment and can be just as effective. An adequate visor is particularly important for people who wear glasses as it helps limit the amount of water falling on the lenses; wearing a peaked cap can help reduce this further. Cuffs should be adjustable, but exposed elastic-mesh fabrics tend to leach water into the coat and up the arms. Simple *Velcro*-sealed flaps are probably the most efficient solution.

The length of a jacket is a matter of personal choice. Longer jackets, known as cagoules, were advocated in the past as being useful for enforced bivouacs but they reduce ease of movement, especially where high steps are required. Thigh length jackets tend to drain water on the thigh area, causing it to become saturated. The action of walking repeatedly presses the leg into contact with the shell clothing at this point, forcing water through the fabric by hydrostatic pressure. A short jacket is excellent when used in combination with salopettes (see *Figure 4.04*) but can lead to a wet waist with ordinary over-trousers.

4.2.3 Over-trousers

The main criterion for a good pair of over-trousers is that they fit correctly. Loose fitting or baggy trousers tend to sag when soaking wet, making walking unpleasant and increasing the difficulty of negotiating more awkward terrain. The ideal length extends to just below the ankle while the crotch area should not contain much excess fabric.

The greater the amount of tailoring in a garment, the higher the price. Trousers with articulated knees and bib and brace style W are luxurious refinements that may offer more to the climber than the walker. Salopettes tend to be too warm for extended use and the need to remove a jacket in order to don shoulder straps is a disincentive.

Zips are an important feature on all types of over-trousers. In the event of a sudden downpour, it is important to be able to don over-trousers quickly. Short zips can make this difficult when wearing boots and once dressed-up people are reluctant to embark on a struggle to take off the over-trousers, when the rain stops. Longer zips make this process much simpler, and full-length zips make ventilation straightforward. However, as with all seams, zips are a compromise, as they are potential leakage points. It can be argued that longer zips are less likely to suffer damage, as the user is unlikely to strain the zip trying to get the boot through. Zip flies for men are of limited value to walkers, as the increased ease of use does not repay the increased likelihood of leakage. On the whole over-trousers with flies are only a bonus for male climbers wearing climbing harnesses.

FIGURE 4.05 TYPES OF GAITERS
PHOTO // STEVE LONG

FIGURE 4.06 TRIPPING OVER POOR GAITER
ATTACHMENTS   *PHOTO // STEVE LONG*

4.2.4 Gaiters

Gaiters are an optional extra but can make a big difference, particularly in very muddy ground, where trousers and socks would otherwise become wet and stiff. Gaiters can be invaluable in heather covered ground, where pieces of vegetation might collect in the socks.

Often simple *stop-tous gaiters*, which simply protect the top of the boot and the ankle, do a perfectly good job, whilst minimising condensation inside. Longer gaiters often become rather sweaty by the end of the day, although breathable fabrics reduce this problem dramatically. Zips on gaiters usually fail long before the fabric, and their replacement with *Velcro* seams on many models seems to be an improvement, being lighter, cheaper and tougher.

The main problem area for gaiters is preventing the bottom from riding up and exposing the top of the boot. Some gaiter and boot combinations work perfectly well without being tied under the boot. Others use rubber seals, but these have a tendency to ride up at the toes and the rubber is easily damaged by rocky terrain.

If a tape, wire or string arrangement is used, any buckles or ties should be on the outer side of the boot to minimise the danger of the wearer tripping over it as well as to prevent buckles or clips catching on each other when the feet are placed together. (*See Figure 4.06*)

In wet conditions, gaiters are best worn underneath over-trousers. True, the trousers get muddy, but rain will otherwise be funnelled into the gaiter and thus into the boot.

4.3 Keeping a secure footing: boots

Footwear worn in the mountain environment should help the walker to move over varied ground as efficiently as possible. It should also hold the foot in a comfortable position without compounding the problems caused by modern living; due to ill-fitting footwear and walking on hard surfaces, many feet have become misshapen causing the collapse of the arch. This can cause problems later on to the ankles, knees, hips and back, so good footwear can be worth the investment.

A well-fitted pair of boots together with foot beds and some modification should alleviate any postural problems. Badly fitting boots can cause friction blisters and can ultimately be the cause of debilitating pain.

Manufactures tend to classify boots in terms of *seasons*. This is useful in trying to decide what type of boot is appropriate for the intended use.

ⓘ **11** Boots for groups
For group issue, the choice of footwear should ideally match the type of terrain frequented; heavier duty boots are more likely to cause blisters and may at times be seen as overkill for lowland walks.

Newly purchased boots and footwear for group issue often cause blisters, as they have not moulded to the wearer's feet. Ideally, a series of progressively longer walks should be taken to acclimatise the feet. It is a good idea to take pro-active measures to minimise the chance of developing blisters, which can ruin a trip. Firstly, tape can be stuck on the normal rub points, particularly the back of the heel, prior to putting on the boots. Boots with high ankle support often cause rub points from around the top of the boot, and protective tape can also help prevent this.

A considerate briefing that encourages party members to request a halt as soon as hot-spots occur can assist in preventing blisters; enquiries at the first break may highlight problems in their early stages.

Boot features and choice

Approach shoe
- Lightweight
- Aggressive tread
- Low ankles

2-season boot
- Waterproof but lightweight
- Flexible sole
- Some ankle support

3–4-season boot
- Tough and waterproof
- Rigid sole
- Excellent ankle support

FIGURE 4.07 BOOT FEATURES AND CHOICE

Boots with soft flexible soles and fabric uppers with limited water resistance can be termed *one-season*. Appropriate for easy path walking and uncomplicated terrain, they may be the best option for a long walk on a hard surface such as a tarmac road. In wet conditions, this type of footwear will result in damp, cold feet.

Boots with a more robust, flexible sole and aggressive tread pattern may be termed *two-seasons*. This type of footwear is suitable for a greater variety of terrain. However, these boots may only give very limited ankle support and therefore demand skilful foot placements, particularly on rocky or greasy terrain. The uppers may have waterproof qualities. Due to the lightness and flexibility of this type of footwear careful consideration of the terrain and experience of the wearer must be taken into account before use.

(i) **12 Boots for leaders**

The leader of a party travelling in the hills needs to have footwear that is effective on all types of terrain and protects the feet from injury or damage. Leaders may be required to look after a member of the party on steep and slippery ground and this is easier when wearing a boot that creates a solid platform. The group's overall safety can depend on the leader's ability to negotiate confidently the ground through which they travel.

The walking leader will need to consider three-season boots for personal summer use on mountains or moors, as these represent a reasonable compromise between comfort and performance.

Whichever boot is appropriate, it is essential that they fit well. The ability of the lacing system to hold the foot in place, especially around the ankle, is very important in preventing blisters. Pieces of closed cell foam can be used to customise a pair of boots if finding a good fit is difficult. These can be used to fill dead space or to help hold the foot in a more stable position inside the boot. It is worth checking where the boot flexes as the foot should be clear of the boot at this point.

When trying on different boots at the shop, aim to find a store that measures feet and fits accordingly. Getting the feet properly measured should help in any fitting. Many people persevere with boots that are too small for them and, contrary to popular belief, blisters are often caused by rubbing due to boots being too tight. Thick socks should be worn when trying on the boots and a snug fit should be regarded with suspicion, because the feet tend to swell with exercise and points of contact can become sore spots on a long walk. There should be a thumbnail length from the tip of the boot to the toe, and a finger should be able to slide between the Achilles tendon and the back of the boot.

Walk around the shop as much as possible. The best shops also offer 'buy and try'; if boots do not fit after wandering around the house for a while, they can be exchanged for another pair.

Foot beds with shock-absorbent properties can increase comfort, especially in stiff four season boots. They can also be moulded to the foot and are designed to hold the foot in its natural position.

Approach shoes are a modern version of the one or two season boot, but with no ankle support. They combine the technology developed for off-road running with excellent friction and varying degrees of water resistance. Additionally they have all the limitations of one and two season boots and are not really designed for use away from paths.

Three-season boots have a stiffer sole unit (indeed, some are fully stiffened) and leather or a leather/fabric upper. These tend to offer better waterproof qualities and may be lined with a breathable membrane fabric. This type of footwear offers greater support and protection for the foot when travelling over rough terrain. They also create a better platform for the foot on steep soft ground. Some types of crampons may be fitted and the boot may be suitable for easy winter walking.

Four-season boots generally have a fully stiffened sole and leather upper. They are suitable for rough terrain and as crampons can be fitted to them they may also be used for winter mountaineering and climbing. This type of boot offers greater insulation and waterproof qualities due to the thickness and construction of the upper. However, many people will find them a little too inflexible and heavy for extended use in summer conditions. The ultimate extension of this type of boot is the plastic shell boot. This is a specialised piece of equipment and is generally considered too cumbersome for general summer hill use.

FIGURE 4.08 BOOT CONSTRUCTION

4.3.1 Boot construction

Boot construction varies greatly. The quality of leather used has a direct effect on a boot's life-span and on how long it will remain waterproof. High-quality leather is expensive and the price of footwear reflects this. It is worth noting that whilst many modern boots can feel very soft and comfortable on first fitting, they may be made of softer, less durable leather whereas boots that take some wearing-in may last longer because of their stiffer construction.

The longevity of a pair of boots will be greatly enhanced if they are cared for properly. They need to be thoroughly dried out after use, but it is important that this drying process should not be too intense. If left overnight, newspaper stuffed tightly inside the boot and changed once or twice during the night will remove most of the moisture.

A wide variety of waterproofing agents is available on the market. It is worth choosing one specifically designed for the type of fabric used in your boots. A boot with as few seams as possible is desirable, since stitches are a potential entry point for water. Seams need to be cleaned of dirt and proofed. A membrane on the inside of the leather may enhance its waterproof qualities, and an absorbent liner will also help remove sweat. Breathable waterproof membranes are generally used in conjunction with poorer quality leathers, so it can be argued that a good quality boot does not need a lining. However, lined boots have proved to give an excellent balance between waterproofing, comfort and cost.

4.4 Protecting extremities: hats and gloves

Keeping the extremities of the body warm can demand a considerable amount of attention. A large percentage of heat is lost through the head – up to 33%. When on the move this is a good way for the body to keep itself at a consistent working temperature, but once stationary on a cold windy moor for any length of time, the benefits of a hat and gloves soon become apparent.

Headgear ranges from a headband covering mainly the ears, through to balaclavas that cover most of the face, head and neck. Comfort is an important factor; wool can feel very itchy against the tender skin of the face, and has therefore been largely superseded by synthetic fabrics for headwear. Wind resistant properties have been incorporated into some headwear, but it should be noted that hearing could be seriously compromised by these properties, as the fabric muffles sound. It is a good idea to carry a choice of hat types for varying conditions; perhaps a headband for a sunny day with a cool breeze plus a beanie for lunch and tea breaks.

When it is cold, dexterity is quickly lost in the fingers due to a closing of the external blood vessels (vasoconstriction). This varies greatly from person to person but can make the execution of even the simplest of tasks painfully difficult. This phenomenon is particularly marked in people who suffer from Reynaud's Syndrome, which causes poor blood circulation in the extremities. The fit and quality of *gloves* can have a marked effect. Gloves can be expensive and sometimes fall apart after a relatively short time. Cheaper models may or may not last but tend not to be well tailored.

For pure all round warmth it is difficult to beat a pair of *woollen mittens*: cheap, long lasting and warm when wet, they also do not take much looking after. If the wearer is allergic to wool then synthetic mittens with a waterproof shell are an option.

Wearing a glove on one hand and a mitten on the other on a cold wet windy day will soon illustrate the mitt's superior heat retention. Put simply, a mitten allows the fingers to share resources, warming the trapped air and minimising exposed surface area (the same principle as a group shelter). Mittens are the ideal hand-wear for group use, but are not very well suited to handling a compass in difficult navigation conditions.

When choosing gloves it is worth spending time trying on several types, as fit is important in order to strike a balance between good dexterity and avoiding tight spots. A classic test for dexterity is to try folding a chocolate bar wrapper into quarters wearing the chosen gloves. The acid test of course is taking bearings from a map on a wet and windy day. One light but effective choice is a pair of gloves made from wind-block fleece. These do not provide much insulation, but give excellent wind protection, and can easily be wrung out in very wet conditions. There are now various completely waterproof gloves available, ranging from washing-up gloves to those made from innovative materials. To date, these are all either sweaty or clumsy, but it is clearly a developing field!

FIGURE 4.09 DRINK CONTAINERS   *PHOTO // STEVE LONG*

4.5 What to carry – group equipment

A well-equipped family or group will have packed equipment for the following requirements:

- Food and drink
- Protection from the cold
- Protection from sunshine
- First aid provision
- Rope (if going into mountainous terrain)
- Emergency shelter
- Spares and repairs
- Something to carry it all in

4.5.1 Food and drink

Few things are more depressing than forgetting one's lunch on a wet, windy day. Lack of food can also jeopardise safety if exhaustion results. There are many high-energy food bars available that give good value in terms of calories for weight. In the short term, calories are the body's main requirement during the day's walk. A balance should be sought between *simple sugars*, which are rapidly broken down to provide energy quickly and *starchy foods* that provide slow-burning fuel. Thus, a good combination for a day might include sandwiches, fruit and cake packed in the rucksack, with sweets and flapjack stored in a pocket.

Re-hydration is essential during a hill day. Again, a balance must be sought between weight and need and this varies greatly between individuals. Larger people may well need to carry as much as two litres, while one litre is more than enough for others, particularly if freely running streams are available. In the British Isles, streams are generally considered a reasonably safe water source if there is nothing within sight that is obviously polluting the water upstream. However, caution should be exercised – particularly in hot climates – because of the risk of *water-borne infections* such as Giardia.

A thermos flask allows warm drinks to be conveniently available; it is for the individual to decide whether the extra weight is worthwhile. Unbreakable flasks are readily available and are a wise choice for walkers that expect their rucksack to take the occasional knock. Re-hydration systems are a popular modern choice of liquid container. These consist of a lightweight bladder with a tube feeder and self-sealing sucking point. Some rucksacks are designed for use with these systems. Regular attention should be paid to maintaining any re-hydration system, since mould can form in the tube and a puncture or damaged nozzle can result in drenched rucksack contents.

A group leader should work on the assumption that at least one member of their party will forget or lose a hat or gloves, thus spares for the group or family members should be carried in addition to spares for the leader. A spare mid-layer jacket should be carried in a waterproof container, in addition to personal fleeces or jumpers used for stops or cooler summit conditions. Re-hydration systems are of limited benefit to a group leader because it will normally be necessary to stop walking in order for group members to access their water bottles.

4.5.2 Dealing with cold conditions

Whilst the choice between cold and warm drink is a matter for the individual, amongst the party a source of warm drinks is highly recommended in case there is the need to raise morale or help deal with mild hypothermia. For groups, fruit juice is again preferable to tea or coffee, which in addition to being diuretic (increasing urination) is not to everybody's taste. A warm drink is also more useful if it is fairly high in calories.

Some groups carry a sleeping bag[3] or duvet jacket to provide insulation for the emergency treatment of hypothermia. A similar weight in fleece jackets or woollen sweaters is far more versatile and will assist the primary aim of preventing hypothermia from developing in the first place. A sleeping bag will reduce further heat loss but it will not actively raise a victim's body temperature, and most sleeping bags are too small to allow a second, warm member of the party to get in to help re-warm the victim. The early signs and symptoms of hypothermia are described more fully in *Cold exhaustion* on page 261.

A sleeping bag or duvet jacket made of synthetic materials is more practical for the wet conditions that inevitably accompany an emergency, as their insulation properties are superior to down when wet. Recent innovation in foil technology has allowed sleeping bag construction to create remarkably light vacuum packed sleeping bags that work in any conditions. These provide an excellent and versatile compromise between weight and function.

---

3 A full-length zip is recommended, allowing easier deployment for an injured person. See *Section 5.3.5 Sleeping bags* on page 133.

4.5.3 Dealing with sunshine

In sunny conditions, various additional items of equipment become very important. *Sunglasses* are vital for protecting the eyes in conditions of bright sunlight, particularly if reflected from a bright surface, such as snow, sand or water. If not protected, blistering of the retina, known as snow-blindness can occur. This is very painful and debilitating, causing permanent damage to the eyes. Although the brain learns to compensate, snow blindness is definitely best avoided by wearing sunglasses with an appropriate level of protection for the environment and altitude. In sunny regions, a spare pair of sunglasses should be carried within the party. Emergency protection can be improvised, by covering the eyes with fine mesh cloth or a mask with eye slits.

In hot conditions *head protection* is also important, especially for people with thinner hair. A peaked cap is light and versatile, offering increased shade for the eyes.

Sun protection cream is vital in sunny conditions. Vanity tempts people to refuse sun cream, but sunburn is invariably the result, leading to painful red and peeling skin with potentially increased susceptibility to skin cancer. Sufficient cream should be taken for the whole party; a leader would be well-advised to budget for this in the trip planning.

Some people wear short trousers in sunny conditions. Longer trousers should however be taken along as spares, and sun cream applied to the legs in sunny weather. People wearing shorts should be particularly vigilant for sheep ticks, which often take advantage of the easier access to tender skin. (See *Section 14.2.5 Sheep ticks* on page 262).

Though less publicised, *heat exhaustion* can be just as serious as hypothermia. In the British Isles, hot conditions are relatively uncommon, but can catch people unawares because of inexperience in dealing with them. Regular and sufficient water intake is particularly important in hot conditions in order to provide the raw material for perspiration. Otherwise the blood gradually becomes more viscous as the liquid is lost, leading to reduced ability to transport oxygen to the organs. Dabbing the head with cool water can help reduce the temperature by taking over the function of perspiration.

Heat exhaustion can deteriorate into heat stroke if left untreated. This is a potentially fatal condition, which develops as the body ceases to maintain its working core temperature. Characteristic signs are dry skin, due to the inability to sustain sweat production, and a full, bounding pulse. Urgent hospitalisation is essential, requiring a stretcher evacuation (see *Heat exhaustion* on page 262).

4.5.4 First aid provision

Every member of the party should carry an 'ouch-pouch' pack of basic first aid provisions for minor injuries such as scratches and blisters. This should include: a personal supply of plasters, a whistle (for attracting attention if lost or separated from the party), sanitary items and sun cream (if sunshine is anticipated). Any prescribed medication should be carried by the individual concerned, and the leader should be discretely informed of its whereabouts.

In addition to personal first aid supplies, sufficient first aid expertise and equipment should exist within a walking party to deal with the remoteness of the situation. An employer has a legal requirement under Health and Safety Executive (HSE) regulations to ensure the provision of a travelling first aid kit containing the following items for their staff:

- A guidance leaflet/card
- 6 x individually wrapped sterile plasters
- 1 x large wound dressing
- 2 x triangular bandages
- 2 x safety pins
- Individually wrapped moist cleaning wipes
- 1 x pair of disposable latex gloves

Since the HSE first aid kit is simply a requirement to protect employees, there is no obligation for a walking party to be limited by this list. The following items are useful optional additions:

- More wound dressings and bandages
- Crepe bandage
- Pocket face mask for rescue breathing
- Cling film (ideal for protecting burns)
- Blister dressing such as Compeed or Second Skin and corn pads (for blisters)
- Wide strip of cotton tape
- Waterproof paper and pencil
- Penknife with tweezers
- Heavy-duty duct tape

As all equipment is a compromise between weight, cost, and versatility, smaller parties and families may not wish to carry all of the items outlined above. As a minimum, items that are difficult to improvise should be carried, in particular, sterile wipes, dressings and latex gloves. Additionally, straps, cling film and duct tape are so versatile that they easily justify their weight.

The party first aid kit should be stored in an easily identified tough, waterproof container. Other equipment within the party may allow additional first aid equipment to be improvised. This includes mouldable foam rucksack internal frames for padding or splinting, walking poles for support or splinting, and rucksack straps for additional splinting ties. For additional advice on first aid, the reader is referred to *Chapter 13 Dealing with injuries*, starting on page 257.

4.5.5 Rope

A rope can be regarded as part of the recommended emergency equipment for a walking party venturing into mountainous terrain. It must be emphasised that in the wrong hands the use of a rope can give misguided confidence, as reliance on a rope is misplaced if knots, anchors or their application are unsound.

FIGURE 4.10 ROPE BEING FED INTO THE ROPE BAG READY FOR DEPLOYMENT   *PHOTO // STEVE LONG*

The rope is best carried fed into a protective bag. This allows rapid and effective deployment if needed, whilst minimising the potentially alarming message to some groups of packing a rope for a mountain walk. (See *Figure 4.10*)

Choice and use of the rope is covered in detail under *12.3 Emergency ropework* which starts on page 216.

4.5.6 Shelter
A *group shelter* is a valuable component of any group's kit when venturing into the hills. This is usually a box-shaped sheet of material constructed from rip-stop nylon, ranging in capacity from two persons to around twelve. For its weight, this is a very versatile piece of equipment.

Once the party has gathered together the shelter can be pulled over heads and everybody sits down, positioning the tallest members in each corner and leaning on the walls to pull the box taut. It is always worth checking a borrowed shelter for rips and to see that the shelter actually fits the party for which it is intended. Having the stuff sack permanently attached to the shelter is useful so that it does not blow away.

There is plenty of anecdotal evidence demonstrating the effectiveness of group shelters, which offer both physical protection and psychological comfort to party members, whatever the situation. Individuals respond better to an emergency situation when remaining in a group and helping each other, than when isolated in individual emergency bags. Morale is easier to maintain, a major factor in preventing the decline into hypothermia (see *Cold exhaustion* on page 261).

Each party member should carry a *personal bivouac shelter* in order to deal with unexpected incidents. These can be used in addition to the group shelter in an emergency or by individuals if they become separated from the main party and require shelter. Lightweight, cheap bivouac bags

FIGURE 4.11 GROUP SHELTER FOR 4–6 PEOPLE   *PHOTO // STEVE LONG*

of heavy-duty polythene are available from most walking equipment retailers. A bright colour (normally orange) makes the bag highly visible for rescue parties (see *5.4 Emergency nights out* on page 135).

4.5.7 Spares and repairs

Once embarked on a journey, a party needs to be self-sufficient. Unless suitable spares are carried then loss or damage of crucial equipment can result in anything from a minor nuisance to a catastrophe, depending on the remoteness of the situation. As always, there is a compromise between the amount of spares carried and the weight involved. Some spares such as cord for boot laces or tape to repair ripped flysheets can be regarded as crucial; others are optional, depending on the destination. When packing it is worth bearing in mind the wise axiom that the more emergency equipment a group carries, the more likely it is to be needed. Head-torches were mentioned earlier as an essential tool for night navigation. (See *Section 2.5 Torches* on page 49).

For day trips, a torch can be classed as spare, because it should not be necessary to use it. However, artificial light can become essential in an emergency and every member of the party should ideally carry a torch. A *spare battery and bulb* for the torch should be carried, to cater for breakage or accidental depletion of the battery. Finding a reliable way to disconnect the battery can minimise the risk of finding your torch glimmering in the bottom of your rucksack just when you need it!

A map and compass are absolutely vital for navigation in poor visibility so spares should be carried within the party. A 1:50,000-scale map showing a reasonably large area is a versatile choice for a *spare map*.

A leader may wish to include the *spare compass* within the party's first aid kit, where it will be easy to find in an emergency.

Spare food should be carried to maintain energy if unanticipated delays occur. This should give a good ratio of energy for weight and should not be consumed under normal circumstances. Mint cake or energy bars are popular choices, since they store well and are seldom irresistibly tempting. Spare drink should also be carried if adequate supplies of fresh drinking water are not likely to be found en route.

In addition to spare clothing and equipment, sufficient kit should be carried to effect *basic repairs*. This may include a penknife with additional blades such as screwdriver and pliers. Spare shoelaces, rucksack tape straps and heavy-duty duct tape are all versatile repair items. Electrical cable ties can also be useful for heavy-duty fastenings. More items may be required for the most remote locations.

4.6 Containers

4.6.1 The rucksack

The basic equipment container for walkers is the rucksack. This should be large enough to hold all of the kit to be carried without having to resort to lashing items to the outside, where they can be damaged, snag on outcrops or branches and become waterlogged in heavy rain. For simple day trips in moorland, a 30-litre sack may suffice; for mountain walks a 45-litre sack will be required; and for overnight camping expeditions a 60-litre sack can be regarded as reasonable. It is easier to take a slightly larger rucksack loosely packed, than trying to cram everything into a tiny bag.

A rucksack should hold its load close to the wearer's back and as high as possible without limiting the ability to turn or tilt the head. This allows a comfortable, more upright posture to be assumed. Weight further away from the back requires the wearer to lean further forward in order to compensate.

The straps should be comfortable and shaped to sit on the shoulders without rubbing. The rucksack length is critical to individual wearers, as the waist belt should sit comfortably around the top of the hips with the shoulder straps comfortably tight. This spreads the load between the hips and shoulders and reduces sideways movement of the sack. Several large capacity expedition sacks have adjustable-length back systems, because correct fitting makes an enormous difference to load carrying.

Most good packs are made with different torso lengths available. A tall person does not necessarily have a long torso (perhaps just long legs) so this should ideally be measured. To determine the torso size, measure along the back from the seventh vertebrae (the largest bump on the back of the neck, when the head is tilted forward) to a point level with the top of the hipbones.

A lid pocket allows items such as sun cream or penknife to be accessible without having to open the main sack and side pockets are useful on overnight expeditions for separating items such as stove and fuel from clothing and food.

Other useful features to look out for include:
- Slim profile, especially if travelling away from paths
- Compression straps to enable a slim profile and to stop the load swinging around. They are useful for carrying walking poles when safety requires both hands to be free
- Double bottom with differentially cut inside layer – this puts weight on the inside layer, significantly prolonging the life of the pack
- Load-lifter straps to pull the load off the top of the shoulders
- An inner malleable frame-sheet helps protect the bag from sharp items and also doubles as emergency insulation or splinting material

A good rucksack should be reasonably water-resistant when new but this will degenerate with use. Completely waterproof rucksacks are available but should be chosen with the emphasis on their comfort and load-carrying abilities in mind.

4.6.2 Packing a rucksack
As a general rule of thumb, equipment likely to be needed early or in a hurry should be packed at the top of the sack or in an outer pocket. Items that can leak should ideally be stored in a separate compartment or at least double-sealed by placing them in an additional waterproof bag.

If mainly on the trail, especially for long distance treks, heavier items packed in the upper portion of the pack create a higher centre of gravity, making it more comfortable to carry. For more rugged terrain packing heavier items close to the back in the middle portion of the rucksack will result in better stability when stepping between boulders or negotiating awkward ground.

4.6.3 Other containers
Suitable inner containers are versatile options for keeping clothing dry in rucksacks. The cheapest method is to use strong rubbish bags – however, these remain relatively fragile and have a limited life span. Proprietary rucksack liners are a good compromise, but the most effective solution is to use waterproof bags, originally designed for water sports. Transparent bags are especially useful, allowing easy identification of their contents.

If a camera is carried, this is best kept on the body, as photo opportunities will inevitably be missed if it is stored in the rucksack. Waterproof cameras are available at premium cost but camera bags are readily available, some allowing a small camera to be stored in a jacket pocket. When carrying a mobile, ensure that it has a waterproof case.

13 A suggested kit checklist

Day trip

Personal kit

- Rucksack
- Emergency bivouac bag
- Waterproof jacket
- Waterproof trousers
- Map
- Compass
- Torch plus spare battery and bulb
- Walking boots
- *Gaiters (not required in hot, dry conditions)*
- Drink
- Lunch
- Whistle
- Hat + gloves
- 1 x spare gloves (for wet conditions)
- 1 x spare warm layer (a fleece/wool top, for example)
- Spare food
- Personal first aid and sanitary supplies
- *Sunglasses and sun cream*

Group kit

- Group first aid
- Group shelter
- Spare map and compass
- Spare fleece or similar warm layer
- Penknife (for repairs)
- Spare hat
- Spare gloves
- Spare socks
- Spare food
- Warm drink or stove
- Rope (if mountainous terrain)
- Small repair kit
- *Mobile phone – turned off for storage*

Overnight

Personal

- Sleeping bag
- Insulating mat
- Spoon, *knife, fork*
- Large mug
- *Bowl*
- Brew kit
- Food
- Spare clothing
- Spare socks
- Possibly shared
- Tent
- Water container
- *Water filter (where pollution is a potential problem)*
- Stove and pans
- Fuel
- Lighter/matches
- Spare lighter (in case of damage to primary supply)
- *Transistor radio – for weather forecast*

Items shown in italics are optional, depending on circumstances

CAMPING AT LLYN BOCHLWYD   *PHOTO // ANDY SAY*

Living in the mountains

Travelling through the hills and mountains brings a sense of independence and freedom from many of the trappings of modern life. All our material requirements can be packed in a rucksack, and with careful planning a reasonable balance can be made between weight and effectiveness, even for expeditions involving nights spent out under the stars. A basic understanding of the demands that strenuous exercise and the upland environment make on the human body is an important ingredient of this process.

5.1 Food and drink

A day spent hill walking demands quite strenuous activity sustained over a relatively long time. The type of energy expenditure on a mountain day is predominantly aerobic, that is, with oxygen supplied to the muscles.

Age, sex and body weight all affect the amount of energy required for exercise, but walking on flat ground at a speed of 4 km/h (2½ mph), a young man weighing 70kg (11 stones) expends approximately 3.7 kilocalories per minute. One hour of walking at this pace will use 220 kilocalories.

Carrying a rucksack, walking at a faster pace, or walking uphill will all increase energy expenditure. For example, the same individual carrying a 7kg rucksack whilst travelling uphill will increase the energy used in one minute to 9.7 kilocalories per minute or 580 kilocalories in one hour. At this pace, it would take about 35 minutes to use the energy contained in one *Mars* bar. Walking downhill on a relatively smooth surface requires considerably less energy.

A reasonably fit group of walkers embarking on the Fairfield Horseshoe in the English Lake District should take about two and three quarter hours to reach the summit and two and a quarter hours to return.

Ascent: **165min x 9.2 Kcal per min = 1518 Kcal**
Descent: **135 min x 5.1 Kcal per min = 689 Kcal**
Total energy expenditure = **2207 Kcal**

This is additional to the energy required to perform general tasks for the remainder of the day.

Being able to move efficiently over mountain terrain will decrease energy expenditure and this in turn will decrease heat production and sweating. The amount of food consumed before and during a mountain day or expedition needs to reflect the body's energy requirements.

Novice walkers often underestimate the amount of energy that they will need to replace, especially if they are used to a sedentary life-style. A daily allowance of *3,500 kilocalories* is a useful starting point for planning a suitable menu, with adjustments for larger bodies, heavy loads or strenuous outings.

For a day trip, sufficient energy input is by far the most important dietary requirement. Intake should be spread throughout the day, with breakfast providing about a quarter of the intake and the evening meal representing a third. The remainder should be consumed in small instalments throughout the day. Several short breaks for food and drink are far more appropriate than a single long lunch break.

For breakfast, cereal followed by biscuits or bread and jam provides a good mixture of *simple carbohydrates* providing instant energy, and starchy *complex carbohydrates* that are broken down more slowly and thus provide energy over a longer period.

Since about half of the energy input should be spread over the duration of the walk, it is important to carry adequate supplies. Sandwiches, chocolate bars, and flapjacks are all excellent sources of energy, as are mixed nuts, dried fruit and raisins.

> **ⓘ** **14** Over-nighting
> Extended trips involving a night or more away from home require planning to ensure that suitable arrangements are made. This is particularly important for leaders of mixed groups of young people, who should also ensure that adequate supervision is available. Both male and female leaders should stay close enough to supervise, preferably in separate rooms immediately adjacent to the children's. On residential trips it is particularly important to be aware of the potential for friendly gestures to be misunderstood, in the legitimate aim of protecting young people from abuse. Simple guidelines such as avoiding being left alone with a child should be adhered to whenever possible and adult participation with children in games involving physical contact should be approached with caution.

After a day's walk, energy replenishment is most effective within two hours of completing exercise. A substantial supper can be enjoyed with the knowledge that the every calorie has been well earned.

For walking trips lasting longer than a day, a balance of nutritional requirements becomes more important. In addition to carbohydrates, the body needs protein, fat, vitamins and minerals. These are provided by food such as dairy produce (containing most of these food types but lacking iron and vitamin C), meat (protein, fat and minerals), and vegetables (minerals and vitamins). Pulses are also a good source for not only protein and carbohydrates but also contain fibre, which is important for healthy digestion.

If the food is to be carried while walking, weight also becomes an issue. It is possible to replenish the body's food requirements from a daily weight allowance of *one kilogram per day*, but this does require some planning. Packaging is 'dead weight' from a nutritional point of view especially as it must also be carried out once the contents have been consumed. Tinned food can often be transferred into a lighter container prior to the expedition.

A comparison of *cooking times* can allow less fuel to be required, thus saving on weight. Dehydrated meals are light, but require considerable fuel to re-hydrate, so boil-in-the-bag type foods are not as extravagant on weight as they might initially appear. Similarly, pasta needs to simmer for less than half the time required by most rice, and instant soups can be prepared more quickly than normal packet soups.

5.1.1 Meeting special dietary requirements

Some people are limited in their choice of food by health requirements, religious or ethical convictions. Others have such pronounced preferences that they would rather go hungry than eat certain types of food. Clearly, everybody needs to be involved in the choice of food, and practical guidance may even be required from a dietician or an organisation for people with special needs, such as the British Diabetic Association (*www.diabetes. org.uk*) or Coeliac Society for gluten-free products (*www.coeliac.co.uk*).

In the British Isles, it is relatively easy to find excellent food for vegetarians. Nuts, seeds, pulses, beans, soya curd and textured vegetable protein provide the basis for nutritious meals that may also appeal to non-vegetarians. Some vegetarians eat dairy produce, which widens the choice, and some include fish in their diet. Again, it is important to consult over personal needs and preferences.

5.1.2 Drink

Re-hydration is absolutely vital to the body's well being during exercise, particularly in hot conditions. The body uses *water* to maintain an optimum working temperature of approximately 37°C (degrees Celsius), through the evaporation of perspiration. Without regular replacement of liquid, the body becomes dehydrated, leading to exhaustion, or more seriously, heat stroke as the core temperature begins to rise. (This is explained in further detail in *Heat exhaustion* on page 262).

Party members should be encouraged to drink moderate amounts of liquid at regular intervals. As with any activity requiring co-ordination, alcohol consumption would be inappropriate and additionally compromise the safety of others. Drinking water containing small quantities of *glucose* and *sodium chloride* (salt) can be absorbed rapidly from the small intestine into the circulation and helps replace salt lost through perspiration. Isotonic sports drinks work on this principle, providing a solution matched to the body's own fluids. These are not always cheap, but it is quite simple to concoct similar (though probably less palatable) drinks based on the same concepts.

The use of sweetened fruit squash, perhaps mixed with a little salt, is recommended since it gives maximum energy for weight.

FIGURE 5.01 A SCOTTISH MOUNTAIN BOTHY
PHOTO // ROB COLLISTER

Very sweet drinks can actually be counter-productive because metabolising the sugar into glycogen uses up much of the water in which it is dissolved. It can also temporarily disrupt the balance between the body's sugar and insulin, leading to the mood swings and hyperactivity characteristic of *hyperglycaemia* (more commonly associated with diabetes). Fizzy drinks bring the additional problem of filling the stomach with bubbles and misleading the drinker by over-riding the sense of thirst. Walkers should therefore avoid these types of refreshment, although swilling the container to expel gas can reduce this last drawback.

Tea and coffee have *diuretic* properties, increasing urination and thus requiring further drink. Warm drinks also require *additional weight* to insulate or heat the water.

A litre container of liquid should provide an adequate reserve for most people's daily requirements – this can be topped up from streams passed en route. Swift-running streams in mountain and moorland provide a reasonably safe source of clean water, provided they do not contain an animal carcass further upstream. In areas outside of the British Isles, a portable water filter may be an essential requirement.

5.2 Hostels and huts

Roofed accommodation to suit most pockets is available in popular walking areas, ranging from hotels through to barns. The standard of accommodation should match the needs of the party and there is no substitute for a personal visit to check on suitability, especially if planning for peak-season weekends or for evening arrivals when it may be too late to find alternatives.

The Mountain Bothy Association, which can be found at *www.mountainbothies.org.uk*, maintains about 100 shelters in remoter parts of the UK (approximately 80% are in Scotland). These offer an alternative to camping and can also provide emergency shelter. The exact locations of bothies are available online, and many association members assist with the maintenance of these delightful cottages and houses. Furniture varies from Spartan to non-existent. Bothies are not suitable for use by large groups because they can easily become overcrowded and damaged. All waste material (apart from firewood) should be taken away from the shelter, and the door should be left firmly bolted but not locked.

5.3 Camping

Choosing a *good campsite* and good organisation are the key elements for a comfortable night, whether using a designated campsite or pitching tents in a wild location.

(ABOVE) **FIGURE 5.02** A WELL-SECURED TENT PEG

(RIGHT) **FIGURE 5.03** COOKING SAFELY AWAY FROM
THE TENT   *PHOTOS // STEVE LONG*

First, a good site must be found to pitch each tent. This should ideally be shelved or flat ground within a gentle slope to allow better drainage. It is desirable that the ground is soft enough to take a tent peg and in an area that offers as much shelter as possible from the prevailing weather conditions. This can take some planning, especially if an approaching frontal system is gradually swinging the wind direction around (see *9.4.1 Weather systems* on page 168). Tents can be blown over by the wind, snapping poles and creating chaos.

On a commercial site, a location reasonably close to toilet and washing facilities is advantageous but this should be balanced against the benefits of a quieter spot if the campsite is busy.

In remote locations, tents should be carefully pitched even in calm conditions in order to withstand unexpected winds overnight. Pegs need to be pushed securely into the ground and angled away from the tent to resist the strain. A rock may be necessary to tap the pegs gently home, but care should be taken as modern tents often have rather light and fragile pegs. Important guy lines can be further secured by placing heavy rocks on top of the peg. Occasionally it may be more effective to secure guy-lines directly to boulders.

Standing camps (i.e. camps used for more than a night) should only be used with the landowner's permission. Hygiene arrangements become even more important and valuables should not be left unattended in a tent.

When striking (dismantling) camp, rubbish should be packed and carried out. Rocks should be replaced in their original locations to mini-mise disturbance to habitats (see *7.2.4 Wildness* on page 153). In wet conditions, a dry inner tent is best stored separately from the wet flysheet to increase the likelihood of a dry second night, whether this is planned or enforced.

5.3.1 Cooking

Many types of stove are available and each has its advocates. Stoves using *re-sealable propane/butane gas mix* are arguably the cleanest and most practical. Full cylinders can be taken to remote campsites and partially used canisters finished in roadside campsites. Empty cylinders should be

16 At the campsite

Water is an important consideration for site location and there should be a source close by. Caution must be exercised when camping near to a stream as these can rise quickly in a storm and break their banks. There are many accounts of campers waking up with a stream running through their tents and even having items washed away. Looking carefully for potential flood spots or evidence of previous flooding, such as marsh vegetation or flattened, lighter-coloured grass, can help prevent problems in the night. A good leader needs to become proficient in choosing a campsite and will often have to make an educated guess from looking at the map – a water supply, relatively flat ground and shelter from the prevailing winds can be identified from the contours and marked watercourses. On arrival however, the leader should be prepared to find drawbacks such as wet or stony ground that the map failed to show.

Pitching a tent requires practice if efficiency is to be achieved in poor weather or darkness. Experience of pitching a variety of tents usually allows pitching arrangements to be deduced even if instructions are not available, but inexperienced members of the party will often need help, if only to prevent the tent from being damaged.

With practice, most tents can be erected quickly, but the procedure can be difficult to remember. It may be possible to colour code poles and sleeves to ease the process. It is always a good idea to practice with a 'dummy run' back at base prior to an expedition. As well as familiarising party members with pitching and striking procedures, this allows any problems such as damaged or missing items to be spotted and dealt with before these defects become a problem.

treated with great care however and under no circumstances should they be incinerated; a dangerous explosion would result.

For group use, the most popular stove is probably the *methylated spirits fuelled Trangia*, because it is simple, stable and easy to maintain. Careful use and supervision is required nonetheless.

Several brands of stove can use a variety of liquid fuels and some can also be successfully connected to a gas cylinder. These *multi-fuel stoves* are often more powerful than simple gas stoves but tend to need more maintenance. They have a tendency to erupt into flames if not pre-warmed correctly using priming fluid or blocks. *Petrol* is a particularly volatile liquid and novices should not use it as a fuel.

Whichever type of stove is used, cooking can be a dangerous exercise if not treated with caution. **It is not safe to cook inside a tent**, and a leader should set a good example by cooking outside, with their group.

Sitting outside to cook in a storm merely results in the individual becoming very cold and wet, so there are times when experienced campers may be forced to cook inside the tent porch due to wind and rain. **This is a potentially hazardous enterprise and great care must be exercised.**

The entrance should be left open to allow hasty evacuation in the event of an emergency and it is vital that fuel hoses or attachments are carefully sealed. Once cautiously lit, the main concern is the stove tipping over so making or buying a stove base can be a sensible precaution. Vigilance is the key and minimising movement around the tent whilst cooking will reduce the chance of an accident.

In the event of a stove *flaring up*, the fuel supply should be turned off immediately if possible. Otherwise, the stove should be ejected from the tent porch and dealt with outside.

Re-fuelling the stove is a particularly risky operation, and should always be performed well away from the tent. The journey to a designated fuel store also gives the stove more time to cool down – reducing the risk of spontaneous eruptions, which have been known to occur, particularly when refilling meths-burning stoves.

A stove is useless if it cannot be lit. Self-igniting switches can be very effective, but an *alternative flame source* should still be taken to cover possible malfunctions.

Matches are difficult to protect in wet weather, and a disciplined approach to returning them to a watertight container is essential. Water-proof matches should be tested, as not all meet their marketing claims. *Cigarette lighters* should be regularly checked for fuel, and the ignition flint, if included, should be kept dry. Any camping party is well advised to carry a *spare stove lighter*.

The *amount of fuel* carried is dependent on the duration of the trip and also the experience of the party. Fuel and time can he wasted by inefficient cooking, so a group is well advised to carry slightly more fuel to compensate for potential problems.

The following suggestions can help reduce fuel consumption:
- Use a second (larger) pan containing water as a lid, placing a well-fitting lid on top of this. Rising heat is thus utilised to warm additional water.
- Store excess hot water in a flask.
- Boil-in-the-bag food is convenient and uses less fuel to cook – partly offsetting the additional cost and weight of this packaging. The bag should be turned over in the pan from time to time to heat throughout the pack. After cooking boil-in-the-bag food, use the water for soup or custard. Eat straight from the bag to avoid pollution from washing-up, and also eliminate the need for a bowl.
- Tins are best opened prior to the trip and the contents transported in a plastic container.
- Pasta and rice can be partially cooked then set to one side with sufficient hot water to continue rehydrating.

An experienced leader should be able to cook efficiently and know how much fuel will be needed. These skills can be passed on to the rest of the party.

5.3.2 Hygiene and safety

Hygiene arrangements are important both for the comfort and health of the individual, group or family in the short term and also for the long-term sustainability of a campsite. Commercial sites should provide toilet facilities and a clean water supply, which should be used by the party.

Upland campsites should be treated with great respect to avoid polluting water and degrading vegetation, particularly in popular areas. These environmental implications are discussed in more detail under *7.4 Sanitation issues* on page 154.

5.3.3 Comfort

Official campsites with amenities on site can provide comfortable living conditions in almost any weather. *Lightweight remote campsites* demand that efficient use be made of the limited resources carried by the walker. Skilful camping will allow a greater degree of comfort to be achieved in any location.

Organisation within the tent can make camping a much more pleasurable experience, especially in wet conditions.

If the *ground is wet*, there is a good chance that water will eventually seep through the groundsheet. If the tent has side pockets, these can be used to keep some items readily accessible and isolated from any pooling water. Placing a bivy bag or flattened laminated maps on top of the groundsheet helps to stop water soaking into the sleeping bag and other equipment. An insulating layer of either closed cell foam or a thin inflatable mattress not only helps keep the camper warm but also acts as a barrier to moisture from the ground. If a short insulation mat is used a rucksack can provide extra cover. These items are discussed in detail on page 133.

For *roadside campsites*, plenty of spare clothing can be easily carried for cooking and other stationary activities. This is impractical in remote sites, where spending much more time operating from within the warmth of the sleeping bag may be advisable to conserve resources.

Boots covered with items of clothing make a good pillow. A torch using LED bulbs provides an effective light source for reading and is much safer than a candle for about the same weight. The torch should be stored in an easily remembered and accessible location when settling down to sleep in case it is required in a hurry; hanging it from a suspension point in the ceiling can work well. A small transistor radio can, for some, make longer autumn nights more interesting and give valuable weather information.

On the return from any camping trip it is worth noting which items of equipment taken were **not** used and why. This may be useful in deciding what to leave behind on the next trip. Reducing the weight of the loads carried can make an enormous difference. A rucksack for a three-day camp including all kit to be carried need not weigh more than 15kg.

Wet kit is best hung up to drip dry. There may be a suitable place for drying clothes at an official campsite; otherwise, it may be possible to suspend items inside the tent porch. Damp clothes are best dried through body heat generated when walking. Gloves can be dried slightly by wearing them to hold the food containers when eating cooked meals.

When supervising a group on a camping expedition there are certain considerations that need to be taken into account. The area where the camp is set needs to be large enough to accommodate the tents and their extended guy lines. Large groups have a greater impact on the environment so it is worth choosing sites carefully, or camping in small groups. The areas around a campsite designated for toilets, washing and collection of drinking water need to be clearly defined. This is discussed more fully under *5.3.2 Hygiene and safety* on the previous page.

5.3.4 Tents

The design of hill walking equipment always involves compromises, and perhaps tents provide the clearest example of the choices that have to be made. *Weight* is of little consequence for roadside camping, so heavier-duty fabrics and poles suitable for family or group use are a very practical option. If the tent has to be carried far to a campsite, however, weight becomes critical. As a general rule, for remote camping *weatherproofing* and weight take precedence as the essential features, while for valley camping with vehicle access, desirable features such as *space* and *comfort* can be given more preference.

Tents vary considerably in price. Bargains can undoubtedly be had, but they should be checked vigorously against the intended use. Remote campsites are not the places to discover that a tent has not been designed to withstand strong winds and rain.

Tents and tent construction

Geodesic tent with its flysheet *(left)* and without its flysheet, showing its construction *(below left)*

Single hoop tent without its flysheet

A small tent for valley use

A large family tent

FIGURE 5.04 TYPES OF TENT AND TENT CONSTRUCTION

FIGURE 5.05 CHOOSE THE COLOUR OF YOUR TENT WITH CARE   *PHOTO // CARLO FORTE*

Weatherproofing

Tents have to contend with wind and precipitation. Generally, the higher the campsites the more extreme weather conditions one can expect to encounter, but even valley base-camps can spring some surprises.

As a starting point, it is only fair to demand that a tent should be *waterproof*. This includes water gathering on the ground as well as from torrential downpours, but there is a limit to the depth of standing water with which even the most impervious tent can contend. A lightweight tent will probably have a *flysheet* made of nylon or polyester, with a waterproof coating on one or both sides – usually PU (polyurethane). The seams should ideally be tape-sealed, although regular application of a glue sealant can be quite effective.

A good clearance between the fly and the *inner tent* will help stop water finding its way inside the tent, particularly if this is maintained during heavy winds and gusts. One method of achieving this is by zipping the two layers together. This also eases pitching and striking, but it is achieved at the expense of extra weight. Some tents feature an attachment point between the two layers level with the side guys, keeping the tension between inner and outer. This should be checked for waterproofing; it is a potential leakage point otherwise.

The *groundsheet* is an important consideration in the balance between weight and performance. A bathtub design incorporating high sides is important when camping on marshy ground. Super-lightweight 2oz PU coated nylon requires careful maintenance and needs re-proofing fairly regularly. One way to overcome waterproofing problems is to line the floor with a plastic bag (for example, a *personal bivouac bag* – see page 134), but this rather seems to defeat the object of reducing weight. Four-ounce neoprene coated nylon is more robust and waterproof, but can de-laminate after heavy use.

Wind can be a source of misery if a tent flaps in a mere breeze and a disaster if the tent blows away. *Windproofing* is indicated fairly directly by the season-rating of a tent, as the criteria used for defining seasons give more weighting to wind strength and precipitation than for temperature. Single hoop tents will not blow away in strong winds, but do have a tendency to flatten down during gusts, and to flap noisily. This type of tent also has a tendency to collect pools of water on the flysheet, due to its relatively low angle at ground level – a potential leakage point.

Tents sold for mountain use tend to be designed to cope with worse weather, but may be damaged more easily by careless handling, such as when pushing the poles clumsily into the fabric. Some mountain tents have snow valances, which are unnecessary extra weight in summer conditions. The valance is a reinforced flap of material designed to be held down with snow or rocks to prevent strong winds blowing under the flysheet.

The toughest tent design for high mountain camping and strong winds is the geodesic dome. The flexible poles cross each other and interlock to give great stability. The inner tent is suspended from the poles and the flysheet is draped tightly over the top. Another advantage of this style of tent is the reduction in the number of guy ropes that are needed. The increased stability is usually achieved, however, with a gain in weight. Additionally most geodesic tents require the flysheet to be fitted after pitching the inner tent and this can result in a soaking if pitching or striking camp in heavy rain, but practice reduces this risk. However, these significant drawbacks have to be weighed against the considerable structural benefits of geodesic designs.

Many variations in tent design can be found, and all have their advocates. Some spring open virtually pre-pitched. This is convenient but should be checked for durability. Some tents have plastic windows, which give better light inside, but must be checked for waterproofing. The potential for the plastic to crack as it ages should also be borne in mind. There are many types of frame structure, and poles vary in weight and strength. A visit to a show site with pitched tents is a worthwhile exercise before making any purchase.

Ventilation

Condensation is a by-product of nylon tents and will be increased by cooking inside the porch. Many tents have 2-way zips, often with a weatherproof flap at the top. Doors at both ends of the tent are useful, and an important safety consideration in the event of a accident involving fire. Some tents have ventilation flaps in the outer skin, usually held open by the main guy line. Good ventilation is particularly desirable in hot weather.

Space

Space is generally only won at the expense of additional weight, although good design can make effective use of all the available room. In bad weather, the tent may have to be shared with the rucksack, unless a suitable plastic bag is carried. In extreme weather conditions a porch may be essential to permit cooking (see *5.3.1 Cooking* on page 126 for safe use of stoves). Ventilation systems should not allow the flysheet to flap against the stove. A second porch is a convenient luxury and inside the inner entrance, adequate headroom is a positive boon in wet weather especially if there is sufficient to allow a comfortable sitting position to be adopted when cooking. For valley camps, standing headroom is a pleasant luxury.

Other features
- Pegs should be strong enough to push into relatively stony ground.
- A suspension point on the inner tent ceiling is useful for hanging a head torch.
- Some tents utilise storage space in the ceiling area – a helpful feature for drying out damp items.
- Mosquito netting is an essential feature if one is likely to encounter these scourges: a fine mesh will be required to keep midges at bay.
- A short length of tubing for repairing broken poles is well worth its weight. This should be about 15 centimetres in length and fit snugly over both broken ends of a snapped pole, allowing them to be joined together again.

5.3.5 Sleeping bags
In areas such as the British Isles, damp conditions are as much a concern as the cold. Down bags should therefore be treated with care as they readily soak up water with consequent reduction of their insulating properties. Synthetic bags are a cheaper and increasingly more viable choice, particularly in emergency use.

A vast range of sleeping bags is available to suit all pockets. They are graded according to the number of *seasons* for which they are comfortable. A *one-season* bag is suitable only for lowland summer conditions. For normal summer conditions, a *two-season* sleeping bag is barely adequate in the hills but can be enhanced by wearing fleece or woollen clothing. *Three-season* bags are ideal for most hill walking requirements in the British Isles from approximately April through to October. *Four-season* sleeping bags are designed to be used in winter conditions.

Various types of construction are available. Some bags are sewn straight through the various layers. This allows cold spots and is generally to be avoided. Other constructions include box quilting and offset layers, which eliminate this problem. The bag should include covering for the head, and ideally a baffle with draw cord around the shoulders to prevent heat loss. A full-length zip is a useful feature if made from good-quality components, affording flexibility in ventilation, and also allowing the bag to be placed around a casualty for emergency use.

The use of a sleeping bag liner allows the sleeping bag to be kept cleaner. Liners are particularly useful for sleeping bags that are lent out for group use, as they can be easily washed. A good liner can make quite a difference to the warmth of a sleeping bag; fleece liners can add a whole season of functionality.

5.3.6 Insulating mats
Various types are available, according to pocket and requirements.

Closed-cell foam pads are light, waterproof, and durable. On the downside, they are bulky, quite expensive, inconvenient to pack, and provide little cushioning on rough ground.

Open-cell foam pads are ultra-light and relatively inexpensive. They compress better than closed-cell foam and cushion well, but they are easily damaged and most significantly soak up water like a sponge.

Self-inflating mattresses are very comfortable, have adjustable air pressure, good body heat retention, compress better than closed-cell and, and are easy to pack. They are expensive, heavier and more slippery than closed-cell pads, and are prone to puncture. Puncture-repair kits are available but these are difficult to use successfully in practice.

For group use, closed-cell mats are the best option, as they are tough and waterproof. For colder conditions, two three-quarter length mats used together provide good insulation for minimum weight increase. Indeed, full-length mats represent something of a luxury for remote camping, especially for shorter people. For valley campsites, a *li-lo*, or even a camp bed provides a very comfortable alternative, if weight is not an issue.

Mats are bulky items and this can be a problem for campers who intend to carry them hill walking. Most mats are intended to be rolled up and inflatable mats can be further compressed by squeezing air out, then sealing the plug to 'vacuum pack' them. Mats are often carried on the outside of rucksacks because of their bulk. However, care should be taken to protect them from damage and rain, ideally by packing in a suitably protective bag.

5.3.7 Bivouac bags

The cheapest bivouac (often referred to as 'bivy' or 'bivvi') bags are made from heavy grade polythene usually measuring about 1.75 metres by 1.25 metres, although lighter, smaller ones are available and would suffice in an emergency. They are adequate for emergency use and can even be incorporated into an emergency stretcher (see *13.4 Assisted movement and carries* on page 247). For planned overnight trips, however, they produce so much condensation that the sleeping bag will become soaked. They are therefore only suitable as a back-up for a night spent under the stars in a lowland site.

'Bivy' bags constructed from waterproof breathable fabrics provide a versatile alternative to camping if the weather is not too severe, particularly if a hooped extension is provided to give headspace. They can also be used to protect the sleeping bag within a tent and provide extra warmth, as well as reducing condensation problems in an emergency bivouac.

The following tips will provide a more comfortable night in a bivouac bag:
- Apply a thin bead of *Seam Grip* sealant on all seams, even if the bag has been seam-sealed at the factory. This increases the chances of keeping water out and protects the seams from damage.
- Use an insulating mat, and place a plastic bivy bag under a breathable bag to assist water resistance.
- Reduce condensation by keeping the head out of the bivy shelter if conditions permit.
- Place boots and/or clothes in the headspace. This keeps them dry and helps lift the bivy material away from the face when fully covered due to wet or cold conditions.
- Condensation will gradually soak the sleeping bags contents, so a down sleeping bag may only be suitable for a single night in cold wet conditions.

FIGURE 5.06 MAXIMISING INSULATION FOR AN EMERGENCY NIGHT OUT

FIGURE 5.07 AN EMERGENCY BIVOUAC
PHOTO // STEVE LONG

- Most breathable bags utilise waterproof, breathable material for the top half and a non-breathable tent-style base. Bivy bags that have half or more coverage of breathable material have less condensation problems, but are more expensive.

5.4 Emergency nights out

Enforced nights out always feel longer and more miserable than ever anticipated. It is preferable to navigate off the hill unless injuries or equipment failure make this impractical. Back at base, the group's contacts will be worried and may even initiate a rescue search, so walkers should make every effort to evacuate themselves, unless this is genuinely felt to be a riskier option than staying put.

If forced to spend the night out, walkers should seek out a site ideally close to a main path and sheltered from the wind. Heat loss into the ground is a particular problem and the walker should maximise insulation using rucksacks and their contents, supplemented by layers of vegetation if available.

Morale is easier to maintain in a group shelter, and keeping everybody together allows the leader to watch for signs of deterioration in any individuals. Occasional food and drink breaks, with musical interludes if the party is willing, will help to make the long night seem less interminable. The party should use all available clothing, making a particular effort to place dry clothing in contact with the skin. Individual bivy bags used within the group shelter will give extra warmth, while still allowing the leader to keep a watchful eye over the whole party.

part **2**

PHOTO // JOHN COUSINS

The upland environment

6

PHOTO // © MY GOOD IMAGES, SHUTTERSTOCK

Where can we go?

All walkers are ambassadors for those who will later follow in their footsteps. A basic understanding of land access arrangements is vital because virtually all land in Britain and Ireland is privately owned. Key elements for sustainable enjoyment include knowledge of land ownership and legislation, as well as an appreciation of the needs of other users. Much of the underlying information is readily available in popular publications and on the internet.

6.1 Interested parties

Despite an average population density of approximately 250 persons per square kilometre in mainland Britain, most of the seventy million inhabitants live in central and southern England and the central belt of Scotland, leaving much of Scotland, Wales, and northern England thinly populated. A similar population pattern is found in Ireland, with most of the population concentrated in the east, around Greater Dublin and Greater Belfast. Although the beauty of our hills and moors is well-known, visitors from Europe and the United States are often surprised by their wildness and the roughness of the terrain underfoot, given their low altitude and limited extent compared to wilderness areas elsewhere. That this is still the case is remarkable. Nonetheless, virtually all land in the British Isles is privately owned by individuals or organisations – even within National Parks.

Our hills are the focus for the recreation of perhaps a million walkers of varying degrees of seriousness, not to mention fell runners, climbers, horse riders, mountain bikers, anglers, paragliders, trials bike riders and 4x4 enthusiasts. At the same time, they are important to the nation, as sources of water, minerals, roofing slate, road stone and renewable energy, be it hydroelectric or wind power. They are important for the maintenance of biodiversity and the continuing survival of many species of plant and animal, for the rearing of livestock, for the growing of timber and (sometimes controversially) for the training of soldiers and the pilots of jets and helicopters. They are the location for large sporting estates based on deer stalking, salmon fishing and grouse shooting. And last, but by no means least, they are the homes of local communities, who have rights and economic needs, as well as deep cultural roots, nourished in some areas by the Celtic languages, in crofting and hill farming. Not surprisingly, there is the potential for conflict between diverging sets of values and widely different world views. Even amongst walkers, there will be differences of opinion – for instance botanists will not always see eye-to-eye with ghyll scramblers.

Given this huge range of pressures on the upland environment, it is a tribute to the democratic process that our mountains and moorlands have become more rather than less accessible and that they are still a source of inspiration and renewal to so many. It should be noted that a significant by-product of the foot and mouth epidemic of 2001 was a wider appreciation of the contribution that tourism – with hill walking in particular – makes to local economies. The epidemic marked a turning point in the relations between many local councils and leisure groups.

6.2 The legal framework

The legal situation differs for the various nations that constitute the British Isles.

6.2.1 England and Wales

Until recently hill-goers only had an explicit legal right to walk on the various Public Rights Of Way: footpaths, bridleways, highways, and on specific **Registered Common Land**. These Rights of Way are shown in red on Ordnance Survey 1:50,000 maps and in green on 1:25,000 maps. Rights of access to open fell existed in many areas but were not enshrined in law.

The situation began to change with the Countryside and Rights of Way (CRoW) Act of 2000, which defined a statutory right of access on foot to uncultivated open countryside, defined as mountain, moor, heath, down – open country and registered common land are now known collectively as access land. The Act was the culmination of a long campaign co-ordinated by the Ramblers Association in which the British Mountaineering Council (BMC) played an active and important part. The CRoW Act states that "… any person is entitled … to enter and remain on access land for the purposes of open air recreation".

However, it was to be another five years before the CRoW Act came into effect on 31 October 2005, because accurate maps of all open access land had to be compiled before the Act could be enforced. In Wales this research was managed by the Countryside Council for Wales (CCW) and in England by the Countryside Agency (CA), who first had to design a mapping methodology which included the definitions to decide what is a mountain[1], moor, heath and down.

Following a review by several Government organisations involved in rural policy and delivery, the Natural Environment and Rural Communities Act 2006 merged those parts of the Countryside Agency charged with environmental activity with English Nature and parts of the Rural Development Service to form Natural England (NE). In Wales the work of the CCW was taken over in April 2013 by Natural Resources Wales (NRW) which also took over the duties and work previously carried out in Wales by the Forestry Commission and the Environment Agency.

The respective websites of the NRW and NE (*www.naturalresources wales.gov.uk* and *www.naturalengland.org.uk*) have much useful information about the access situation, and many useful links, including the latest maps of open country as defined by the CRoW Act. It should be remembered that the conclusive maps are subject to legal disputes in some areas and will be reviewed every ten years, in consultation with local access forums.

The overall result of the CRoW legislation was that walkers are no longer restricted by law to specific paths on more than four million acres of wild land, in return for consideration of other users' needs. Schedule 2 of CRoW legislation lists activities that are not covered by the new right, and CRoW does not allow for use of motorised vehicles or intentional damage to wildlife and plants. Some integral parts of the outdoor experience for many people such as camping, swimming in non-tidal waters and lighting fires are also specifically exempted from the access rights.[2] With regard to swimming and camping, it is best to pursue a policy of 'out of sight, out of mind' away from water catchments, as was the case before. Fires are more problematic. There is something archetypal

1 'Mountain' was defined by CA as "all land over 600m above sea level and other upland areas comprising rugged and steep land, crag, scree, fell, or other bare rock and associated rough vegetation".
2 Dartmoor National Park allows wild camping within the 1985 amendment to National Park legislation.

about sitting round a campfire, but a fire out of control can be hugely destructive and moreover dead wood in upland environments is an important source of nutrients and shelter: walkers should respect the sensitivities of landowners and managers in this regard.

The CRoW Act does not give permission for commercial activities on open access land but that most activities undertaken by groups under instruction (such as teaching navigation, hill-skills, or similar) are not regarded as being strictly 'commercial' under the guidance, especially if the group involved is from a charity, educational group, local authority or voluntary organisation. Activities organised for promoting or teaching an adventurous outdoor activityare unlikely to be undertaken or organised for commercial purpose under the terms of the Crow Act.

At the time of writing (2013) the government of England has started to exercise the new powers given by the Marine and Coastal Access Bill (2009) for the creation of a corridor of access land around the coast of England, extending legal access rights into the 30% of our coast that is currently inaccessible at high tide. In Wales, the Welsh Government created an All Wales coastal path and in late 2013 started a consultation on reviewing all the access legislationand rights in Wales with a view to improving and increasing the amount of land available for responsible outdoor recreation. At the time of writing this process was still ongoing.

6.2.2 Scotland

In Scotland there are almost 7,000 rights of way, but very few are sign-posted, and they are not shown at all on OS maps. In practice, the public has long enjoyed access to most of the large areas of open land owned by the National Trust and the National Trust for Scotland, and enjoyed unhindered *de facto* access to many other mountain and moorland areas, albeit with more areas limited in stalking seasons than south of the border.[3]

The traditional rights of access (including wild camping) became statutory after the Land Reform (Scotland) Act of 2003 received royal assent on 25th February 2003. Access rights can now be exercised over most land and inland water in Scotland provided that visitors behave responsibly by following the Scottish Outdoor Access Code (SOAC). Specific exclusions are detailed in the Scottish Outdoor Access Code and include gardens immediately surrounding a property, greens on a golf course and areas such as building sites and working quarries.

The SOAC is based on three key principles which apply equally to the public and to land managers:

• **Respect the interests of other people.** Acting with courtesy, consideration and awareness is very important. If you are exercising access rights, make sure that you respect the privacy, safety and livelihoods of those living or working in the outdoors, and the needs

---

3 In Scotland the stalking season is 1 July – 20 October for red stags, 21 October – 15 February for hinds – over half the year potentially, with additional time on some forest estates for roe deer. In England and Wales, the open season for red stags only excludes 1 May – 31 July. Grouse shooting restricts access on some moorland between the 'Glorious' 12 August and 10 December.

of other people enjoying the outdoors. If you are a land manager, respect people's use of the outdoors and their need for a safe and enjoyable visit.

- **Care for the environment.** If you are exercising access rights, look after the places you visit and enjoy, and leave the land as you find it. If you are a land manager, help maintain the natural and cultural features which make the outdoors attractive to visit and enjoy.
- **Take responsibility for your own actions.** If you are exercising access rights, remember that the outdoors cannot be made risk-free and act with care at all times for your own safety and that of others.

The access rights also exclude activities such as hunting, shooting or fishing. The use of motorised recreation or passage is barred, except by people with a disability using a vehicle or vessel adapted for their use.

Local authorities retain the right to exempt land from access rights for short periods and to introduce by-laws.

6.2.3 Ireland

The situation in Ireland, both North and South is more uncertain. Farmers are legally entitled to forbid access and there have been a couple of highly publicised cases of confrontation. However, if walkers are friendly, and sensitive about where they park and what routes they choose, there will normally be no objection to small groups and families walking on moorland or hill. Large groups, particularly commercial groups, may generally be less welcome and such parties should always seek prior permission. Dogs are not welcome and loose dogs may legally be shot if seen in the vicinity of farm animals.

Within the Republic of Ireland, there are six National Parks; although public access is permitted, the primary aim of the parks is conservation, and there is currently no legal right of entry. Similarly, although Coillte, the state forestry company, maintains an open access policy, the public has no legal right of entry. Concern over public access prompted a strong and successful campaign in 2013 against Government proposals to sell future harvesting rights to Coillte's estate. There are 43 national way-marked trails, totalling over 3,300 kilometres, plus many other local trails, all of which are open (see *www.irishtrails.ie*). These trails are based on permissive access agreements; none is legally a public right of way. Under the Walks Scheme introduced in 2008 landowners on certain trails are paid to carry out maintenance work on the section of trail crossing their land. While this scheme has generated goodwill amongst those who benefit, it was not available to landowners who facilitate informal access and the scheme has been closed to new entrants since December 2010. Comhairlena Tuaithe, the national body with responsibility for access, is currently piloting a Mountain Access Project in two areas, Binn Shléibhe near Clonbur, Co. Galway and the MacGillycuddy's Reeks in Co. Kerry. The Mountain Access Project seeks to secure access to a defined area through the voluntary agreement of all landowners, by agreeing entry points with the landowners, providing any necessary parking, stiles etc, providing clear information to recreational users and indemnifying landowners against any claims that might arise from recreational activity on their land. While this model has the potential to provide a solution to the difficult issue of access, progress with the pilots has been slow. A private members' bill proposing a right of access to the countryside was debated in the Dáil in June 2013 but there is considerable resistance and it appears unlikely that this will progress much further. Mountaineering Ireland, the representative body for walkers and climbers, aims to improve and secure on-going access, with initial emphasis on securing access to state-owned land in the Republic and Northern Ireland.

In Northern Ireland there are few public rights of way in upland areas and landowners remain deeply concerned about public liability. Nevertheless, provided walkers behave with courtesy and common sense, access to the hills is usually not too difficult. In the Mourne Mountains, by far the most popular area, access is generally easy with well-established car parks and routes through enclosed land on to the hills. The Ulster Way, which traverses the six counties of Northern Ireland, has access difficulties in some areas but most of the popular areas are open. Outdoor Recreation NI has developed a number of waymarked routes and publishes the *www.walkni.com* website, which is a useful source of information on walking in Northern Ireland.

While changes in the law with regard to access and occupiers' liability in Northern Ireland have been recommended, to date access has not been high on the political agenda. The new Outdoor Recreation Action Plan for Northern Ireland (2013) recommends a review of the existing Northern Ireland access legislation in order to make it easier to assert public rights of way, to create access to open country and to achieve a right of access to all public land.

For an update on the access situation in the Republic and Northern Ireland, check the website of Mountaineering Ireland – *www.mountaineering.ie*

The Leave No Trace message is promoted throughout the island of Ireland. Leave No Trace Ireland was established in 2006 by a number of organisations with a shared interest in encouraging responsible outdoor recreation. Leave No Trace is based on an education programme which helps people understand the impact of their activities and make better choices when they use the outdoors. See *www.leavenotraceireland.org*

6.3 Getting on with our neighbours

Rights do not come without responsibilities. Walkers now have an explicit right to walk over much of the wild land of Great Britain. In return, they also have a responsibility to treat the land with respect and those who own or manage it with consideration. To a large extent, this is a matter of common sense and basic courtesy, but it is enshrined in both the Countryside Code and the SOAC.

In the light of the CRoW and Land Reform (Scotland) Act 2003, it is essential to recognise that there is no right of access over cultivated farmland except on public rights of way. Both give guidance for control of dogs; in the CRoW act dogs must be kept on short fixed leads at all times near livestock and between 1 March and 31 July elsewhere to protect ground nesting birds, while in Scotland 'close control' is acceptable, meaning the dog remains to heel and responds to commands. In rural areas, these considerations outweigh any social benefits of bringing any dogs to accompany a group. Failure to remove dog dirt in all public places will be an offence throughout Scotland and subject to local bylaws elsewhere in the British Isles.

6.4 Information sources

South of the Scottish Border, the most accessible sources of information on access are Ordnance Survey maps. Ordnance Survey maps show public rights of way and the boundaries of National Trust land. 'Explorer' maps (1:25,000 scale) now show access land, but it should be noted that this is a 'broad brush' depiction that includes 'excepted land' such as land within 20 metres of a dwelling or stable. However this information, can – and does – change. In this respect the map is an item of equipment worth updating on a regular basis, rather than waiting until the old one disintegrates.

Walkers also need to be aware that landowners can restrict access to specific areas for up to 28 days in a year for any purpose (but not at weekends or public holidays), which may mean changing plans during a walk. Longer restrictions are possible if they can be shown to be necessary for land management or reducing fire risk and public safety and NRW and NE can make constrictions for conservation reasons. Upcoming notified and longer restrictions are shown on the online mapping mentioned above (*http://magic.defra.gov.uk/MagicMap.aspx* and *www.ccw.gov.uk*). On the ground, signs depicting access land may be erected, or in rare

FIGURE 6.01 ACCESS LAND SIGN

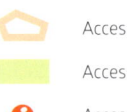

Access land boundary and tint

Access land in wooded area

Access information point

FIGURE 6.02 SYMBOLS ON OS 1:25,000 MAPS

instances a crossed version of the icon may be used for exclusions or restrictions.

National parks have a range of services to help the visitor. Each park has at least one information centre and a ranger service and most have a Youth and Schools Liaison Officer who will be happy to advise visiting groups.

In the British Isles the three mountaineering councils (*British Mountaineering Council*, *Mountaineering Council of Scotland* and *Mountaineering Ireland*) all work hard to maintain and improve access for walkers and climbers. They can offer advice and information and like to be informed if any serious problems are encountered.

In Scotland, the SOAC describes the parameters for access, but specific details require further research. The former *Hillphones* service has now been replaced with web-based information on deer stalking. Heading for the Scottish Hills (*www.outdooraccess-scotland.com/outdoors-responsibly/access-code-and-advice/scottish-hills/heading-scottish-hills/*) is organised by the Mountaineering Council of Scotland and Scottish Natural Heritage (SNH – see *www.snh.org.uk*), on behalf of the National Access Forum, and gives detailed stalking information and contact details for those Estates who are members. Although the service does not cover all stalking in the Highlands and does not include the hind cull, it is an important step towards improving co-operation between walkers and the sporting estates. A leaflet explaining the scheme and giving relevant phone numbers is widely distributed in shops and magazines but failing that, the MC of S and SNH can supply copies. There is a wealth of advice and information about access throughout the Outdoor Access website. It is the walker's responsibility to ensure they have all the information available to them on stalking before they set out on their walk.

Natural England and Natural Resources Wales (and their predecessors) have published various leaflets about access in England and Wales. Their respective websites(*www.naturalengland.org.uk* and *www.naturalresourceswales.gov.uk*) have much useful information about the access situation, and many useful links, including the latest maps of open country as defined by the CroW act.

In 2012 Sport Northern Ireland and the Northern Ireland Environment Agency published two 'Enjoy the Great Outdoors' leaflets – a general guide for recreational users and a guide for responsible dog owners (available on *www.outdoorrecreationni.com*).

In 2013 Comhairlena Tuaithe published 'Recreation in the Irish Countryside', a public information leaflet for landowners and recreational users (available on *www.countrysidecouncil.ie*).

PATH EROSION *PHOTO // ELFYN JONES*

Protecting it
for the future

Our wild places are the results of a fragile balance
between the changing forces of nature and the demands
of successive generations of landowners and users.
Government policies represent the will of the people,
but it is the responsibility of every individual to play
a part in preserving this heritage for the future.
It is possible for all of us to help find the balance
between healthy recreation and unnecessary
impact on delicate ecosystems.

7.1 The balance of forces

"I often wonder how many people realise what battles have been fought to keep this fine region as little blemished as it is. How many are conscious of the perennial pressures that come from would-be exploiters and their philistine projects?"[1]

FIGURE 7.01 NATIONAL TRUST SIGN
PHOTO // STEVE LONG

The distinguished naturalist, Bill Condry, wrote those words about Snowdonia many years ago. However, they could have been applied to any upland area in the British Isles and they are even more relevant today than they were then. The pressures to develop the upland environment for profit are enormous. Inappropriate planning applications are dressed up emotively as answering a local or a national need or creating jobs; all too often, they are successful.

The uplands of Britain have been awarded many designations, designed to protect their special qualities. *Sites of Special Scientific Interest* (SSSI), national parks, *Areas of Outstanding Natural Beauty* and *National Scenic Areas* (Scotland) give our wilder landscapes a degree of protection, but only a degree. The interests represented on national park committees sometimes allow long-term damage to be inflicted for short-term benefit. Moreover, whilst a park authority can apply stringent planning controls to housing, it has little control over agricultural or forestry developments. National park officers do a fine job with very limited resources but they have always been under-valued by government and are fighting a constant rear-guard action. Similarly, the title of *National Nature Reserve* or Site of Special Scientific Interest has not always been sufficient to protect specific habitats. During the nineteen-eighties, when government agencies simply did not have the funds to compensate landowners, SSSIs were being destroyed at the rate of one a day. Matters have improved since then but much has been lost.

Upland farming in the latter quarter of the twentieth century was steered by per-head subsidies for livestock that has led to extensive over-grazing, and by short-term policies encouraging drainage, re-seeding, road-building, hedge clearance and fencing. This activity was funded by the Common Agricultural Policy (CAP) and promoted by the Department of the Environment, Food and Rural Affairs (DEFRA). The government agencies responsible for conservation at the time (*English Nature*, *Countryside Council for Wales* and *Scottish Natural Heritage*) opposed these policies but had little power to fund alternatives. The CAP delayed the economic decline of livestock farming in the uplands but it has resulted in a rapid and irreversible loss of habitats and a steady

1 *The Snowdonia National Park*, The New Nationalist Series, 1966.

FIGURE 7.02 CONSTRUCTING A ROAD ACROSS A HILL TOP   *PHOTO // NATIONAL TRUST*

degradation of the landscape. However, it is heartening that over the last few years the emphasis has shifted from productivity at all costs to agri-environmental schemes that encourage conservation and good practice in land management under the stewardship of less fragmented agencies for environmental matters reflected by the changes in title to Natural England and recently in Wales to Natural Resources Wales. In particular, moves away from per-head subsidy appear to have been reasonably successful in encouraging moves back towards less intensive grazing.

There are ways in which individuals can help to make a difference. One is by supporting watchdog organizations like the Save the Cairngorms Campaign, Friends of the Lake District or the Snowdonia Society, who also do their best to encourage good practice through farm award schemes, dry-stone walling competitions and litter clearance. Another is to write letters about specific issues or developments. Letters to local councillors, national park officers or MPs do make a difference, particularly in deciding whether a controversial planning application should be called in for a public inquiry. Yet another way is to support bodies that protect wild land or an important habitat by buying it. Examples are the *Royal Society for the Protection of Birds*, the *Woodland Trust*, the *John Muir Trust* and the *County Wildlife Trusts*, who are all now significant landowners. The biggest players of all, the *National Trust* and the *National Trust for Scotland*, own huge amounts of land all over the United Kingdom – although it might be argued that their purchasing power may have undermined the ability of local farmers to purchase property on the open market. Although often leased to tenant farmers, Trust properties are managed to conserve the landscape and all that lives and grows on it whilst allowing public access, a balancing act that is achieved, on the whole, very successfully. The walker wishing to help conserve the landscape that he or she enjoys could do worse than join one of these charitable trusts.

7.2 The impact of people on the uplands

Without a doubt, the greatest impact on the uplands over the last thirty years, both visually and in terms of habitat destruction, has been from commercial forestry and agriculture, the latter in the form of drainage, access roads, new fencing, over-grazing and the use of quad bikes on wet, boggy terrain. In addition, masts for radio, TV and telephones and, more recently, wind turbines have been proliferating even in protected areas.

Ski areas have a profound impact on the few sites in Scotland where commercial skiing has been developed, with their uplift facilities and car parking. These are superimposed on important and fragile ecosystems. Environmental protection restrictions associated with the funicular scheme (the Visitor Management Plan) constructed on Cairngorm at the turn of the century have reduced the choices available to walkers for gaining entry to this area – at the time of writing access to the Cairngorm summit during the summer months from the top station is only allowed under the direct supervision of a ranger!

Less obvious visually, but of great significance ecologically, has been the acidification of lakes and rivers thanks to acid rain, exacerbated in some places by conifer plantations, whilst high levels of nitrogen and ozone in the air are beginning to affect vegetation. It can only be a matter of time before global warming begins to affect arctic alpine plants, especially in southerly regions like the Brecon Beacons and Snowdonia. By contrast, the effect of walkers on the upland environment has been relatively small. Nonetheless, the number of walkers and climbers visiting the mountains and moors of the UK in thirty years has roughly quad-rupled because of increasing prosperity, leisure time and ease of travel nation-wide. This has led to congestion on the roads, especially in the summer, and demands for road widening schemes. Parking has become a problem at weekends throughout the year in popular locations, with park and ride experiments an inevitable response.

7.2.1 Paths

All over the British Isles, the walking boom has resulted in sheep trods becoming tracks, paths becoming quagmires and major paths becoming eroded scars visible from miles away. Reducing and managing the impact of millions of pairs of feet is important if some sense of wildness in the hills is to be retained and if walkers are to co-exist with land managers, wildlife and plants.

Walkers can help to reduce erosion by resisting the temptation to walk on the grass at the edge of a path. This is understandable when the path is muddy or stony, but trampling causes the grass to die, allowing the topsoil to wash away and the path to grow steadily wider. Wearing gaiters makes it easier to walk on wet or muddy paths, thereby preventing damage to path margins and the widening of eroded paths. Similarly, following the zigzags of a path in descent as well as ascent, rather than cutting corners, reduces the gullying that can destroy the whole path.

Although getting off the beaten track is an important part of the outdoor experience for some, leaders of groups need to ask themselves

FIGURE 7.03 DIFFERENT APPROACHES TO FOOTPATH WORK   *PHOTOS // ELFYN JONES*

whether the benefit to their charges justifies the impact that they will undoubtedly have. The answer will depend on the size, level of experience and maturity of the group and the nature of the terrain, but leaders need to be clear about it in their own minds. In general, the less experienced the group, the less it will benefit, and the larger the group, the more damage it will cause. On the whole, parties of novices from schools, centres or youth groups do not need to explore away from paths in order to have a worthwhile experience.

When going off-road or even on small paths, footwear can make a difference. Experienced walkers can wear light boots or even approach shoes, which will have relatively little impact, whereas less experienced walkers will need the ankle support and edging capabilities of a heavier boot, especially in wet conditions.

Another way to reduce the impact of a group away from a path, provided it is not precluded by safety factors, is to spread out rather than walking in single file.

7.2.2 Footpath repairs

Early attempts at footpath repairs were not always successful in terms of standing the test of time, blending with the landscape or even in persuading walkers to actually use them. Much has been learned over the years, however, and nowadays most work is skilfully and sensitively carried out, using appropriate local materials to produce paths that are well drained and user-friendly. It is, however, labour-intensive work and expensive.

One way in which walkers can put something back is to support the work of the *Access and Conservation Trust* (ACT), which has been formed by the national mountaineering councils. As well as giving financial support it is possible to take part in one of the working holidays that the National Trust, the John Muir Trust and the *British Trust for Conservation Volunteers* organise for their members. Typically, work includes dry stone walling, tree planting, rhododendron bashing and litter clearance as well

FIGURE 7.04 A CAIRNED PATH   *PHOTO // STEVE LONG*

as footpath repairs. Instead of visiting summits and covering miles, participants expend an equal amount of effort coming to know a small location in intimate detail, learning new skills and gaining new insights into the land as they do so. Many walkers have found the change of focus provided by such holidays extremely rewarding.

7.2.3 Cairns

Man-made piles of boulders known as cairns can be found throughout the uplands of the British Isles. Some are very old. Many of the large mounds of stones found on the summits are Bronze Age burial sites dating back to a time when the climate was warmer and drier than it is now and people lived high up in the mountains. The tradition of adding a stone to a summit cairn probably goes back a very long way.

A small cairn, which marks a path junction or a descent gully, or where a path crosses a boulder field, serves a useful purpose and few would quarrel with this. However, the proliferation of cairns way-marking paths that has occurred over the last thirty years is unsightly, unnecessary and, sometimes, downright confusing. Nor can there be any justification for attempts to create new paths by cairning. Systematic but responsible dismantling of new cairns is to be encouraged, replacing stones on rocky ground, preferably with lichen intact and in similar orientation to surrounding rocks. It should be remembered, however, that some old cairns are important historical monuments, so destroying these particular cairns could be regarded as an act of vandalism.

Dartmoor has suffered harmful erosion due to the widespread popularity of various treasure hunt exercises known as letter boxing. Written clues or rubber stamps are hidden in peat hags or within cairns and walls, resulting in repeated erosion from people seeking the hidden artefact. In recent years the 'digital' version of this pastime – geocaching, has the potential to increase this erosion dramatically. These activities are best reserved for urban locations where plants and wildlife do not lead such a precarious existence.

FIGURE 7.05 HIGH- AND LOW-VISIBILITY TENTS *PHOTO // CARLO FORTE*

7.2.4 Wildness

For many people, much of the pleasure of hill walking stems from a sense of wildness and emptiness. British hills are neither wild nor empty in an absolute sense, even in the far north of Scotland; but relative to life in the cities, they most certainly are and that sense is one that can be enhanced or diminished by our own and other people's behaviour. Leaving litter behind is an obvious example of an action that impinges on the enjoyment of others. Scratching of graffiti on rock, throwing stones into lakes, trundling boulders downhill and unnecessary shouting are all examples of behaviour that is upsetting to others whilst also damaging the environment and disturbing wildlife. This type of activity is most common among young people and is usually a thoughtless expression of energy and exuberance rather than malicious vandalism. It can easily be pre-empted, for instance, by a group discussion beforehand on the purpose and meaning of national parks followed perhaps by a timely reminder. That same energy can be usefully harnessed in the cause of conservation by, say, a litter sweep of a popular summit or taking down a few superfluous cairns.

Other, less obvious but still significant behaviours that detract from a sense of wildness in the hills are physical damage such as the creation of fire rings or stone circles where tent pegs have been weighted down or transient impact from using brightly coloured clothes and tents – or both, in the case of unnecessarily large groups. It is astonishing how a green tent is all but invisible even at close range whereas an orange one stands out like a beacon. It is for good reason that greens and browns are the preferred colours for deer stalking.

The use of mobile phones is another contentious issue. Nobody can object to carrying a mobile for emergency use (bearing in mind that there remain many places where it is not possible to pick up a signal) but it is more considerate to keep it switched off – perhaps stored in the first aid kit. In a high lonely place, the magic of the moment is destroyed by a ringing telephone and the return to urban values that it represents.

7.3 Habitat protection and recreational needs

It is surprisingly infrequent for access to the hills to be restricted on conservation grounds. Partly, this is because many walkers are conservationists (and *vice versa*). They derive pleasure from the birds, plants and rocks they see around them and 'tread lightly' as a result. However, it is also because land managers have discovered that, in busy areas, creating and maintaining good paths is the best form of protection for plants and wildlife. The vast majority of walkers prefer to stay on well-defined paths, so trampling of vegetation and disturbance to birds and mammals does not have to be an issue.

Another factor is that conservation bodies have learned from bitter experience in places like Glencoe and Ben Lawers that publicity, ease of access and visitor centres are the kiss of death to wild country. The Cairngorm plateau, with its thin soil and easily damaged communities of lichens, mosses and arctic alpine flowers, is another habitat that has suffered severely since access became relatively easy [2]. Tempting though it is to recoup money spent on land acquisition by providing facilities for the public, mass tourism is simply not in the best interests of wildlife. The RSPB has achieved a compromise in Scotland, heavily promoting the osprey site near Loch Garten, but managing unostentatiously a sizeable swathe of the Cairngorms in the Abernethy estate. The John Muir Trust does nothing to hinder public access to its land, but does nothing to encourage it either. Another recent development has been a move towards restricting vehicle access on some former tracks, resulting in longer approach walks. Such policies could be construed as elitist, but at present, they keep visitor numbers to a level that is acceptable in terms of both conservation and retaining some degree of wildness, without resorting to the heavy-handed management practices of some American wilderness areas.

7.4 Sanitation issues

Going to the toilet in the great outdoors is something many people are rather coy about discussing, but it is a problem area and it is essential that it is addressed. The problem is obviously most acute when wild camping, but even day walkers can be caught short and it is all too common to find human excrement and toilet paper beside, or even on, a path. Consideration for others demands that a toilet site should be at least fifty metres away from a path or camp, and preferably not in a cave, sheepfold or ruined building that is likely to be visited by others. However, it is vital that the site should also be at least fifty metres away from a stream or lake. Gut pathogens such as *E coli 0157* and *Cryptosporidium* can be transmitted through contaminated water, and within the last few years, Giardia, a parasite that invades the gut with unpleasant consequences, has become endemic in the mountains of New Zealand, almost certainly as a result of human faecal contamination. It has long been present in North America and many developing countries, making the treatment of water by boiling,

2 The effect of the new funicular railway to within 500 metres of Cairngorm summit has so far been limited by strict access regulations but the dual standards implicit in allowing guided parties may undermine this *status quo*.

FIGURE 7.06 TROWEL AND CIGARETTE LIGHTER   *PHOTO // STEVE LONG*

filtering or with iodine obligatory. If hill-goers are not to be deprived of the chance to drink pure mountain water, so unlike the chlorine-laden liquid that comes from taps (and, contrary to popular belief, very rarely contaminated by dead sheep), they must take this issue seriously.

Toilet paper takes an exceedingly long time to biodegrade. Walkers should either carry a lighter to burn it, or avoid using it altogether; *sphagnum moss* is an effective alternative. Sanitary towels and tampons should be brought home in a poly bag – even if buried they will be scented and dug up by animals. A trowel will allow faeces to be well buried in a hole at least six inches deep. This is particularly important around popular remote campsites; the bacteria in the soil are essential to break it down. Placing a rock over the burial will deter animals from digging it up, but merely placing a rock on top of a turd slows the process down. The trowel needs to be strong; cheap ones bend easily in fibrous upland grass. There is a stainless steel folding model on the market, which is light, compact and no hardship to carry. It is not cheap but costs less than most other items of emergency equipment and is far more likely to be used!

An alternative approach is to carry out toilet materials in order to dispose of them on return to civilisation. This is certainly possible, but there are many difficulties. A suitably tough container is needed, and a reliable disposal system is required back at base. Otherwise, the risks to hygiene outweigh the benefits to the mountain environment.

7.4.1 Washing

Washing, whether of self, clothes or pots and pans should never be done directly into a watercourse, even if biodegradable soap is used. It is far better to use a pot for washing and dispose of the dirty water away from the bank. Food supplies such as boil-in-the-bag minimise the need for washing up and contrast very favourably against old favourites such as bacon and sausages. There is a strong case for not taking soap of any sort into the hills. It is by no means essential in terms of hygiene and can not only affect insects and fish directly, but can also alter the chemical balance of water that is low in nutrients. This can lead to eutrophication, or enrichment, and the growth of algal bloom, which can be harmful to wildlife.

On the other hand, skinny-dipping in an upland tarn or in a pool of a mountain stream, like drinking mountain water, is one of the great joys of hill walking. Despite pronouncements in some quarters, the pollution it causes is minimal and perfectly acceptable in terms of the local ecology – but beware, this is a potentially hazardous activity; see *12.6.1 Lakes* on page 238.

BUTTERWORT   *PHOTO // ANDY SAY*

Understanding
the environment

The moors and mountains are home for many inter-
dependent creatures and plants, some at the extreme
limits of their survival range. Learning about these
environments can be a source of lifelong pleasure,
and helps us to seek a positive balance in our own impact.
These moments of spiritual well-being are all too rare
in modern life; the mountains offer us the freedom to
contemplate our role.

8.1 Ecosystems

Ecology is a relatively new science that looks at plants and animals not in isolation but in terms of their relationships with each other and with their environment. An ecosystem is the sum of these relationships in a particular place. Planet Earth is one enormous ecosystem but the term can also be applied to small, intimate localities. The analogy is often drawn with a spider's web – movement at any point on the web can be felt everywhere else. As John Muir put it long ago, "When we try to pick out anything by itself we find it hitched to everything in the universe".[1] Humans are a natural part of many ecosystems, but since the industrial revolution, their influence on the rest of the earth has become disproportionate. Many environmentalists feel that the huge problems facing the world stem not just from industrialisation and population growth but also from an underlying philosophy that views the earth as a commodity to be exploited rather than a community to which humans belong.

The mountains and moors of the British Isles mean a great deal to a lot of people. Nevertheless, they are ecosystems that have been badly damaged by human activity. The bare, open landscapes that are valued so highly are to a large extent man-made, and in terms of ecology and biodiversity they are in Fraser Darling's memorable phrase, "devastated terrain"[2].

The process started long ago. When Neolithic peoples first began to cut down and burn trees, domesticate animals and significantly alter their environment six thousand years ago, the British hills would have been wooded to 600 metres above sea level in many places. Despite the climate becoming colder since then, the hills would still be tree-covered up to 450 metres in some places, with scrub vegetation growing much higher, had the land been left untouched. However, humans have always needed timber for fires, houses, boats, carts, fences, bows and a host of other uses. As time went by, trees were felled to smelt iron and to clear the ground for crops, and grazing livestock began to inhibit regeneration.

The net effect was for forest cover to decrease steadily. In the more populated, southern parts of Britain, a sophisticated system of woodland management (coppicing) was developed during the Middle Ages to provide a sustainable supply of timber, but this does not seem to have been used in the north and west, where the hills gradually became denuded of trees. Once the tree cover had gone, the characteristic heavy rainfall leached nutrients from the soil, mostly acidic already because of the underlying geology. In time, the soil became waterlogged and blanket peat bogs began to form. The end result was a habitat in which only a few specialised plants and animals could survive and an overall loss of biodiversity. This was especially true in the west of Ireland and the highlands and islands of Scotland, where the colder and wetter conditions accelerated the metamorphosis.

During the 18th and 19th Centuries the process was taken a stage further by the *Clearances* in Scotland and the *Enclosure Acts* of England and Wales, both of which led to heavier and more systematic grazing of the hills by sheep rather than cattle, making woodland regeneration all

1 *The Wilderness World* of John Muir (ed. E.W. Teale).
2 *The Highland and Islands* New Naturalist series. (Fraser Darling).

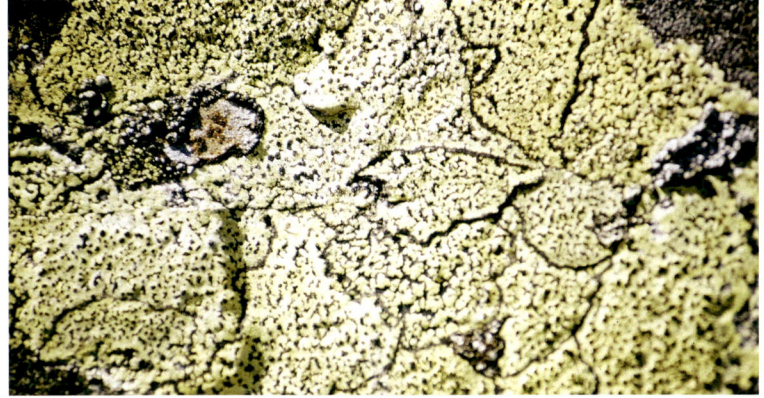

FIGURE 8.01 RICH TEXTURES OF *RHIZOCARPON GEOGRAPHICUM* – GEOGRAPHIC LICHEN

but impossible. The situation has been exacerbated even further in the last forty years by the acidification of lakes and rivers and by overgrazing encouraged by a system of per-head subsidies for sheep. Because sheep, as one ecologist has put it, are not lawnmowers, but highly selective feeders, the effect of overgrazing is to damage and ultimately reduce both heather moorland and the areas of more nutritious grassland. This in turn affects those insects, birds and mammals that prefer those habitats, reducing biodiversity even further. Global warming is yet another factor likely to have an increasing effect in the future.

However, the picture is not all doom and gloom. On the positive side, there are now numerous incentive schemes to encourage lower levels of grazing, the planting of native trees and the exclusion of sheep and deer from woodland. There are also some visionary long-term projects such as *Trees for Life* in Glen Affric and Carrigfran Wildwood in the Southern Uplands, which aim to restore the glens and lower hills to a more natural state. On the other hand, a totally 'hands off' approach will not always favour bio-diversity. In some areas, ecologists favour a regime of light grazing which will prevent specialised habitats such as heather moorland and chalk downs land from reverting to forest.

8.2 Natural history for all

Walkers head for the hills for many different reasons but the most common are a desire for fresh air, exercise, companionship, wide open spaces and beautiful scenery. Coming from an urban background and culture, most Britons have little knowledge of natural history and only for a minority is it a prime motive for hill walking. Yet natural history programmes on television are enormously popular and most people, whatever their age, will take an interest in what lives and grows around them if it is presented in an appropriate way. Receiving a lecture or being bombarded with strange-sounding names is an instant turn-off for all but a few – however, the success of environmental films and dedicated TV channels demonstrates how enthusiastic presenters can share their feelings of wonder, amazement, sorrow and anger to inspire people and awaken their curiosity.

FIGURE 8.02 *DRYAS OCTOPETALA* – MOUNTAIN AVENS   *PHOTO // ROB COLLISTER*

Few outdoor leaders will be trained biologists or ecologists, but that should not inhibit them from sharing with others their own enthusiasms and specific interests. It will be a sorry leader who has no such interests at all. The most important skill to develop, however, is not identifying species or rock types but simply noticing detail, large or small, in the landscape, and having noticed it, bringing an active attention to bear, exploring not only with the eyes but through smell, taste, touch or hearing as well.

People learn in different ways and are attracted to different things. Take a moss-covered boulder, for instance, beside a woodland path. Most walkers will be chattering away so busily that they will not notice it at all. Once it has been pointed out to a group and looked at more closely, some will remain totally unmoved but among the others, there will be a wide range of responses. Some will be curious. How does the boulder come to be there? Why is it covered with moss? How does moss grow on bare rock? Others may be struck by its shape, texture and location, as if it were a piece of sculpture. Others may be more intrigued by the number of different mosses growing there, the intricacy of their varying forms (a magnifying lens can be useful here – even a compass lens will help) or the subtly differing shades of green. Others again may be entranced by the cool, damp springiness beneath their hands or against their cheeks.

Admittedly, adults may be more responsive to a mossy boulder than the average group of teenagers, but there is no lack of alternatives to engage the imagination and attention of all but the most resolute cynic. Most youngsters are fascinated by insectivorous plants like sundew and butterwort (again, a magnifying glass will help, enhancing the spectacle of a midge trapped in sticky dew), which leads naturally to considering why the soil should be so poor in nutrients that plants have adapted in this way. The solitary rowan tree growing from a vertical crag has the drama of a survivor about it which, once noticed, begs many questions. The aerial acrobatics of a raven or a buzzard being mobbed by crows are eye-catching events, worth taking time out to watch (binoculars help) and can lead on to other considerations about animal behaviour.

It is the act of noticing and appreciating that is important, for not only does it enhance the pleasure of a day in the hills, adding an extra dimension to it, but it must also lead to a more caring attitude towards that place. Being able to answer questions is less important, though it would be an opportunity missed if a leader did not take the trouble to find out the answers subsequently. Putting a name to a plant comes last of all, (especially if it is Latin), though it can be fun for a group to invent its own names. For the linguistically minded, however, nomenclature can also provide a fascinating insight into natural history.

Deliberately structuring periods of silence into the day can encourage awareness and observation. Obviously, a leader needs the goodwill and co-operation of the party for these strategies to work and some people will always find it hard to keep quiet. Most, however, will be surprised at how much they see and hear. Even more effective is to create opportunities for individuals to sit quietly and alone, observing the natural world around them and becoming a part of it. Such vigils, which can vary from ten minutes for young children to a four-day vision quest for adults, nearly always provide a powerful experience.

Care for the particular leads to concern for the general. Interest in a moss-covered boulder or a sundew or a rowan tree can lead to greater understanding and a more caring attitude towards the whole mountain. Caring for the mountain not only modifies behaviour on it, but leads to understanding of how its problems reflect wider global issues. Only a more widespread concern about these issues, especially in the West, will force politicians to take them seriously. The potential influence of the out-door leader in promoting awareness and concern, particularly in the young, cannot be overstated.

9

PHOTO // JOHN COUSINS

The weather

The inhabitants of the British Isles are famed for their obsession with the weather. Located at the meeting point of several major weather systems, these islands get more than their fair share of variable weather, giving their inhabitants never ending opportunities to discuss it.

9.1 The weather's impact on walkers

The weather has a profound effect on the walking environment. So an overall impression of what the weather might do for the duration of every walk or expedition is an essential part of the planning process. The final decisions about the itinerary can utilise this information to make best use of the prevailing conditions, after considering the following interconnected factors:

9.1.1 Wind speed and direction

The wind can have a tremendous effect on morale and safety. Strong winds can make conditions feel considerably colder than the air temperature (the wind chill effect), and pin a party down if caught unawares on an exposed ridge. An accurate weather forecast reduces the chances of a party being surprised by gales.

9.1.2 Temperature

How cold is it going to be, especially in that wind? Choice of clothing and spares should be modified according to the temperature. Contingency clothing for a cold autumn day will be more substantial than spares taken on a summer stroll.

9.1.3 Precipitation

Rain or hail preceding or during the walk will have a profound effect on the party. Morale is often lowered by rainfall, particularly in the absence of good quality waterproof clothing. Precipitation also affects the going underfoot; wet rocks can be very slippery and consequently progress will be slower. In the hills precipitation may not just mean rain; even in summer campers in the hills may awaken to a light covering of snow, necessitating great care during the return to civilisation.

9.1.4 Visibility

Low cloud makes navigation considerably more challenging. It may be possible to plan a route that keeps under the cloud base for better views and easier route finding. However, navigation skills are needed within the party to cope with unexpected lowering of the cloud base.

9.1.5 The future

Sooner or later, the weather will change! Sometimes weather systems move a little faster or slower than weather forecasts predict, so some understanding of weather-related phenomena can enable the hill walker to spot warning signs of impending change and act accordingly.

9.2 Weather forecasts

Forecasts come in many types for different regions and users. Whilst a city businessman decides whether or not to carry an umbrella to work, a fisherman's life may depend on an accurate prediction of the sea state. The hill walker's decisions also vary, for example from deciding to walk the Ballachulish Horseshoe clockwise, anti-clockwise or avoiding it altogether.

Hill walkers need to know where they can obtain forecasts and how relevant the information is to their particular situation. Forecasts are available from the following sources:

FIGURE 9.01 SCREENSHOT OF WEATHER WEBSITE

9.2.1 Internet
The Internet holds the greatest wealth of weather information. Accurate and in-depth forecasts can be obtained for just about anywhere in the world and sometimes even a live web-cam view can be obtained directly from the summit. Many sites are dedicated specifically to mountain areas. There is such a plethora of sites and change is so rapid that it is pointless to list useful sites here other than the UK Met Office at *www.metoffice*.gov.uk. Useful links can easily be book-marked and updated and several smartphone apps link to live weather forecasts, allowing a data-enabled phone to receive weather updates even when camped in remote places if reception is available.

9.2.2 Television
Television forecasts are readily obtainable for most households, but are generally quite limited in their relevance for hill walkers, as the forecast is normally designed for the bulk of the population, who work in the towns and cities. However, these forecasts can give a useful overview of weather patterns, particularly if attention is paid to the weather maps. Some channels, for example BBC Scotland on a Friday evening, may provide a weather forecast for hill walkers on a specific evening for the weekend.

Local television often includes weather bulletins for farmers and these can give very useful information for walkers but since they are regional in nature they do not really help anyone at home planning a trip away from their immediate locality.

9.2.3 Telephone/fax
Various companies offer excellent weather forecast services for voice or fax. Hill walkers should take care to obtain forecasts produced specifically for mountain areas. Normally a number is dialled, followed by a specific suffix for a particular range of hills. It is worth checking the cost of these calls since some are commercially run and priced at premium rates.

9.2.4 Newspaper
Newspaper forecasts vary in quality. Generally the more serious newspapers also carry the most detailed forecasts and include regional variations as well as weather maps for the British Isles and Europe. Newspaper forecasts give useful information about weather systems and the movement of air masses, but give little information specific to the hills and mountains.

9.2.5 Posted bulletins

Provided by many tourist offices, mountain shops and outdoor centres, these displayed weather bulletins are often the most specific and accurate forecasts of all. However, some local knowledge may be required to establish where they are located and also viewing times, which may well be limited to opening hours. Sites of other local bulletins may sometimes be obtained from walking and climbing magazines.

9.2.6 Radio

National radio stations give little useful information specifically aimed at the needs of hill walkers. Most radio forecasts focus on the weather for major population centres, so the most useful forecasts for hill walkers are local stations or Radio 4's *Shipping Forecast*. Stations such as Nevis Radio give local forecasts while the shipping forecasts give an indication of approaching weather patterns, if the listener is aware of the locations of the various shipping areas. Radio does retain the advantage that immediate information can be obtained during overnight expeditions, initially from a vehicle radio, or with a lightweight FM radio at remote campsites.

From all these sources a wealth of information is available to assist planning a trip. Effective filtering of this material can allow hill walkers to make informed choices, even with minimal understanding of meteorology. Sometimes an accurate forecast enables hill walkers to avoid the worst of the weather by making an early – or perhaps a late – start, for example to avoid a cold front passing through the area. A basic understanding of the main weather systems allows the observant party to spot tell-tale signs of a weather system that is moving faster or slower than forecast.

9.3 Understanding weather

9.3.1 The atmosphere

A blanket of gases some 1,000km thick surrounds the earth and protects it from the extremes of temperature that are found beyond. Known as the *atmosphere*, this mantle is predominantly calm and stable but the 10km in contact with the earth contains most of the inherently unstable water vapour and is consequently forever changing – bubbling in the heat of the sun like a gigantic cauldron.

The lower layer of the atmosphere produces all our weather and is known as the *troposphere*. Its outer limit, the *tropopause*, can be likened to a membrane that prevents this layer from spreading upwards.

9.3.2 Areas of different temperature

Air that remains stationary for any length of time gradually forms a fairly homogenous *air-mass* that mirrors the *relative humidity* and *temperature* of the earth's surface with which it is in contact. There are many reasons why some air masses can be warmer than others, both locally and globally. When the warm moist air of one air mass meets the cooler, drier air of another, the vapour condenses into clouds and provides the potential for precipitation.

FIGURE 9.02 HOT AND COLD AIR MASS DISTRIBUTION AROUND THE GLOBE

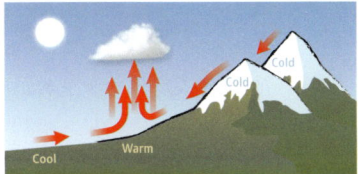

FIGURE 9.03 AN EXAMPLE OF FACTORS LEADING TO LOCALISED WARMING

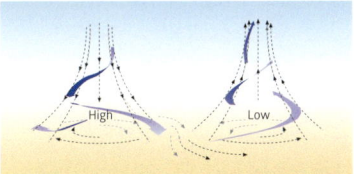

FIGURE 9.04 AIR MOVEMENT IN HIGH AND LOW PRESSURE

9.3.3 Areas of different pressure

It is common knowledge that warm air rises. Rather like removing a weight, this reduces the pressure bearing down on the Earth below. The rising warm air is deflected sideways by the rotation of the Earth (known as *Coreolis Force*) so it spirals upwards in an anticlockwise direction.

On the other hand, cold air sinks and is squashed against the surface of the Earth. This results in an area of higher pressure, and the column of descending air spirals in the opposite direction (clockwise), spreading out ('diverging') at the base. This divergence provides the air that moves into the void left behind by rising air in neighbouring areas of low pressure.

9.4 Creating wind, cloud and rain

Imagine the act of exhaling warm steamy breath on a cold, frosty morning. As it meets the external cold air, the steamy air is cooled and condenses into a cloud. Similarly, cloud and rain result when warm steamy air comes into contact with colder air. In the earth's atmosphere, when warm and cool air masses meet, the warm air is pushed upwards and cooler air is drawn in to fill the void; this movement is one of the factors that creates wind. On moving upwards the warm air cools and clouds are formed by condensation.

One or more of the following three factors usually causes this upward movement and hence *condensation*:

- **Weather systems:** One air mass lifts another. These are large systems that sweep over the whole country, usually in the form of depressions.
- **Convection:** Warm, moisture laden thermals rise and cool. This occurs on both large and local scales.
- **Mountains:** Damp air is lifted over mountains and cooled.

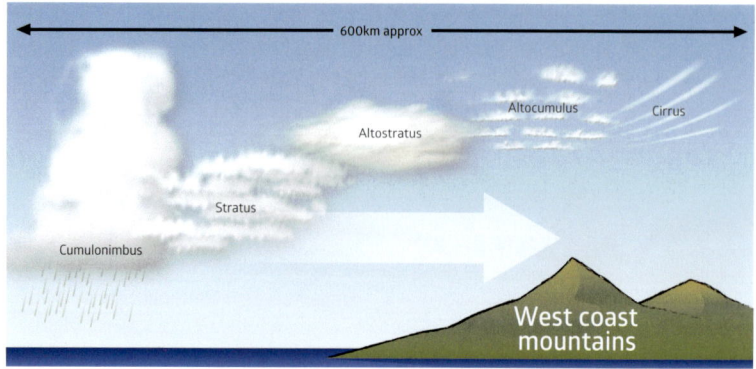

FIGURE 9.05 WEATHER SYSTEM APPROACHING THE UK FROM THE WEST

9.4.1 Weather systems

Air masses range in temperature world-wide, from the Poles to the Equator. The line where these different masses of air meet is known as a *front*. Borrowing a military title is a rather appropriate analogy, because a battle for domination ensues. Perhaps the simplest example of a front is the *Polar Front*. Here the cooler air from the North Pole meets the warmer air from the south. This meeting or Polar Front is often found in the region of the British Isles and its specific location to the north or south of the country can create significant variations in weather conditions. This mixing of air masses has an enormous influence upon the weather.

Differing air masses will eventually form an homogenous mixture. In the meantime, they sit alongside each other in the same way that adding cold water to a hot bath leaves a chilly layer at the bottom – unless it is actively stirred up.

At the Polar Front the air masses begin to mix when divergence at altitude increases, resulting in less air flowing into the column than is flowing out. This reduces the total weight of the air and the pressure it exerts at ground level therefore falls. At surface level, air flows into the base of the column of air to fill the void left behind. Now the cycle of a depression has formed, as warm air begins to flow upwards and cool air is drawn in at the base of the air column.

In Western Europe, frontal systems (often called *depressions*) generally travel eastwards after forming over the Atlantic. This is why wet weather tends to approach from the west.

Warm fronts

A warm front is a mass of warm air advancing towards cooler air usually due to larger air movements in the atmosphere. Warm air rises, and slides over the cooler air. The warm, moist air is lifted and progressively cooled, forming high wispy clouds at first, and then ever increasing layers of thick cloud as more moist air is forced upwards.

Weather signs:
- A halo round the sun or moon suggests the presence of moisture in the form of ice crystals high in the atmosphere. Watch to see if this thickens.

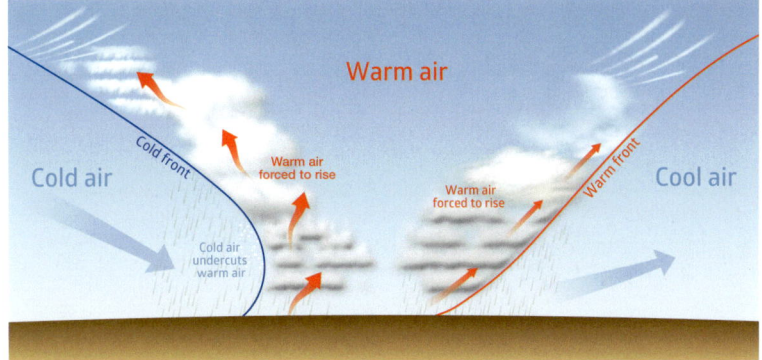

FIGURE 9.06 CROSS-SECTION THROUGH A DEPRESSION

- High wispy *cirrus clouds* or *mares' tails* develop as the leading edge of the warm air is cooled.
- Layers of cloud, called *stratus*, develop to cover the whole sky eventually.
- These layers of cloud becoming steadily thicker, and descend as it starts to rain or drizzle.
- The whole sky remains covered during the passage of a warm front, and it is likely to rain or drizzle persistently for some time.

Warm fronts are usually followed by a calm period preceding an even more dramatic cold front. This calm period is characterised by an easing of the wind and bright weather with good visibility. Clouds often begin to tower (*cumulus clouds*), but as the warm air mass is not being driven rapidly upwards at this point, the clouds do not usually cool sufficiently to cause much rainfall.

Cold fronts
A cold front is a mass of cool air advancing towards warmer air. Cold air sinks, and dives under the warm air. It then forces the warm air upwards, like a snowplough forcing its way underneath. As the warm air is lifted, it cools down. Its moisture is forced to condense to produce clouds and precipitation. This happens much more quickly than in a warm front, and the effect is consequently more dramatic.

Weather signs:
- Sudden blustery showers of heavy rain, and possibly hail.
- *Cumulonimbus* (meaning *towering rain*) clouds sweep across the sky in belts
- Clear sunny spells between the showers
- Strong, gusty winds, with a possible change in direction
- Distinct drop in temperature
- Cold fronts bring the most dramatic weather encountered in mountains, sometimes with dangerous lightning storms. Minimising the danger of lightning strike is discussed under *12.5.1 Lightning* on page 236.

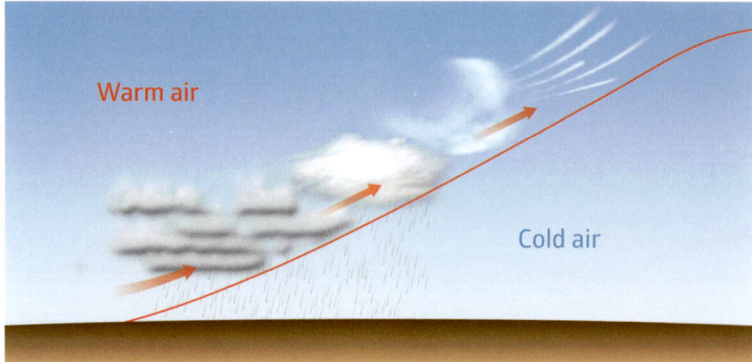

FIGURE 9.07 A WARM FRONT

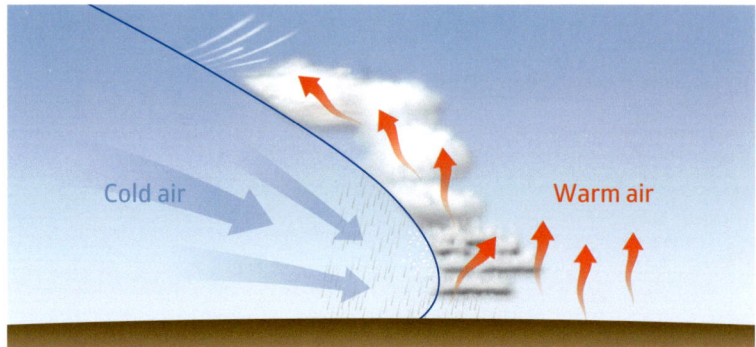

FIGURE 9.08 A COLD FRONT

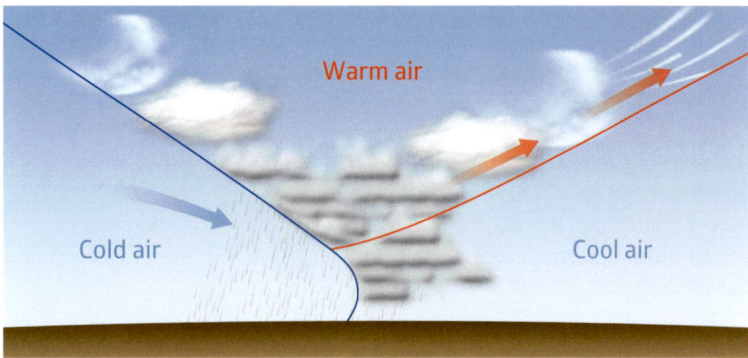

FIGURE 9.09 AN OCCLUDED FRONT

Occluded fronts

In the later stages of a depression's life cycle, the whole warm sector is usually lifted from the ground and replaced by the advancing cold air which piles into the air that was ahead of the warm front. This meeting point, known as an *occluded front*, has characteristics caused by the relative temperatures of the two cool air masses. Usually the following air is colder and therefore undercuts the air in front. This is known as a cold occlusion, similar in behaviour to a cold front, with strong winds and rain. Sometimes (usually in winter and spring) the following air is warmer and

FIGURE 9.10 POCKETS OF AIR RISING AND COOLING

FIGURE 9.11 A THERMAL ABOVE A HOT SUMMIT

therefore it is forced to rise up and over the coldest air, resulting in a warm occlusion. This behaves much like a warm front, with rain and drizzle.

Occlusions usually mark the decline of the storm, so the wind and rain gradually decrease. However, like all weather fronts, the weather will be more pronounced in the mountains because of the increased lifting effect.

FIGURE 9.12 WARM DAMP AIR BEING LIFTED OVER MOUNTAINS

9.4.2 Convection

On a clear day, a south-facing hillside and its summit will warm up in the sun. These warm the air, which then rises to produce localised warm air currents called *thermals*. On a day with strong thermals, it is often possible to watch gliders using the lifting force to spiral upwards.

As air rises, pressure is reduced. Put simply, there is less of the earth's atmosphere above it to squash the air. A thermal therefore carries warm, moist air upwards, expanding and cooling as it goes. As the air is cooled, the condensation rate increases until *dewpoint* is reached and visible droplets collect to form clouds. These droplets become steadily larger, like moisture condensing on a window pane. Soon they become so large that their weight causes them to slide down the pane – or in this case – to fall out of the sky as raindrops.

Once the cloud sheds rain, the thermal mass is cooled, the moisture is gone, and the whole process can start again. Thermals can be very powerful on hot summer afternoons, causing electrical imbalances leading to lightning storms.

9.4.3 Mountain weather *(orographic lifting)*

Weather forecasts often mention hill fog, regularly illustrating that the weather is worse in the uplands than elsewhere. This is especially common over the mountains close to the west coast of Britain and Ireland.

As a westerly wind sweeps in from the Atlantic, the western mountains are the first thing it meets. These force the warm wet air up and over the tops of the hills.

FIGURE 9.13 TYPICAL MOUNTAIN WEATHER CLOUDS OVER THE ENGLISH LAKE DISTRICT

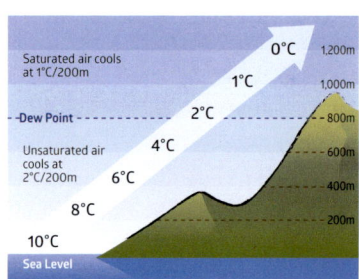

FIGURE 9.14 RISING AIR, DEW-POINT AND TEMPERATURES

FIGURE 9.15 CLOUDY FOOTHILLS AND A RAINY SUMMIT

Pressure and temperature

Ascending a mountain, the pressure decreases as the height of the air column pressing down on the Earth's surface decreases. There is also a steady reduction in temperature as molecules collide less frequently. (Pressure and temperature are directly proportional for a fixed volume of gas.)[1]

Unsaturated air cools at the *dry air lapse rate* of 1°C per 100 metres. Air that is condensing into cloud, and possibly also into precipitation cools at half this rate because of the heat produced by the process of condensation. This is known as *saturated air*, which cools at half the rate of dry air, i.e. 1°C per 200 metres.

The critical height here is the dewpoint (at 800m in *Figure 9.14*, above). The height of this can vary depending on the temperature of the air at sea level. At this point, the condensation rate exceeds evaporation, leading to the formation of the visible droplets that we see as clouds.

This fine mist becomes thicker and thicker as the height increases and the temperature continues to drop. If the dewpoint is slightly above the tops, a misty cloud may be seen hanging over a summit.

1 High pressure results in more frequent collisions between molecules, generating more heat.

Rain shadows

As the moist air is lifted over the mountains and some of the excess moisture falls as rain, it inevitably becomes drier. As this drier air sinks down the far side of the mountains it warms up. The evaporation rate exceeds the rate of condensation and the skies clear.

As moist air reaches the coast, the lowlands and beaches may be clear of cloud. Westerly mountains, however, force this moist air upward to form mist, hill fog, localised cloud and rain. In Snowdonia, the Moelwyns would typically be damp on such a day, with similar precipitation in the Lake District, the Mourne mountains, and Lochaber.

By the time the air mass reaches the eastern areas, much of its moisture has already fallen as rain, and the clouds start to break up. Not surprisingly, the Cairngorms are often drier in these conditions, and regions like the South Downs have an excellent sunshine record.

9.5 Weather maps

Weather maps, or synoptic charts, plot the differences in pressure and use symbols to represent the reported or anticipated weather at a given time. Lines called isobars represent the areas of similar pressure. These are similar to contour lines on a map – except that they join points of equal pressure on the earth's surface (corrected for sea level). Isobars are grouped more closely where the pressure is falling rapidly, known as a steep pressure gradient. The contour metaphor can be extended to winds; a steep pressure gradient results in strong winds. Just as a ball rolls faster down a steeper slope, air movement is faster when there is a marked difference in pressure.

As a rule of thumb, lots of information on the weather map suggests plenty of weather activity. Areas of little information suggest calmer weather.

9.5.1 Winds

Air will always flow from areas of high pressure to fill areas of low pressure.

It follows that the cooler air, which is heavy and spiralling downwards, will flow outwards as it spreads over the surface of the earth. Likewise, the areas of warmer air spiral upward and suck air in to fill the space left behind.

The following rules help to interpret the wind speed and direction from a synoptic chart:
• Low pressure air masses rotate anti-clockwise and the winds blow slightly inwards from the isobars.
• High pressure air masses rotate clockwise, and the winds blow slightly outwards from the isobars.
• The closer the isobars, the stronger the wind.

9.5.2 Analysing weather maps

A simple analysis of a weather map allows hill walkers to understand the mechanisms behind the weather forecast. This allows the walker to build an awareness of any changes that develop. Weather forecasting is not an

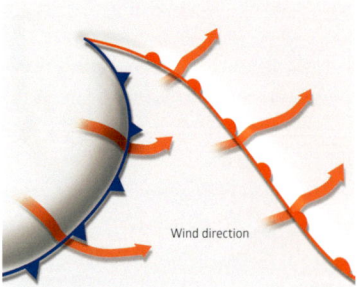

FIGURE 9.16 A 3-DIMENSIONAL REPRESENTATION OF A FRONTAL SYSTEM

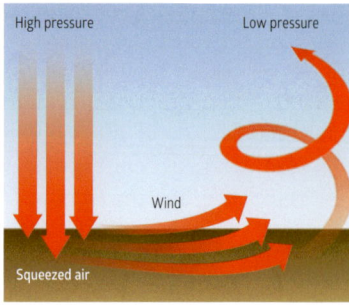

FIGURE 9.17 AIR SQUEEZED FROM HIGH TO LOW PRESSURE

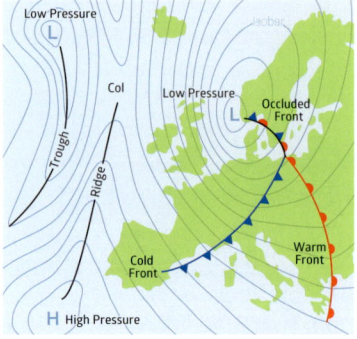

FIGURE 9.18 A WEATHER MAP SHOWING FEATURES

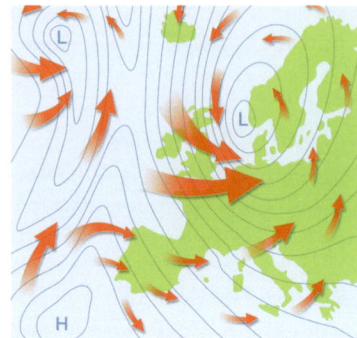

FIGURE 9.19 A WEATHER MAP WITH WINDS

exact science, and sometimes weather systems change speed or direction due to unforeseen factors.

With practice, the key components of a weather map can be quickly spotted. Low and high pressure zones can easily be identified and the spacing of isobars gives an indication of wind speeds.

For frontal systems the key information is:
• The type of front, that is, warm air rising over cold air or cold air diving under warm.
• The direction of movement. The best charts include the past direction travelled in addition to the anticipated direction.
• As a rough rule, the more a front deflects the line of an isobar, the more dramatic the resulting weather will be.
• Any occlusions, where two fronts have combined. This is a sign of frontal systems starting to stabilise and decline, although in the short term it may bring prolonged rain and cloud.

9.5.3 Moving air masses
A weather map that shows the direction of movement of weather systems gives a simple indication of where air masses have travelled. Air that has travelled over an ocean will naturally be relatively moist, while air from a continent will be drier. Air masses that are being pushed northwards from further south will be relatively warm, while cool air from the north will be gradually warming as it travels southwards.

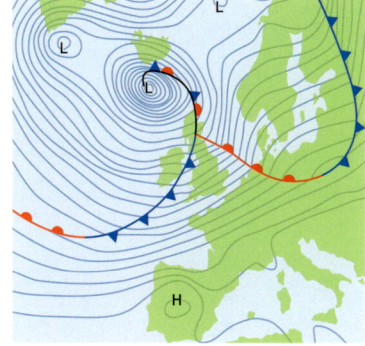

FIGURE 9.20 A SATELLITE PHOTO OF A 'MODEL' DEPRESSION *(LEFT)* WITH THE SAME INFORMATION PLOTTED ON A WEATHER MAP *(RIGHT)*

9.6 Localised weather

Most weather features drawn on the charts are countrywide. The mountains may exaggerate their characteristics, but the entire country will be affected by the associated weather. The shape of the ground can influence the weather,

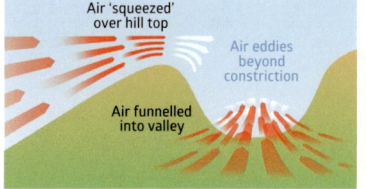

FIGURE 9.21 FUNNEL EFFECT AND EDDIES

and form mists and fogs. Mountains can create their own weather by lifting and cooling the air mass, and also due to the localised effects listed below:

9.6.1 Funnel effect
The hills can funnel the winds, resulting in dramatic localised variations. As the air is squeezed between the hills and the tropopause, it is forced to accelerate through the narrower gap. Summits and saddles are therefore often much windier than surrounding country. However, powerful eddies can form on the leeward side, resulting in strong winds flowing in a different direction to the main weather pattern – this is one aspect of weather forecasting where local knowledge can give a significant advantage.

9.6.2 Banner clouds
High winds squeeze over the summit, squashing the air over the top. On the lee side of the ridge, the air expands, cools down, and condenses into a banner cloud. This effect, giving warm sunshine on one side of the ridge, and cool clammy mist on the other, is often associated with high pressure.

FIGURE 9.22 THE FORMATION OF BANNER CLOUDS

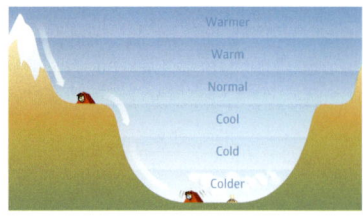

FIGURE 9.23 A TEMPERATURE INVERSION

9.6.3 Fog, frost and inversions

As cool air sinks, it can pour into hollows and become trapped by its own density, with a layer of warm air above. This effect is called a temperature inversion, a relatively common phenomenon in the autumn.

Valley fog in the mornings and hazy hill fog on ridges and peaks is associated with high pressure, which allows temperatures to fall dramatically during the clear night due to convection.

Weather signs:
• Layers of mist in the bottom of valleys, the morning after a clear or frosty night. Notice how this fog disappears quickly in the sunshine, and lasts longer in the shade.
• Sheets of hazy hill fog pouring over ridges as the cooler air spills over into the next valley. It will probably be beautifully sunny elsewhere.

9.7 Making the best of the weather

Safe, enjoyable travel usually involves an element of good timing. An accurate weather outlook can allow a walk or expedition to go ahead, be modified, or if necessary be scrapped. On the day of the trip a weather forecast allows walkers to plan a route that makes the best use of the weather.

9.7.1 Recognising the development of bad weather

Weather systems bring a sequence of descending clouds as a front approaches. Observation of the developing clouds can therefore help walkers anticipate weather changes or compare the clouds with the weather forecast and predict changes in its timing.

A very simple introduction to clouds is included below. Readers wishing to learn more about this are referred to *A.1 Bibliography* on page 266.

At a very basic level, a succession from high wispy clouds (*cirrus* types) through to progressively lower layers of clouds (*stratus* types) is a clear indication of an approaching warm front. The higher *stratus* layers, known as *cirrostratus*, often form a halo around the sun or moon, so a halo around the moon is often a good early warning of rainfall arriving by the morning. The time taken to progress from *cirrus* to *altostratus* (recognisable as the cloud layer becomes sufficiently opaque to block the moon/sun halo) is generally similar to the remaining time before rain arrives.

When a low pressure system is approaching, the high altitude winds move in a different direction to air movements below. The practical application of this is known as the *crossed winds rule*: cirrus clouds oriented in a different direction to low clouds or even the smoke from a chimney stack are a reliable indication of changing weather.

Recognising the passing of a warm front will allow the prediction of a cold front that is likely to arrive after perhaps a day of more settled weather.

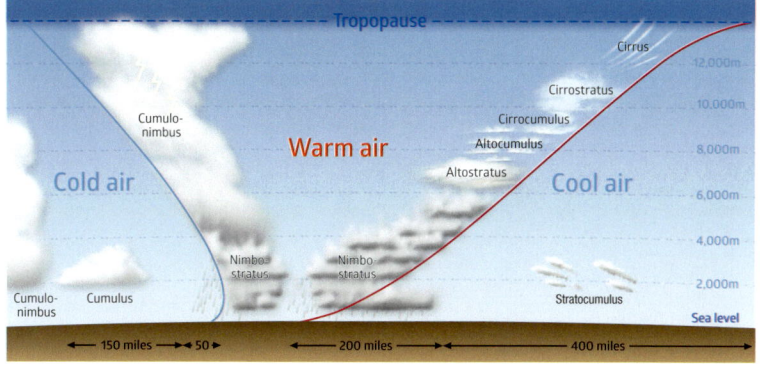

FIGURE 9.24 CROSS-SECTION THROUGH A DEPRESSIONSHOWING CLOUD TYPES

'Cotton wool' shaped clouds (known as *cumulus*) show cells of rising air. If they do not continue to expand vertically the air mass is reasonably stable, but in unstable conditions the clouds will tower upwards to form *cumulo-nimbus*[2] clouds that may even spread outwards as the rising air hits the *tropopause*. These can bring thunder and lightning storms, often associated with hailstones, which are formed by the cooling of raindrops, forced upwards within the cloud by the powerful spiralling updrafts. Eventually the weight of the hailstones overcomes these updrafts and down they come.

In showery conditions, the blackening clouds can often be seen developing on the horizon, allowing plenty of time for waterproofs to be donned.

9.8 Problem weather

9.8.1 Heat waves

The British are notorious for underestimating the debilitating effect of heat exhaustion and dehydration, which can have very serious and even fatal consequences in a heatwave. Weather planning allows the group to plan a realistic itinerary, avoiding steep climbs during the hottest hours and seeking the breezy or shady slopes.

Mad dogs and Englishmen go out in the midday sun.

9.8.2 Strong winds

Wind in the mountains is generally much stronger on the summits than at sea level, because wind accelerates through the smaller gap between the land and the top of the atmosphere. Wind speeds on the summit of Ben Nevis average three times faster than in Fort William. A similar effect is common in saddle features, making these places to hurry through rather than linger. Even a simple regional forecast from a national newspaper will give sufficient warning for a leader to avoid precipitous ridges if strong winds are predicted in the lowlands. It may be possible to sneak up to the summit on the lee (downwind) side but sometimes strong eddies prevent this.

2 Nimbus: latin for rain.

Types of clouds

CIRRUS

ALTOSTRATUS

STRATUS

CUMULUS

VALLEY FOG

APPROACHING FRONT

It is reasonable to expect winds to be two to three times stronger on summits than at sea level. Sometimes, however, the summits can be calm despite wind in the valleys. This is often the case with temperature inversions. Local knowledge can give additional insights to localised eddies which are not apparent from weather maps.

9.8.3 Precipitation

Sometimes an accurate forecast enables hill walkers to avoid the worst of the weather by making an early – or perhaps a late start – for example to avoid a cold front passing through the area. A basic understanding of the main weather systems allows the observant party to spot tell-tale signs of a weather system that is moving faster or slower than forecast.

9.8.4 Summer storms

In summer, a prolonged period of high pressure can result in humid conditions that are dissipated by afternoon thunderstorms. An early start is advisable, or at least an early finish. If towering clouds begin to develop, this should be seen as a warning to evacuate any summit, sharp ridge or exposed rocky terrain before the lightning begins to strike.

part 3

Party management

PHOTO // STEVE LONG

Planning to
look after people

A leader's responsibilities can range from a nominal role within a group of equals, through to the challenges and rewards of caring for a party of novices. Awareness of the often unspoken needs of other members of the party is an essential attribute of a successful leader, while the practical considerations of fulfilling these various requirements demand many qualities in addition to the practical skills described earlier in this book.

Leadership brings its own challenges and rewards. Leading a peer group might bring the satisfaction of a shared adventure – perhaps an exciting battle against the elements, whereas the rewards of leading a group of novices are often far more subtle. The inexperienced party looks to its leader to communicate an awareness of the potential hazards, to plan an appropriate itinerary and to place the requirements of the group above individual personal wishes. A successful leader should be able to build upon a varied wealth of personal adventures in order to balance these demands.

10.1 The party

10.1.1 Prior knowledge

Within any group of people, a jostling for position commences and subconscious links and alliances are formed until some form of pecking order is established. This can rarely be achieved without a degree of conflict, but once accomplished the group can work more effectively as a unit.[1] A leader needs to be aware of these dynamics within a group and how they may be affecting individuals. Of course, any leader who fails to become respected and trusted by dint of knowledge and experience, is in for a rough ride.

Prior knowledge of a party's experience, ability and expectations is a great advantage when planning any walk. Knowing expectations and weighing them against the group's ability helps the planning process. Some leaders plan their routes months beforehand and may even be required to do so by their local authority, school or organisation. This has the advantage that the group dynamics can be well developed and understood and other issues such as levels of fitness and personal equipment can be tackled. On the other hand, some leaders meet their groups for the first time on the morning they are due to go walking and have to make assessments on the spot. A high degree of flexibility is needed, enabling plans to be adapted rapidly to give the best day in the circumstances.[2]

10.1.2 Individual factors

People vary in many different ways: physically, mentally, personality, culturally, knowledge and experience. Therefore the design of the activity, the equipment, information and environment should take account individual capabilities and limitations as far as is reasonably practicable.

Physical differences can be the most obvious, but this is not always the case. People have different body shapes and sizes but different levels of strength and capabilities may not be immediately apparent.

Vision, hearing and manual dexterity can also vary widely and in some cases e.g. where colour, vision or visual acuity is important it is necessary to test people's capabilities. Sometimes all that is needed is a different strategy for communication – for example somebody who is colour-blind is more likely to be able to distinguish the 'large bush' than the 'red bush'.

1 See Tuckman's *Stages of Group Development, Forming Storming Norming Performing* model
2 John Adair introduced the concept of *Action Centred Leadership* and his model of the relationship between task, individual and group has influenced all subsequent research in group management. Further information and other models are provided by the books listed in *A.1 Bibliography* on page 264.

FIGURE 10.01 TWO VERY DIFFERENT PARTIES   *PHOTO // (LEFT) ANITA LONG, (RIGHT) ROB COLLISTER*

Mental abilities vary from person to person and these will need to be assessed by the party leader. Other factors may affect mental abilities e.g. stress, illness, medication, injury etc.

People also have different personality and cultural traits, which can make a difference to the type of activity that they are suited to and may be important where there are specific safety requirements. Additionally, people have different knowledge and experience on which to draw.

Although the Data Protection Act 1998 places duties on employers to ensure confidential and appropriate handling of 'sensitive personal data', which includes data about a person's health, any group member or leader has a duty of care to inform the others if their condition has or may have an impact on the risk assessment for the activity. The key issue is not the impairment but its effect. Disabilities that have relatively transient impairments such as migraines, diabetes, asthma and back pain can present severe barriers if the adverse effect on the individual is substantial.

10.1.3 Party size

There are no specific national recommendations on staff-to-student ratios for leading groups on mountains or moorland. Generally, the larger the party, the harder it is to communicate, often forcing leaders to resort to a didactic style of leadership in order to keep control. This can limit room for individual expression and the large numbers may impact on the experience and the wilderness itself. The venues for large groups will therefore have to be very carefully selected.

The ideal is to limit parties to a size that allows the leader to count everyone at a glance. In moorland a maximum party size of around ten people still allows the leader to keep a reasonable degree of control. In rugged terrain smaller ratios are essential unless the route is well within the capabilities and experience of the party. The leader needs to be in an appropriate position to protect every party member if the group crosses rock steps where potential slips need to be prevented – this would become unmanageable with a large group. Larger parties are much better sub-divided into more manageably sized groups, each with its own leader.

In many cases it is not possible to recruit sufficient leaders to reliably allow this degree of autonomy.

In theory 'a problem shared is a problem halved', but assistant leaders, trainee leaders or responsible adults do not necessarily have a great deal of knowledge or experience. Leaders must be very clear about their responsibilities and whether or not these can be shared. If assistants are in any way an unknown entity then they are best counted as additional members of the group.

Advertising for assistant leaders can pay dividends. There are many people around who have attended *Mountain Leader* and *Hill and Moorland Leader* training[3] courses and are trying to gain experience working with groups.

10.1.4 Equipment

Ensuring that the party is suitably equipped is essential. Novices need to be told in advance what to bring, but the leader should never make the assumption that they have actually brought it. With many inexperienced groups, a formal kit inspection may sound over the top, but it will nearly always reveal something important that has been left behind, or some heavy 'luxuries'. Equally, items of clothing can be dropped or lost during the day, or become useless once wet. The wise leader carries not one but several spare hats, jumpers and pairs of gloves.

10.1.5 Specialised equipment

It is increasingly common for people to use equipment on the hill that is required for their safe mobility, ranging from walking poles and prosthetic limbs through to four-wheeled bicycles and motorised wheel chairs and scooters.

Prosthetic limbs

Standard prosthetic legs are remarkably versatile, although it helps if they have 'active' feet, i.e. carbon fibre or similar. Essentially these are feet which have a bit of spring in them, to make it easier to cope with rough and variable terrain. Components need to be protected against possible ingress of dirt, water, etc. Most amputees will use trekking poles for stability. Standard trekking poles can be used, although the flick lock system is more secure and may be found easier to adjust with teeth. It is also possible to cut off the handles so that the poles can be custom-mounted to a pair of prosthetic sockets.

Wheelchairs

Access to the hills for wheelchair users should not be confused with three or four wheeled downhill bikes, although it is natural to expect an increasing number of disabled cyclists to use these vehicles on designated tracks. It is also anticipated that an increasing number of people 'pushing the boundaries' of terrain that a wheelchair has been designed to negotiate

---

3 Formerly *Walking Group Leader.*

and a wider range of specialised and customised vehicles to be introduced.

For the purposes of this book we have made the assumption that users of off-road wheel chairs enjoy the same legal status (in terms of Rights of Way) as pedestrians, and as such can make use of public footpaths and designated Right to Roam land.

There is no specific reference in the Equality Act to any aspect of rights of way management and, as yet, no body of case law that can be referred to in the application of either the Equality Act or the DDA to rights of way.

(*www.defra.co.uk*)

Most wheelchairs, power chairs and scooters are designed for 'everyday' use by people of an average weight. In general manual wheelchairs have a high centre of gravity and need good surfaces with small gradients; small wheels are designed for tarmac and concrete so are difficult to move on stony tracks. The rider needs to be fairly fit or have attendant pushers and pullers. A balance must be drawn between robustness and weight, especially for more rugged tracks. In recent years manual wheelchairs for rough going have been designed, some with adaptive mechanisms for improved and easier propulsion. A lower centre of gravity is more stable but has less clearance.

Electric scooters or power-chairs designed for general mobility in a town environment may be suitable for some easier rambles. Some power-chairs and scooters have limited clearance and power, plus they can be readily damaged on rough tracks. Scooters with medium to large wheels and batteries of at least 50 amp-hour capacity are best. Most scooters have handlebar controls, but there are models that use a joystick or more elaborate control systems for those with upper body disabilities.

'Off-road' electric scooters are the 'Land Rover' equivalent of the shopping scooter, being designed for rough country with greater power, ground clearance and strength than town models. They are manufactured by a number of British companies as well as imports.

10.1.6 Fitness

Fitness for hill walking is quite specific and it is likely that even a group of fit youngsters will tire sooner than they expect. There is a huge difference between what people think they can do and what they can actually do! It is also easy for a leader to fall into the trap of pushing the party hard to give them a really full day. Planning a shorter journey with plenty of stops, setting a comfortable steady pace and talking about the area will give most novice groups a more worthwhile and enjoyable experience. The ideal speed for any party is one that allows conversation to be conducted without struggling for breath.

Varying degrees of fitness and ability within the group is always a potential problem. Sensitivity, flexibility, creative problem-solving and the ability to entertain the group may be needed to give everyone an enjoyable day. Slowing down the faster group members by giving them tasks or engaging them in conversation (perhaps geology, flora or history) whilst the slower ones catch up and regain their breath, is one way of keeping the group together. Another method if the conditions and the terrain are suitable is to split the group for short periods. A useful strategy is to send faster members up to a certain point by a longer route – preferably accompanied by an assistant leader, whilst the leader walks with the slower ones. This has the potential for misunderstandings, so everyone has to be absolutely clear about the rendezvous and the leader needs to be confident of the outcome.

10.1.7 Aspirations

Within any party aspirations vary, and not all will be realistic. The aspirations of some must never be allowed to jeopardise safety or enjoyment for others. Conversation with each individual is needed to clarify goals, clear up misunderstandings and prevent disappointment. The larger the party the less likely it is that a leader can achieve this with everyone.

10.2 Aims

Planning a day on the hill should begin by formulating the aims of the day. These should be discussed and agreed upon by all concerned, otherwise the trip will become just another coercive, disenfranchising experience. These aims can be seen as providing a skeleton, which is then fleshed out with practical information such as weather conditions, wind direction, logistics and party fitness. For example, if the group's main aim for the day is to improve map reading skills, choosing an area with a variety of navigation points, where communication is easy, will be more appropriate than an exposed mountain ridge, however exciting. On the other hand, if the aim is simply to enjoy an outdoor ramble but a strong cold wind is blowing, a forest walk may be the order of the day.

It would be unwise to assume that any expedition will go according to plan, no matter how well prepared. Quite often plans need to change, sometimes within minutes of starting. This tends to happen when the leader has no prior knowledge of the group and the individuals within it, the weather has changed for the worse or the day has started later than planned. This is when the ability to be flexible and adaptable becomes essential. Planning shorter alternatives and escape routes is a fundamental step in the preparation, and this process should continue throughout the actual trip. The focus of the day may have to switch within minutes, from aiming for a summit to helping a party member descend to safety because of an asthma attack, for example. Leaders who are building their experience may find it helpful to think through possible scenarios and prepare a stock of options that can be used when circumstances change.

10.3 Terrain

Consideration of terrain and how weather conditions might affect it inevitably raises questions about the personal experience of the leader, as well as the group. Qualifications serve as an indication of competence but they must go hand in hand with current experience of the type of terrain likely to be encountered if a leader is to operate safely and confidently. Skills develop or degrade over time depending on how regularly they are used. Leading groups on the moors requires very different skills to leading groups in the mountains. If an incident occurs, does the leader have the skills required to deal with it?[4]

10.4 The route plan

Planning a route in advance allows potential problems to be identified and corrective measures to be taken, minimising their impact. It allows an estimate to be made of the amount of time required to complete the proposed trip. This can be balanced against the available daylight hours and the weather forecast. A route plan also allows an outline to be left with a friend or contact, allowing constructive contingency measures to be taken if the party is seriously delayed. On the other hand, overly rigid recording of plans can stifle flexibility. A leader should feel free to modify the route in the light of developing conditions, but major changes such as an alternative venue should be communicated to the central contact before embarking on the walk.

The route plan should reflect the factors identified above, namely the fitness of the party, the aims, the terrain, and (at the final planning stage) the weather forecast. For expeditions involving an overnight camp, an indication of the approximate location of the intended campsite can be particularly helpful in the event of unexpected problems. It has been known for a family to require urgent contact with a member of a party during a camp. Again, a leader should not feel obliged to follow the plan at all costs, so if the campsite is more exposed to prevailing winds than anticipated, then a move may be justified.

10.4.1 Route cards and tracings

Route cards are a traditional format for assisting and recording the planning process and remain a valuable tool whether produced by hand or by using computing technology: the underlying process and concepts are similar for both digital and physical versions.

The first stage is to sketch out a proposed itinerary on a physical or digital layer superimposed over a map. In recent years route-planning software has become available using map data that allows a route to be quickly drawn over the map, and calculations made automatically using a customised version of Naismith's rule. With additional modifications for lunch and tea breaks, this can be printed or sent by email to interested parties. The track can also be exported onto a GPS unit[5] for use during the expedition, and conversely a GPS track from a trip can be exported back to the map for reviewing. These tools are very powerful providing that they are combined with a thorough and thoughtful examination of the map: a reasonably large monitor is therefore advisable for planning.

A day's walk is typically divided into a series of natural divisions known as legs. It should not be necessary to divide the day's walk into more than ten legs, and fewer may suffice.

4 See Tannenbaum and Schmidt's *Continuum of Leadership Styles*.
5 Global Positioning System, the details of which can be found on page 38.

Route card

O.S. Sheet **51**   Group **D of E. Gold**   Date **4/10/02**   Time out: **10.00**   Finish time: **16.00**

Leg	From	To	Bearing (mag)	Distance (km)	Height (m) Gained	Height (m) Lost	Time Distance	Time Height	Time Descent	Time Breaks	Total time	ETA	Description	Escape route
1	NN 615249	617255	N	0.6	40		9	4			13	10.13	Glenbeich Lodge Track	Return
2	617255	606277	320°	2.7	400		88	40		10	88	11.41	2nd stream, then ridge → ·571	Return
3	606277	595286	318°	1.6	110		24	11		5	40	12.21	NW → ·638	Return
4	595286	592276	218°+	1.2	50	10	18	5			23	12.46		S → Track
5	592276	577277	W	1.5	115	60	23	12	1	60	76	14.00	→ Meall Buidhe summit	W → Road
6	577277	576284	NW	1	44	50	15	6			21	14.21	Ridge → shoulder then N → summit	NW → Track
7	576284	583305	N→NE	2.3	0	395	35			10	45	15.06	To Forest Track	N → Track then W
8	583305	583222	NE,SW	2.4	10		36	1	2	5	37	15.50	Track → Road	Finish Route
9														
10											(Beinn Leobhainn)			
11														
12														

It gets dark at: ....**19.00**..............

Central contact name: .....**Iain Peter**........... Phone number: .....**01234   567890**............

Variations on Naismith's rule. **→**   Highlight rates used

Walking rate: (horizontal)	
Fast	5km/hr
Average	4km/hr
Slow	3km/hr
Extra slow	2km/hr

+

Uphill rate in metres/hr:		
Fast	900m/hr	= 15 m. in 1 min
Average	600m/hr	= 10m. in 1 min
Slow	300m/hr	= 10m. in 2 min

Steep descents: Add 1 min for every steep descent of 10m

Total distance: **13·3 km**   Total height gain: **670 m**

Party member names: **Steve Long, Mike Turner, Neil Johnson, Martin Chester, Louise Thomas**

Special notes: **Minibus 3.   Midge repellant.**   **O.K.   MP**

FIGURE 10.02 EXAMPLE ROUTE CARD

An example route card is included above. The card has a tabular structure with information entered into a series of rows and columns, with each row dedicated to an individual leg. For each leg the destination grid reference is noted along with a short description, such as 'stream junction' or a place name. The total distance for each leg is measured; this can be done with a piece of string or by marking smaller sections along the edge of a piece of paper as in *Figure 10.03* opposite. A variety of dedicated map measuring devices is available; as with digital mapping it is important to check that the correct format for distances has been noted (i.e. miles vs. kilometres). Most mapping software is capable of exporting the data in this format, which eliminates much of the legwork involved in measurement and mathematics – but again this more 'disengaged' compilation of data should not be allowed to undermine careful examination and consideration of the underlying terrain.

Height gained during each leg is added up. Height loss is normally ignored as descent time generally balances out over the course of a day at about the same speed as on flat ground. Using Naismith's rule, (described in *Timing* on page 65) the total time anticipated for each leg can be estimated. Additional time should be allowed for rocky sections, short breaks and for map reading pauses. A reasonable estimate is to add ten minutes for each leg, with a further half-hour lunch break added to a leg ending at around midday – longer lunch breaks are generally best avoided as the party will often become chilled. A running total gives a good indication of the trip's time requirement and this can be balanced against available daylight and other logistics. A short description of the route, handrails to be followed[6], terrain to be covered and important bearings allow navigational strategies to be planned at leisure. The route card should include escape routes for the various stages for the walk;

6 See *3.3 Following linear features* on page 58.

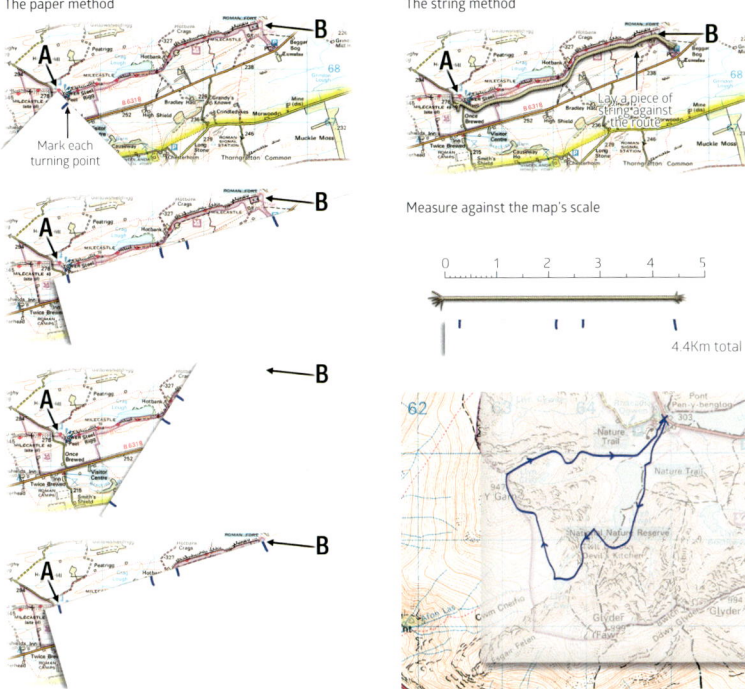

The paper method

A **B**

Mark each
turning point

A **B**

A **B**

A **B**

The string method

A **B**

Lay a piece of
string against
the route

Measure against the map's scale

0   1   2   3   4   5

4.4Km total

62

FIGURE 10.03 MEASURING DISTANCE WITH STRING OR PAPER

FIGURE 10.04 AN EXAMPLE OF A ROUTE TRACING

contingency plans for a rapid evacuation or alternative route if conditions or events necessitate such changes.

Various spreadsheet packages are also available that automate much of the maths involved in producing a route-card. These should not be seen as a substitute for examining a map and the terrain through which the proposed trip will pass.

As a formal exercise, *route cards* are an excellent planning format and are particularly useful for inexperienced leaders developing the ability to plan a day from the map. A route card can be a useful aid if carried on the trip. If the party is moving faster or slower than anticipated, the running time total on the card makes it easy to spot and take any necessary action. A route card may also include important bearings for particular legs, allowing the leader simply to enter the bearing on the compass rather than struggling with a flapping map on a windy summit.

Despite the value of route cards as a planning medium, the tabular structure is difficult to transfer to a map for anybody trying to evaluate a planned route. A route that looks perfectly feasible on the card, for example, might involve crossing a major river without a bridge. A route card therefore has little value as a means of communicating a planned journey to other people.

The ideal format for showing a planned route is a printed map with the track, (whether on paper or on a monitor) or a route tracing. Several options are available for tracing a map. The proposed route can be drawn as a line on a laminated map using a marker pen. Even without mapping software, a printed map can be photocopied or scanned, and the route marked with a highlighting marker pen. Even without specialised navigational software a scanned map has the advantage that it can be emailed to a supervisor or contact. It is also possible to import and geo-tag scanned map data into specialised mapping software; either proprietary or using open-source data, and this can be represent a considerable saving for the more computer-literate navigator.

Alternatively, tracing paper can be laid over a map and the line drawn on this. In order for this information to have any meaning, identifiable points must be marked so that the tracing can be superimposed on a similar map. It is usual to mark four sets of intersecting grid lines as crosses with the grid numbers written alongside. The tracing should include features such as campsites, areas for navigational exercises, and a list of crucial timings with perhaps estimated arrival times at various points.

10.5 Leadership

The adage that 'good leaders are born and not made' is no longer taken very seriously. True, not everyone can or wants to lead others. For the outdoor leader, a healthy confidence grows gradually with broadening personal experience and increasing familiarity with the leadership role. However, self-confidence must be tempered by empathy, judgement, intelligence and humility – otherwise a dictatorship arises. Proficiency in practical skills such as navigation and route finding develops only through experience in a wide variety of terrain and conditions. Leaders likewise require opportunities to practice and acquire party management skills and the ability to recognise and respond to differing abilities and needs within a group. Both sets of skills are essential for a leader to be effective. Above all, leadership demands the maturity to give priority to a group's needs as opposed to the wishes of a few individuals or pursuing a personal agenda.

10.5.1 Communication

Effective communication involves a flexible use of language that can be clear and concise at one moment yet able to develop an idea or elaborate on a feeling at another. It can involve subtle adaptations to the speech patterns and body language of another. This two-way process requires good listening skills – listening not simply to content, but also to why it is said and how it is expressed. The use of a phrase such as "I really shouldn't …" often betrays a willingness to be persuaded, whilst "I don't want to …" means just that – yet superficially both phrases seem to have the same meaning. In return, it has been proved that there is a huge gulf in motivational power between use of the conjunctive 'and' rather than 'but'.

Active listening may be about questioning, paraphrasing and summarising in order to reach the meaning behind the words. Moreover, body language and position relative to the rest of the party can say so much without words at all.

Successful communication demands consideration of how we present ourselves to a specific person or group in terms of dress, posture, seating or venue. A leader who strides out at the front of a group or family has

> Communication is a crucial area, at the core of so-called 'people-skills'.
> Yet, because it is less easy to teach than technical skills, it can be neglected.
> Many simple techniques for managing groups can be learned and practiced,
> and to this extent, people can learn to become more effective leaders.
> A simple example is making a conscious effort to use people's first names.
> This can help build rapport and is a powerful, persuasive tool if used subtly.
> The implicit empathy can bring a leader valuable support in a crisis.

obviously assumed control, and this would be characteristic of an autocratic style of leadership. On the other hand, a leader who takes advantage of opportunities to mix at various times with the other members of the party, empowers other members to make simple route-finding decisions, and demonstrates an interest in getting to know people better. Finally, a leader who stays at the rear of the party, even when navigating through complex terrain, sends a clear message that they have abdicated responsibility for route-finding decisions.

Body language can be very expressive, and because it is usually subconscious, can be more honest than words. For example, somebody who insists that they 'do not have a problem' whilst firmly crossing their arms across their chest and avoiding eye contact (or perhaps staring aggressively) is demonstrating a closed attitude, which is at odds with their words.

Effective leadership during a walk achieves a successful balance between the needs of individual members of a group, the social dynamics within the party and the aims for the trip.[7] This demands honesty and empathy. *Prejudices* need to be challenged both within oneself and the party, but by education rather than by confrontation. We cannot force change upon others, but we can use our own behaviour as a tool to challenge preconceptions about the limitations of other people. *Anti-social behaviour* is usually tackled most effectively by a quiet word in private, although sometimes a leader might have to make an initial response in front of the rest of the group, rather than imply endorsement of prejudices by failing to be seen to disagree.

10.5.2 Decision making

Leadership can be a lonely and thankless task. The quality of an expedition can be dramatically altered by the leader's decisions about whether to intervene or to allow the party to make and learn from mistakes: the most expedient choice is not always the best for genuine education. With an inexperienced party, the leader usually has to tackle these choices unaided by discussion since to broach the subject will inevitably change expectations and behaviour. Inner worries often cannot be discussed

---

7 The use of *Neuro-Linguistic-Programming* (NLP) in the field of personal development has contributed greatly to the understanding of communication skills; how language and behaviour reflect beliefs and viewpoints (paradigms), and how effective and flexible communication can promote change. NLP practitioners use a pragmatic approach to various models and maps of the human mind. The most effective dissemination of information in this fascinating and developing field tends to be seminar-based, because it does not transcribe well to the restricted format of publications. However there are many internet links available to anybody who wishes to learn more about this approach to communication and relationships.

(i) **17** Communication for leaders

Briefings

In the outdoors, briefing a party before departure and at appropriate times throughout the day is essential. For example, negotiating a route through bog or descending a scree slope may be second nature to the leader but are likely to need thorough briefing for novices.

In windy or wet conditions, leaders need to ensure that everyone can hear and see them: auditory masking from the environment or from activity will affect people's ability to hear and therefore retain information. The leader should move to a quiet area or wait until the noise reduces. A good method is to create a *semicircle* around the leader with backs to the wind, rain or sun. Prioritising communication requirements will enable the leader to take advantage of safe ground to have these chats, which should be preceded by taking a moment to think about what needs to be covered and how it should be conveyed. Communication should be direct and simple using clear, concise instructions that avoid idiomatic phrasing. It is good practice to confirm that information is understood, perhaps by asking group members to summarise salient points. A good leader will adapt and change methods of communication if they are not satisfied that the message was understood.

Beware of *overloading* everyone with information, as people will soon 'switch off'. The way these instructions are given will determine the attitude of the party to the situation. A delicate balance needs to be struck much of the time between being too casual and too alarmist.

In high winds the line of sight is an important consideration as the leader may need to wave to attract attention of group members if shouting proves ineffective. Light direction can also be an issue: if the sun is out and shining on the leader's face the students can see facial expressions and will gain all the information the leader is transmitting – this is particularly important for group members with hearing impairment (see *10.6.4 People with hearing impairment* for more information). Conversely if the sun is shining into the group's eyes communication will be disrupted. Eye contact is important for effective communication, so the leader should remove sunglasses for briefings.

without undermining the confidence of other party members, and the leader may have to assume an air of assurance in order to support other members, even if personally racked by doubt. Yet on the other hand, bottling up these feelings can lead to recriminations and mistrust if things do not turn out well – body language will often betray unspoken doubts.

For any situation, two factors will assist a leader enormously. The first is personal experience of similar or comparable situations, which allows a pragmatic and realistic perspective. The second is empathy with the party members and their needs; what could be a routine discussion for one

Coaching

Many hill walking skills can be passed on to less experienced party members simply by setting a good example, because subconscious observation pays an enormous part in the acquisition of new skills. But sometimes in the interests of safety or efficiency it is expedient for a leader to take a more active role in helping or speeding the learning process. Helping other people to become more skilful requires a range of skills that a leader will build over time: observation, analysis and communication.

A deceptively powerful tool is the use of questioning in order to help the less experienced members of the party reflect and to make their own adaptations – sometimes the collective creative force can be so powerful that the leader is inspired to adopt the same solution!

Sometimes an observant leader will notice that party members are persisting with techniques that work for the urban environment but are inefficient on the hill. For example, rucksacks are a familiar urban accessory but often carried on only one shoulder, a style that is inefficient at best and with dangerous potential to unbalance the walker or slip from the shoulder. The leader might tackle this in one of many ways, ranging from a well-timed and diplomatic question through to a demonstration of the technique used to don a heavy sack: bending the knees to insert a shoulder, followed by a rapid straightening of the legs to 'bounce' the sack upwards as the other arm and shoulder is inserted into the second shoulder strap. Alternatively a suitably competent peer might be invited to demonstrate.

Reviewing

Reflection is an important part of any learning process, and effective leadership facilitates opportunities to review. Sometimes just providing a little space for reflection can strike the perfect balance, whilst for other circumstances the leader may choose to take a more active role in reviewing. This can range from a metaphorical pat on the back through to a formal reviewing session, depending upon the situation.

Rest breaks offer a good opportunity for group members to share feelings about the journey. Depending on the maturity and experience of the group, the leader may choose to give a briefing about any hazards or 'no go' areas that are anticipated on the next leg of the journey, or invite suggestions from the group, developed from the review.

After delegating tasks, a few words are required to confirm completion. Feedback for improvement is best communicated in positive terms, focussing on both areas of success and on an action plan for successful development. After a challenge or crisis, debriefing is important in order both to close tasks and to allow people the opportunity to express their fears and doubts. This can profoundly influence the long-term effects of the incident.

party might lead to emotional disintegration for another, for example. A leader should always consider the consequences before taking an action or making a statement.

10.6 The law

Responsibilities in relationships with other people are no different when walking than any other aspect of one's life. The law is designed to support individual rights and liberties, and should thus be seen as an ally. Unfortunately, the rare cases when people have been injured through the actions or omissions of others in the hills have invariably been highly publicised, and this can lead to a distorted pre-occupation with worst-case scenarios.

10.6.1 Legal liability

As in all aspects of life, walkers owe a legal *duty of care* to other hill users who may be affected by their actions or failure to act. Leaders have an additional responsibility for the party within their care, as they can be reasonably expected to have a greater awareness of *potential hazards* than the rest of the group.

The extent of the duty of care required is naturally dependent on the age, expertise and experience of the other people involved. As maturity increases, individual autonomy and awareness also develop. A leader can expect experienced *adult* group members to make informed choices about their destiny, but should exercise tighter control on a group of novices. *Children* lack the worldly wisdom to be able to make balanced judgements about risk; they are more likely to be swayed by peer group pressure and perceived rather than actual risk. So a leader carries the responsibility of assessing risk on their behalf.

Activities that carry increased risk of injury require greater care to prevent foreseeable accidents occurring. Required equipment should meet the accepted standards for the activity. Thus, a walking leader would be entitled to veto a trip around the Carn Mor Dearg arête for a relatively inexperienced group wearing plimsolls. The responsibility for selecting appropriate footwear falls upon the experienced member of the party, who should know that for this group these shoes would dramatically increase the risk of ankle injury or falling.

....

Leaders working with young people must fulfil the requirements of the **Adventure Activities Activity Licensing Authority** (AALA), for any commercial providers of a range of activities that includes hill walking. These providers should therefore hold a current licence, which demands accountable systems of risk management and suitably experienced and qualified leadership. At the time of writing the future of licensing across the UK is uncertain but the Health and Safety Executive has advised that it is 'business as usual'. Further information can be found on the AALA website: *www.hse.gov.uk/aala/index.htm*

....

(i) **18** Position of the leader within the party

The leader's *physical positioning* within the party will vary depending on leadership style and terrain. Autocratic leaders usually position themselves at the front of the party whilst a democratic style involves the leader circulating amongst the group. On trickier ground, the leader may take a position to the side of the party, ready to step in at any point either to take control or to protect where necessary.

It is essential that the leader has the ability to read the ground ahead, identify the risks posed for that particular group in the prevailing conditions and adopt a position that allows the appropriate amount of protection to be offered for each member of the party. There are several possible methods. The simplest is a *braced position* between the individual and potential danger such as a small drop, offering an emotional shield and giving a sense of security. This, along with calm vocal re-assurance is adequate for most situations. Some awkward steps may require more active *spotting* or supporting. Spotting is described in more detail within the context of *Risk Management* starting on page 213.

Offering assistance from above is never as effective as from below unless an emergency rope is being used. Holding a rucksack strap from above may have a re-assuring affect but would require considerable strength and balance by the leader if the individual were to slip.

It may be appropriate to teach party members how to spot for each other on awkward steps, particularly if they have prior experience of this terrain. However, the leader should not regard this as a substitute for close supervision, because a slip might result in several party members getting injured.

In this day and age, every leader needs to be aware that inappropriate physical contact can have social and legal implications, but the key word is 'inappropriate'. It makes sense to brief the party on what spotting or even combined tactics may involve beforehand. It would be wise to heed the warning from anybody who declines to accept this assistance, and adopt a different solution to manage hazards.

10.6.2 Practical considerations

A walking leader should operate within the *guidelines* set by the supervising authority or employer. Even informal leaders are advised to ensure that adequate insurance cover has been arranged for legal liability, to protect other people on the hills and also specifically for the group under their care. If working for an organisation that does not provide *insurance cover*, the leader should consider arranging independent professional liability insurance for the level of risk inherent to hill walking.

A walking leader must be able to demonstrate a reasonable level of care and in these circumstances written evidence is very useful. Simple *proforma* documents facilitate planning and give proof of a standard of planning.

> **19** Party members with sensory impairments
>
> Deafness and blindness can vary for each person. The nature, severity and onset of sensory loss are individual to each person, as are the technical intervention and methods of language and support. The relationship between the leader and any group members is therefore particularly important and care should be taken to discuss strengths and weaknesses openly and with empathy. The leader should bear in mind that other additional needs may well exist whether they are physical, sensory, medical, learning or behavioural.
>
> Whilst some people may have been blind or deaf from birth, others may have experienced sensory loss in later years and still be adapting to changes. Problems with vision or hearing can develop suddenly, for example the loss of a contact lens or spectacles, or a malfunctioning hearing aid. The following specific suggestions may help groups to manage any special needs effectively.

Sample proforma templates for trip planning and medical care have been included in the appendices of this book.

Risk management is a continuous process, and written documentation helps demonstrate that this is in progress. Written guidelines and safety procedures demonstrate an awareness of standard procedures. The choice to depart from guidelines should never be made lightly – on the other hand they should not undermine a leader's authority to exercise dynamic risk assessment of the specific situation. Near misses and accidents should always be reviewed in order to prevent similar or worse mishaps occurring if foreseeable in the light of previous incidents.

Legal problems usually stem from inadequate communication. Regular planning meetings with the group and also parents of younger party members allow adequate dialogue and realistic expectations to be developed.[8]

10.6.3 Party members with a disability

The definition of a person with a disability is 'someone with a physical or mental impairment which has a substantial and long term adverse effect on his or her ability to carry out normal day to day activities'.[9] The definition includes a wide range of people with differing levels of ability, and care should be taken to ensure that everyone is treated fairly. The disability in question should only considered in terms of health and safety, and not used in a way that would discriminate.[10]

Any risk assessment should take into account the health and safety of all persons, identifying the hazards and evaluating the risk. As with any group this is based on the simple question 'who might be harmed and how?' and in this case should include an objective appraisal of vulnerable people within the group. Control measures put in place should be realistic and proportionate to the risk to the individual.

---

8 In the unfortunate event of an accident the importance of visits to the casualty and their relatives should never be underestimated.

9 See *Equality and Human Rights Commission* for full details.

10 Discrimination is covered under the Equalities Act 2010 and defined by the Equality and Human Rights Commission.

10.6.4 People with hearing impairment

Mountains can be a noisy environment on a windy day. Therefore the suggestions for effective communication on page 194 are particularly important for people with impaired hearing. Not all deaf people have a high level of English, so select words carefully.

Depending on the number of leaders it may be necessary to move around frequently within the group or organize the positioning of individuals carefully within the group. It can be difficult to gain the attention of a deaf person so it may be necessary to address their peripheral vision by waving or by shining a torch in order to gain their attention, or by contacting a delegated assistant who is in their sightline.

Depending on the aims of the trip, the leader may need to convey technical information, in which case it is helpful to have handouts prepared. The use of 'bullet points' and also leaving fair amounts of white space can help the readers to digest information. Simple images, both diagrams and metaphors convey information very efficiently. A tough 'wipe board' carried on the hill can be extremely effective.

In sign language it is the use of hand signals that is most obvious to the lay person. *Non Manual Features* (*NMF*) however are hugely important because 'body language' is a shared communication system. Facial expression is particularly important so it helps if during briefings the leader's face is not hidden behind a scarf, head-over or sun glasses. Beards can interfere with 'lip pattern' for lip readers so are best kept trimmed.

If a deaf person is lip reading or using an interpreter then they will be unable to take notes or watch a demonstration simultaneously. The classic coaching model of a clean demonstration followed by an explanation is particularly effective and should be followed by some free time if necessary for note-takers.

Some groups may wish to bring a communicator or interpreter for support: it is important to consider specifically the implications of the communicator's participation: their skill level and experience of the mountain or moorland environment, available equipment and also their organisation's policy on risk management. Any communicator or interpreter will need an awareness of relevant vocabulary for upland landscapes, so that they can ensure the correct context is used when rendering language.

10.6.5 People with visual impairment

Many decisions about managing risk on the mountains are developed by noticing significant changes in surrounding environment, and therefore people with visual impairment will vary both in confidence and also their awareness of specific hazards. If a guide dog accompanies the walker particular care should be taken in the vicinity of other animals, which may react significantly; sheep might bolt towards a hazard for example, whereas cows and ponies can become quite aggressive, particularly if protecting young.

Assigning a sighted person to each walker with impaired vision in a group can be an effective way both to manage hazards and also to develop social cohesion within the party. A sensible precaution when crossing steep hillsides is for the sighted person to walk on the outer side of the path.

ⓘ 20 Remote supervision

Unaccompanied journeys are powerful learning experiences for trained parties. The leader is removed from the group, allowing the party to make their own decisions. At the appropriate stage of development this can be enormously empowering, and celebrates the party's acquired resources. The **Outward Bound Trust**, the **Duke of Edinburgh's Award Scheme** and some local education authority centres have used this technique for many years and many organisations view it as a key component in their outdoor education programmes.

With *careful supervision* and *planning*, a group can benefit tremendously from this type of experience. The feeling of isolation with no perceived outside expert to fall back on stimulates resourcefulness; social as well as practical skills are developed experientially.

Unaccompanied journeys are potentially the most difficult and challenging work a leader can undertake. They require careful judgement, a good deal of preparation and training, and a finely tuned contingency plan for any mishaps or emergencies that may arise. Above all, it takes courage and vision not to intervene too readily, when things do not go according to plan.

On the other hand, it is important not to abdicate responsibility entirely; the leader still owes a duty of care to the group. The level of care shown by the leader is demonstrated through the skills they have passed to the group, the planning and preparation of the unaccompanied journey, as well as the ground observation and the amount and type of remote supervision given. The leader needs to be sure that the group is sufficiently skilled, well-prepared and equipped and that clearly-understood safety protocols are in place. Training needs to be given in navigation, basic first aid, camping, safety issues and emergency procedures. Unfortunately, the most important attribute of all, common sense, cannot be trained. Contingency plans for unexpected problems should be discussed, with perhaps the provision of aide-memoirs to help deal with a crisis. Clear guidance should be given about the use and misuse of mobile telephones, which can undermine the feeling of self-sufficiency if used inappropriately.

Helpers should pay particular attention to low-hanging branches or other obstructions which can easily trip or injure a partially sighted or blind walker, even on a well-surfaced pathway.

For some people peripheral vision can be very limited, particularly at dusk and into darkness, so an early finish to the day is advisable.

All hill walkers have a moral responsibility to assist other people in difficulties, but this is not a legal obligation. Leaders should always give priority to the safety of their charges and make this their primary consideration when helping others.

The level of supervision provided needs to be appropriate for the group and terrain. Areas of potential navigation problems and dangerous terrain need to be identified and highlighted.

Various methods of remote supervision are available:
- **Shadowing** is the monitoring of a group by the leader, with or without the knowledge of the group members. The planning of the route is a key element in successful shadowing. A group following a funnelling feature such as a valley is easily observed in clear weather from the top of a neighbouring ridge. (Binoculars are essential for this method.)
- **Check points** can be utilised where the leader can meet or observe the group at known points along the route.
- **Message drops** can be used at unmanned checkpoints. The group leaves a message, suitably water-proofed, to record the time that they passed through. However, care should be taken to avoid littering the countryside; it is all too easy for these messages to become dislodged – while the answer blows in the wind, the communication fails! It is a good idea to 'date-stamp' messages so that other walkers do not inadvertently remove them with the laudable intention of removing litter.
- **Two-way radios** or **mobile phones** are another option, but reception strengths would have to be tested in advance, and effective contingency plans made for equipment failure. This method is sometimes used in conjunction with issuing the group with a GPS device.

10.6.6 Negligence

Claims of negligence are actually remarkably rare for outdoor activities. Generally these have been civil liability cases where there is a claim for compensation as a result of the alleged negligence of the leader. However, if a fatality occurs or intent to harm is perceived, then criminal proceedings might be initiated.

There are a several defences against a negligence claim:
- **The accident was unforeseeable**, such as a huge boulder falling down on a well recognised path which lacked a previous history of significant rock fall.
- *Volenti non fit injuria* (no harm is done to those who consent). If a consenting adult is aware of and has accepted the risks of undertaking an activity and injury occurs with no apparent negligence on the part of the leader, then that leader cannot be held liable. For example, an adult group member sneaking off to explore mine workings, which the leader had warned the group about, would be deemed to have made a voluntary decision to ignore a clear warning about danger.
- **Contributory negligence** – the plaintiff is partly responsible for the accident as well as the defendant, for example an experienced person starting up a loose gully with a party above them. Loose stones are

(i) **21** Leaders, negligence and the law

Leaders who work within the limitations of their personal experience and manage groups effectively have nothing to fear from the law. Unfortunately there have in recent years been some well-documented cases of negligence claims against outdoor leaders in both the civil and the criminal courts. The legal consequences of negligent leadership are now a significant consideration for everyone who intends to take groups out into the hills. A leader can never unconditionally guarantee the safety of their charges and so it needs to be remembered that the leader is required to demonstrate a reasonable level of care, work within the accepted norm and embrace both legal and moral responsibilities.

Leaders who have been trained and assessed under the appropriate leadership training scheme[11] can demonstrate a conscious effort to fulfil the above conditions. They are better equipped to operate as leaders, since their assessment ensured that they understood the accepted norms of the day.

Having passed any assessment it is then essential to stay current by regular activity, continued discussion with other experienced leaders and through further training opportunities. Last but not least, the leader needs to be *fully-insured* against personal liability. Active membership of a local walking club will help a leader to keep in touch with new developments and ideas, whilst membership of the relevant national mountaineering body[12] provides up to date news and information and helps fund the many good causes such as continuing access negotiation.

an obvious hazard and the plaintiff chooses to take the risk with no safety equipment such as a helmet – in such a case it would be difficult for the plaintiff to argue that rock-fall was unforeseeable.
• **A break in causation** – someone goes to hospital for a minor injury but there is then an error at the hospital. The event that caused the minor injury did not cause the hospital's mistake.

Leaders with a duty of care for people with disabilities may well find that their experience and expectations are challenged by the attitude of their group members towards risk. There are role models within all walks of life who have challenged socially accepted limitations and hill walking is no exception. A disabled person will generally have the best awareness of their physical capabilities and also of any specialised equipment used for self-transport so it is important that both the leader and the participants share their special experience and knowledge in order to decide what is realistic. Care should be taken to ensure that everyone is treated fairly and the disability in question is only considered in terms of health and safety, and not used in a way that would discriminate.

11 See *Appendix X* for details of Mountain Training's schemes for leading walking and mountaineering activities.
12 British Mountaineering Council, Mountaineering Council of Scotland or Mountaineering Ireland.

Specific responsibilities

The leader's responsibilities are not solely confined to the individual and the group. They extend to the parent or guardian, where appropriate, and to the overall manager, organising authority or committee. Leading in the outdoors involves *legal*, as well as *moral* obligations. A leader is acting in *loco parentis* to any individuals under eighteen. This, in law, implies that the leader owes an even greater *duty of care* than to an adult; he or she must exercise as much care as a parent would reasonably be expected to take.

It is necessary to obtain *parental consent* for any journey that is proposed for young people under eighteen. Parents or guardians have to be informed in detail of the aims, nature and possible route of the walk, and should thus have a reasonably realistic understanding of the aims and inherent risks.

A *consent form*[13] should be based on a comprehensive consideration of potential eventualities. It should be very clear and honest about the type of terrain expected and the nature of the experience. Once these forms are signed, there is little room to manoeuvre if circumstances change so it is important that they are inclusive. Medical forms are also a requirement, not only to inform the leader of any potential problems that may occur on the hill but also to show that they have taken all appropriate measures to pitch the activity at the correct level for their group. Consent forms are a necessary pre-requisite, but they are no substitute for a face-to-face meeting with parents and guardians; allowing uncertainties and misconceptions to be aired and discussed. It is all too easy for a consent form to be misinterpreted, and for signed agreement to be based on ambiguity.

Responsible organisations select their leaders with considerable care. Any claims for compensation would be passed up the chain of responsibility to employer or facilitator, who is ultimately responsible for the activity undertaken. Leaders therefore owe a high degree of responsibility to their employer or supervising authority as well as to their party. It is important that leaders are aware of the authority's operating guidelines.

10.6.7 Leadership roles for people with disabilities

All leaders have strengths and weaknesses – their leadership role focuses on their *abilities*, rather any disability. It is vital that the leader is able to exercise decision-making judgements and to undertake a realistic appraisal of their own abilities. The leader should ideally be able to make unassisted progress on the chosen itinerary, so a reconnaissance trip is highly recommended. For more adventurous expeditions it is important that contingency plans and back-up are carefully considered. As always the leader should build up experience and confidence gradually: however there can be little doubt that a disabled leader can be an inspirational role model for both able-bodied and disabled groups.

13 A sample consent form is included on page 274.

10.6.8 Leadership roles for people with medical conditions

Taking on leadership roles is entirely feasible for anybody with a well-controlled medical condition. There is no legal requirement to disclose a medical condition and therefore it is perfectly permissible for anybody to lead a group, provided that they fulfil the normal requirements for leadership and insurance: as always the legal and moral duty of care to the party members is critical. In these circumstances the guidelines of the *Driving and Vehicle Licensing Agency* (*DVLA*) forms a good basis for advice, which must then take personal circumstances into account.

Medication

Leaders who rely on medication to control a medical condition should ensure that an adequate supply is available for the duration of the trip, plus extra as contingency.

Hazards and risk management

Adventurous activities by definition carry an element of uncertainty. There is always the possibility that the endeavour will not be successful, or that in exceptional circumstances a participant may be injured. However, the satisfaction gained from planning a trip and then testing oneself to travel efficiently through challenging terrain is an important factor in the enduring attraction of walking in wild places.

Learning to manage risk is one of life's greatest lessons, and accepting responsibility for one's actions is arguably one of the defining characteristics of maturity. These are important elements in the almost universal recognition of the educational value of adventurous activities. Underlying these worthy justifications is the knowledge that adventure brings excitement and fun.

Risk management is the process of making informed decisions about the things that can harm people in order to minimise their potential and to balance them against the outcome. The following sequence needs to be examined:

Identify the hazards	
Decide who could be hazards harmed by them, and how	Recognise hazards
How likely is it to go wrong?	Assess risk
Is the risk level acceptable? (Group decision …)	Value judgement
Is there a need for further action?	Action
Monitor and re-evaluate this process	Review

The issue of value judgement provides a subtle difference from a workplace risk assessment. The fact that a course of action is more exciting or enjoyable is generally unacceptable in industry, but is one of the defining factors in why people go walking in the hills. This paradigm clash is why tabloid pundits frequently brand hill walkers as irresponsible. It is important that any risk is adequately assessed in order to give a meaningful balance between activity and harm. The leader has a duty to ensure that the group is aware of the potential risks rather than encouraging a *gung ho* approach based on a naive faith that everyone is invincible. This requires a realistic appraisal of one's own motives, followed by a balanced account that explains the risks honestly without giving unnecessary cause for alarm.

11.1 Risk assessment

Assessment of risk is required at various stages of a trip in order to make an informed judgement about the balance of human, environmental and timing factors.

Generic hazards are inherent in all hill and mountain walks and are factored into the initial planning.

• **Who is going?**

The size of the party is an important consideration and special requirements such as medical conditions and behaviour problems should be noted at this time. The need for suitable assistants should also be examined, especially if an overnight trip for children is planned.

The maturity of party members is a subtle balance between worldly wisdom and specific experience of upland environments. A confident adult may have less awareness of hazards and personal limitations than, for example, a participant in the Duke of Edinburgh's Award Scheme. Self-assurance in other walks of life is not necessarily transferable.

- **Where are they going?**
Plenty of information about the venue can be gained in advance by an experienced walker. The general nature of the terrain can be found from maps and guidebooks. Travel arrangements should be carefully examined and potential problems minimised. It may well be possible to gain further information by contacting a local youth and schools liaison officer or tourist office.

- **When are they going?**
The time of year gives a rough indication of likely conditions, including number of daylight hours, average rainfall and temperatures. These are by no means certain but allow preliminary planning. The information can be supplemented closer to the event by obtaining a medium or short term weather forecast. Other potential hazards can, to an extent, also be forecast, such as the increased likelihood of encountering other parties on popular routes during weekends and school holidays.

- **Why are they going?**
A risk assessment should be balanced against the aims of the trip. Thus, for example, the risks of an exposed mountain scramble would outweigh the benefits for a group of novice walkers, but might well be appropriate for climbers seeking an exciting journey through mountain terrain. Environmental considerations should also be reviewed at this stage in order to limit the damage to potentially sensitive areas.

Site-specific hazards may not be apparent on a map or at initial briefings and might only become discernible upon arrival.

A reconnaissance trip can help reduce the likelihood of unpleasant surprises but is by no means essential for an experienced walker. In any case, some hazards, such as a damaged bridge or a collapsed path may appear subsequent to the site visit.

On-going assessment is vital for successful risk management. A good walking leader will vary the level of supervision they provide for different groups in different conditions in order to provide an appropriate balance of safety and personal empowerment of individual group members.

11.2 A practical risk management system

Traffic lights are an everyday example of a risk management system, and the three colour code system is used below to help explain the process.

The *green stage* consists of planning, research and training; thus minimising unexpected problems.

The *amber stage* is the ongoing process, anticipating or reacting to changing circumstances. This will include navigation skills, changing levels of supervision, appropriate use of safety equipment and revision of route choice.

Finally the *red stage* consists of the worst case scenario; dealing with incidents and accidents. This can include first aid, emergency evacuation, use of emergency equipment and, if necessary, calling for outside assistance.

The amber stage will tend towards either green or red depending on the circumstances. If not managed well, any change towards green can only be a lucky coincidence. It is important to reflect afterwards on decisions made (or missed) during an expedition so that lessons can be learned – some hazards only become obvious when a series of factors combine.[1]

This colour code is used throughout Part III.

11.2.1 Categorising hazards

Hazards can be categorised into three interlinked components:
• Human
• Environment
• Timing

Successful management of risk aspires to place the right *person* in the right place at the right *time*. However, it will never be possible to eliminate risk entirely, and individuals within a group must accept a degree of responsibility for their own safety, depending on their age, maturity and prior experience of the activity.

Human hazards generally stem from inadequate communication. Sometimes dialogue in advance with authorities such as the Social Services might be important to pre-empt behavioural problems or other special needs. The importance of face-to-face planning meetings, and briefing sessions for parents in the case of minors, cannot be over-emphasised. Unfortunately this is not always practicable, and in such cases, a well-planned briefing before departure should be regarded as the minimum requirement.

This should discuss the following issues:
• Aims of the trip
• Anticipated terrain and weather
• Clothing and equipment
• Food and drink
• Medical conditions, allergies, illness
• Meeting time and place
• Transport arrangements
• Costs
• Anticipated hazards and action
• Individual and collective responsibilities
• Code of behaviour
• Central contact (who will hold details of itinerary and completion time)

---

1 Risk assessment is sometimes likened to a 'one-armed bandit' slot machine: several 'lemons' may line up without even being noticed. One more lemon can tip the balance and lead to disaster. Reflective practice seeks to identify any 'lemons' overlooked during the trip, in order to avoid relying on the happy intervention of good fortune on future trips.

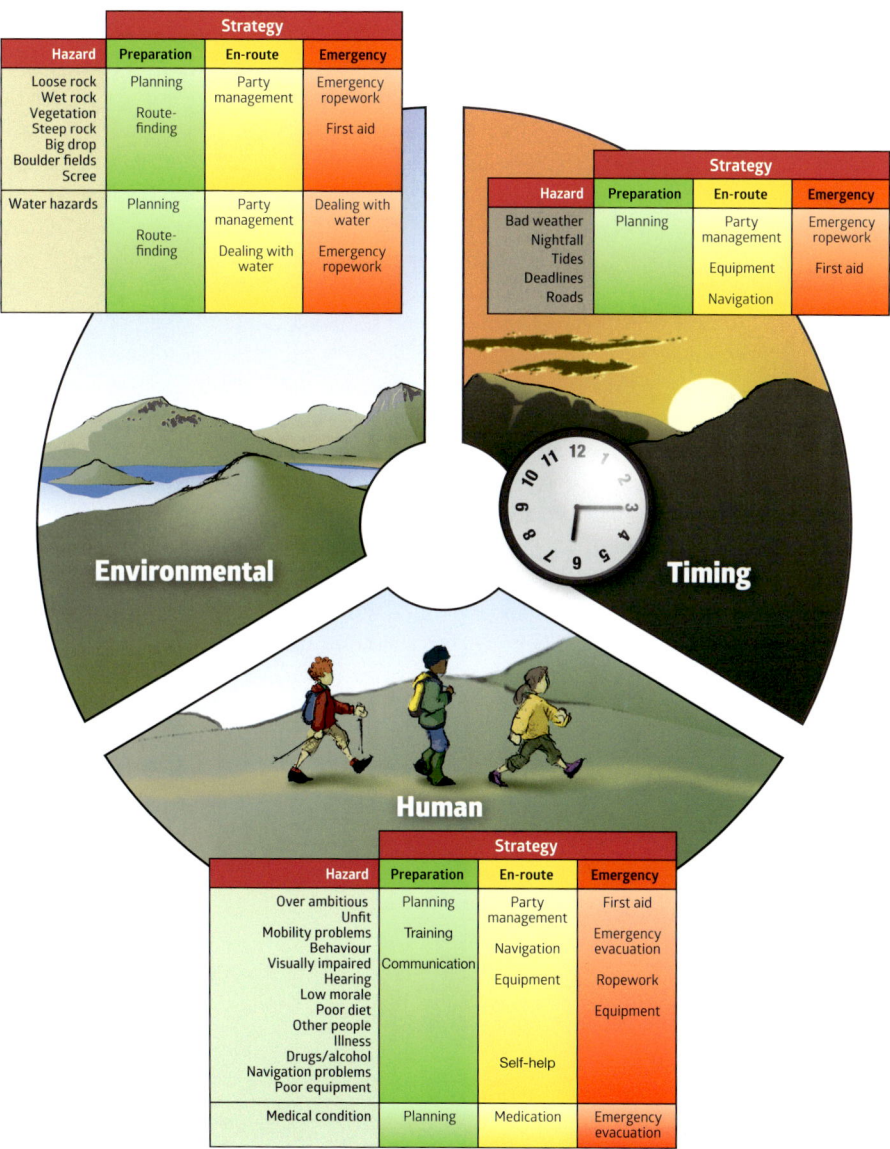

Environmental

Hazard	Strategy		
	Preparation	En-route	Emergency
Loose rock Wet rock Vegetation Steep rock Big drop Boulder fields Scree	Planning Route-finding	Party management	Emergency ropework First aid
Water hazards	Planning Route-finding	Party management Dealing with water	Dealing with water Emergency ropework

Timing

Hazard	Strategy		
	Preparation	En-route	Emergency
Bad weather Nightfall Tides Deadlines Roads	Planning	Party management Equipment Navigation	Emergency ropework First aid

Human

Hazard	Strategy		
	Preparation	En-route	Emergency
Over ambitious Unfit Mobility problems Behaviour Visually impaired Hearing Low morale Poor diet Other people Illness Drugs/alcohol Navigation problems Poor equipment	Planning Training Communication	Party management Navigation Equipment Self-help	First aid Emergency evacuation Ropework Equipment
Medical condition	Planning	Medication	Emergency evacuation

FIGURE 11.01 HAZARD COMPONENTS

11.2.2 A central contact

The days of leaving a route card on a car windscreen are long over. Firstly, there is no guarantee that anybody will act on the information, and secondly, thieves are given an accurate indication of how long they can work on the vehicle. Sadly, leaving belongings in a vehicle for the party to use on their return is no longer a safe option.

An important contribution to dealing with unexpected problems is identifying a *central figure*, who can be contacted by the group and also by their families if necessary. Most responsible authorities or employers will insist on this as a pre-requisite for any trip. This person should be briefed about when and how to contact the emergency services and how to deal with the press if approached. A central contact can also disseminate information to all family members, for example, if the group sends just one call or text to warn that their return home will be delayed.

The central figure should be a responsible adult who can be contacted at any time if necessary. This is vital for organised groups with formal leadership, and also highly recommended for informal groups. The group should arrange when they will notify the contact that they have safely returned from the hills. This should include a reasonable leeway for minor delays or perhaps problems gaining telephone contact. An agreed additional leeway should be arranged, after which time the rescue authorities should be notified.

Planning arrangement for the trip should include the collection of party member names and family contact arrangements to pass to the central figure, and in return, the telephone number for this central contact should be circulated to family members and also the overseeing authority if applicable. A sample planning pro-forma is included in *A.3 Planning* on page 269.

22 Hazards and the leader

A full discussion of the above issues allows the group to make an informed choice about the planned activity. It may be that additional training or a modified itinerary is called for in order to reduce the perceived risk to an acceptable level. The leader should retain the *right to veto participation* of any group member who does not accept the code of practice drawn up by the majority, or at least modify the plans if agreement cannot be reached.

Some problems with *group behaviour* cannot be anticipated, so leaders should continually monitor interactions and adapt management strategies as necessary.

Planning and observation also allow environmental problems to be identified. Some hazards can simply be avoided altogether, for example by walking in moorland rather than mountains so that most if not all rocky ground is avoided. At a more local scale, individual water hazards or broken ground might be bypassed, or at least negotiated with a degree of supervision that reduces the risk to an acceptable level. A group leader should guard against enthusiasm or ambition causing the party to underestimate the hazard or over-estimate their abilities. This is particularly important in the case of inexperienced or immature group members, who may express willingness to tolerate a high level of risk due to misunderstanding the potential consequences.

Changing environmental conditions may increase or reduce the potential for injury. Inexperienced groups will be less likely to anticipate these dynamics and thus it is essential for the leader to make observations on their behalf.

Planning can minimise the problems arising from timing issues. The number of daylight hours available is an important starting point for planning any itinerary. Closer to the date, use of local weather forecasts minimises the potential for unexpected wet rock, windblown ridges and lightning storms.

Contingency plans should take account of the unexpected, so a lightweight torch, waterproof jacket and over-trousers, spare clothing and a portable shelter such as a group survival unit are all sensible precautions that will not encumber a party unduly.

PHOTO // ELFYN JONES

Specific hazards

All adventure involves a reasonable level of calculated risk, balancing the party's strengths against the challenge of the excursion. When there are less practiced walkers within a group, the leader needs to maintain an enjoyable balance between interest and safety at the appropriate level for the party. However, changing circumstances can upset this equilibrium; the leader needs to recognise early warning signs and take appropriate action to protect the party from hazards.

FIGURE 12.01 MOVING ALONG A SHARP RIDGE

12.1 Steep ground

Party management on steep ground is an issue that has been revisited at various points in this book. For walking leaders without relevant experience in this type of terrain, the management strategy is simple: avoidance. They should confine their leading activities to areas where craggy terrain is absent or easily identified and circumnavigated. Mountain walkers will often operate in complex ground where experience in weaving a safe route is demanded, and decisions about managing safety on exposed steps will require judgement and foresight. There are times when it is not possible to achieve a satisfactory level of safety just by briefing and positioning of the leader within the group, and further skills are required.

FIGURE 12.02 SPOTTING

12.2 Spotting

Spotting is a term used for the art of safeguarding other party members by strategic positioning and attentive fielding; requiring considerable judgement and empathy. The *spotter* effectively blocks a potentially serious drop by standing between the scrambler and the edge, while remaining vigilant in order to steady a slip or pre-empt a tumble. Usually the party leader personally provides this role, but may sometimes delegate it to a competent deputy if route finding is difficult.

A mature, competent party may each take it in turn to *spot* for the person above, but the leader may well have to prompt this and provide suitable training. On narrow ridges or in constricted gullies, each person might safeguard the person above in ascent or descent, and thus make a series of steps safely manageable. However, this should not risk a domino effect sweeping the whole party off. This method can be very effective in relatively low risk situations for both novices and experienced party members. The party leader however, cannot delegate responsibility for overall safety in this way, and should not expect the system to ensure safety on steps where a slip could have serious consequences.

Spotting is only a suitable method for safeguarding party members if the spotter is not thereby placed in a hazardous situation. It must be possible to take a stance that is secure enough to allow a slip to be fielded without risk of the spotter being knocked over a dangerous edge. There is enormous variation here; a position that allows infant school pupils to be easily safeguarded may be too precarious for protecting an obese adult. As a rule of thumb, if one hand is needed to maintain contact with the rock, effective spotting will be compromised.

A leader should be wary of adopting a position that obstructs the best line of ascent; this can make progress more difficult for party members and is likely to annoy them or at worst increase the risk of a slip.

Whilst the choice of appropriate places to use spotting effectively requires a balance of many factors, the physical process is relatively straightforward. The aim is to prevent any slip becoming catastrophic, either by preventing a loss of balance developing into a fall, or by steering a falling scrambler to a safe area and away from potential danger. It is particularly important to stop the head or back hitting the ground in the event of a slip. The spotter's hands should be ready to support or catch someone before momentum builds. This is particularly important for weaker members of the party, for whom the hands should follow a few inches away from the upper back.

It should never be necessary to push or even touch the person unless they actually slip. Over-protective behaviour can be very patronising, and inappropriate touching is potentially open to interpretation as abuse. The party should be warned that contact would be inevitable in the event of a slip. A real slip may demand reflex reactions despite vigilance and it is possible that quite intimate contact may result. Effective communication will minimise the chances of this being misinterpreted.

In mountainous terrain, narrow ridges sometimes dictate movement in single file. There may be little potential for safeguarding each other, and thus the leader will probably recommend a more conservative style of movement if the situation is particularly exposed. There are a few precipitous ridges, such as Crib Goch, where in adverse conditions, movement *à cheval* (sitting astride the ridge and waddling along) may be necessary. As always, personal example by the leader can influence the party's willingness to follow this advice.

12.3 Emergency rope-work

The possibility that a rope might be required to deal with an unexpected situation is one of the defining characteristics of mountain terrain, and is thus a skill expected of any mountain leader.

12.3.1 Choosing a rope

As with all equipment, the choice of an emergency rope is a compromise between weight, bulk and effectiveness. The rope should be *strong* enough to hold a person's weight easily even if shock-loaded, and *stretch* sufficiently to absorb the potential impact loading of somebody slipping. It should be fairly *resistant to abrasion*, and *thick* enough to be gripped easily.

Kernmantle construction ropes manufactured to Roped Access or Climbing standards (CEN and UIAA[1]) comfortably fulfil the above requirements. Kernmantle construction consists of a load-bearing core of plaited strands, protected by a woven outer sheath. Because professionals use these ropes for safety protection, they are covered under European regulations by quality assurance systems. Climbing ropes are slightly more elastic than roped access

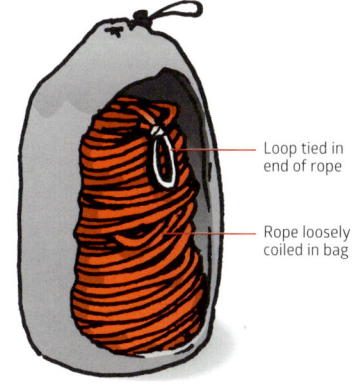

Loop tied in end of rope

Rope loosely coiled in bag

FIGURE 12.03 FEEDING ROPE IN/OUT OF A ROPE-BAG

ropes in order to deal with the potential for leader falls, but both types are perfectly adequate for hill walkers. A diameter of between nine and eleven millimetres is generally recommended: thinner ropes may be strong enough but are too difficult to grip effectively in many situations, and are more prone to catastrophic damage on sharp edges.

The length of rope carried will always be a compromise between weight and effectiveness. Situations can be readily conceived where 30 metres of rope would be required, so this is generally recommended as the minimum length to carry. Rope can be purchased from a reel but advice should be sought from the suppliers about its intended function. Because it is vital that the user knows the rope's history, second-hand ropes should be treated with great caution.

12.3.2 Storing the rope

The rope must be trustworthy in emergency situations and should therefore be inspected for damage before storing carefully in a dry place protected from sunlight. A visual inspection will reveal any damage to the outer sheath, and running the rope through the hands will reveal any deformities: a damaged rope should be discarded, as it is at best unpredictable.

Ropes should be readily deployable for use, avoiding any tangles. There are many ways to coil a rope, but all have the disadvantages of taking time to uncoil and they also leave the rope vulnerable to chemical or ultra-violet damage. Acids in particular cause devastating damage to a rope that may not become apparent until used.

The best way to store and carry a walker's emergency rope therefore is to feed the dry rope carefully into a protective bag. Tangles are avoided by starting from one end of the rope and pushing contiguous short lengths into the bag working up towards the other end, which is packed at the top of the rope-bag, possibly with a loop pre-tied. A rope stored in this way can be pulled tangle-free from the bag as required. When not in use

1 UIAA – The Union of International Alpine Associations (or International Mountaineering Federation) manages a worldwide standard for mountaineering equipment to ensure that gear is fit for purpose if the manufacturer's recommendations are followed.

FIGURE 12.04 TRADITIONAL ROPE COILS

the rope should be dried, then stored in its bag in a clean, dry, chemical-free location away from bright sunlight. On a mountain walk, a rope-bag stored near the top of the leader's rucksack allows reassuringly rapid deployment if necessary.

A rope bag has the additional advantage of being discrete; a novice party might otherwise be quite alarmed to see a rope being packed as part of the equipment for an introductory mountain walk.

The ability to coil a rope still has some applications for walkers, particularly for improvising carries, described on page 247. A brief description of traditional mountaineers' coils is therefore included here.

Coils are made by laying spans of rope as loops into one hand[2]. A span is made by extending both arms at right angles to the body, with a strand of rope running between the hands. Alternatively, coils can be made around the neck, each extending to about waist level. All but about 1½ metres of the rope is coiled in this way. To lock off the coils, the first end is doubled back upon itself to form a loop about 30cm in length, and the other end is whipped several times around all the loops, working back towards the doubled-end loop and pulling each whipping turn tight. There should be about six whipping turns. Finally, the end is threaded through the loop, which is tightened by pulling the loop end through the whipping turns.

12.3.3 Using the rope

The main purpose of a walker's emergency rope is to provide physical protection to party members where a potential slip cannot be adequately safeguarded by other means. This is very much a worst-case scenario; good route choice, navigation and party management should generally prevent this situation arising in the first place. There are times, however, when perhaps a party member might be intimidated by vertigo on an easy slope above a long drop, and psychological support can be given with the rope.

Alternative routes should be considered before resorting to roped protection; for example, a rope used in ascent often tempts the party into more dangerous ground ahead. Use of the rope is more likely to be valid

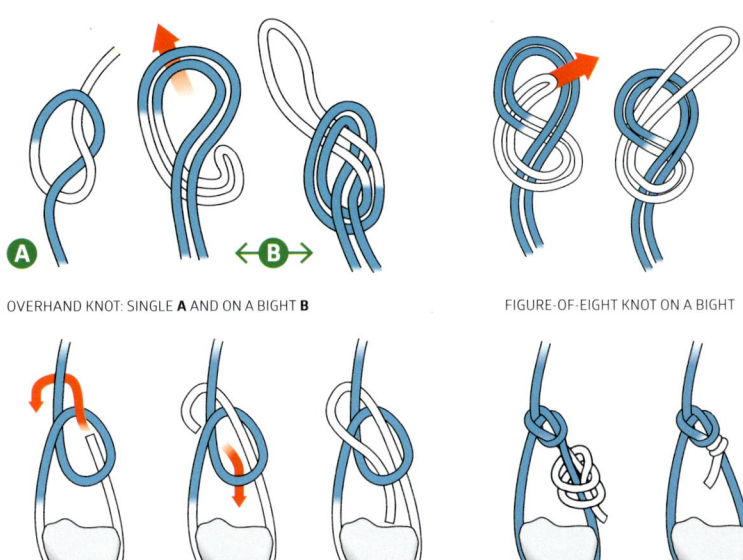

OVERHAND KNOT: SINGLE **A** AND ON A BIGHT **B**

FIGURE-OF-EIGHT KNOT ON A BIGHT

BOWLINE KNOT

LOCKING KNOT FOR BOWLINE

FIGURE 12.05 SOME BASIC KNOTS

when an unexpected hazard blocks a descent route, such as ice-glazing (verglas) on an otherwise straightforward rock slab.

Mountain walkers who are not regularly using a rope are best advised to learn a minimal number of safe rope techniques and to concentrate their attention on learning to recognise suitable anchors – secure objects to which the rope can be attached. Key skills are the ability to *attach* the rope to a person and to a sound anchor, and to *halt a fall* successfully by handling the rope with an appropriate belaying method.

Leaders should ensure that their rope-handling skills match currently accepted practices, by undertaking suitable training and assessment such as that provided by the *Mountain Leader Training Scheme*. If a leader is not confident that their rope-work is adequate to match the situation, outside assistance should be sought rather than trying to muddle through.

12.3.4 Attaching the rope

A simple *fixed loop* is perfectly adequate for attaching the rope to a person or a rock spike. This will normally be near the end of the rope, with a tail projecting by about 20 centimetres to guard against the knot creeping undone while not being long enough to trip over. The knot should be easy to tie and check by visual inspection, and should be re-checked periodically to prevent it working loose with prolonged use. Pulling the knot tight upon itself will help minimise this tendency.

The basic *overhand knot* (shown with other basic knots in *Figure 12.05* above) is perfectly adequate; this is constructed by doubling a length of rope back upon itself to form a loop about one metre in length. The knot is made by looping the doubled end around itself to form a circle and threading the tip of the loop back through this hole. This can be draped over a spike, or fixed to a person by getting them to step into the loop and adjusting the position of the knot until it is reasonably tight around the waist. As an indication, the nervous walker should also be able to insert their fist into the loop – but only just.

Climbers may prefer to use a *figure-of-eight knot* through familiarity – however, this is slightly harder to adjust. Another popular knot is the *bowline*, which should be used with caution as it is susceptible to being mis-tied and because unsafe variations look superficially similar. A *locking knot* should be regarded as essential for a bowline, to prevent it inverting if pulled apart by snagging. Locking knots are also desirable, but less critical, for finishing other knots.

12.3.5 Confidence roping

Occasionally a party member will be so intimidated, above a convex slope for instance, that they will freeze up and be unable to proceed. This phobia[2] is difficult to predict in beginners, (although their behaviour elsewhere may give intimation) but their fear is often not open to negotiation. Perhaps a combination of empathy, encouragement and physical shielding (or *spotting*) will allow the party to continue, but otherwise the leader will need to re-examine the aims of the day and either avoid the passage or resort to use of the rope to improvise a perceived safety net for the nervous participant.

A few metres of rope is pulled out of the rucksack and attached to the nervous or injured person's waist by fastening a loop and adjusting it to fit. This rope is gripped by the leader, who endeavours to remain directly above – adjusting their position to keep the rope tight in order to provide both physical and psychological support.

Efficient use of this technique may provide sufficient encouragement without attracting undue attention from the rest of the party. A sensitive approach is required in order to prevent ridicule, perhaps exacerbating the situation or breeding resentment.

Confidence roping should be rehearsed in descent – after all this is when the intimidating vertical exposure is most apparent in the field of vision. The waist loop knot is best slid around to the back and the leader endeavours to remain directly above the assisted walker.

Confidence roping requires practice in order to become effective – this is best obtained with a willing partner in safe terrain. The distance between the pair will be adjusted slightly on different terrains but should be kept as short as practicable to minimise rope stretch and the effects of inertia once a slip has started. A small loop tied in the rope about 1½ metres – a full arm span – from the victim may be found to provide a convenient handhold. At times, it may even be appropriate for the leader to hold the waist loop directly. The leader should adopt a dynamic posture with the knees and arms bent, and eye contact maintained as much as possible. The most effective posture can be found by loading the rope (by getting the victim to lean forward heavily), and resisting this force. Dialogue is of

---

2 Sometimes referred to as vertigo or more correctly acrophobia.

FIGURE 12.06 CONFIDENCE ROPING IN DESCENT   *PHOTO // STEVE LONG*

course essential, but the leader should also encourage support from the victim; some people feel more comfortable with a very tight rope while others feel that they are being pulled off-balance.

While zig-zagging uphill, the rope is always held in the downhill hand. This leaves the uphill hand free to hold onto rocks or boulders for supplementary support, and also prevents the leader being swung around by a sudden slip from their charge. If a hand is needed for more than simple balance, the terrain is probably too difficult for this technique and the leader should rethink the strategy. Eye contact has a dramatic effect on the effectiveness of this technique, and the leader should look back at their partner as often as the terrain allows, in order to gauge their reactions to the situation and also to instil confidence.

Traversing routes often present a problem. If possible, the leader will follow a parallel path above the victim, but otherwise will have to keep the distance between the two as short as possible, in order to minimise the potential of a pendulum fall.

The type of terrain where confidence roping is used is quite critical. It is ineffective in boulder fields where the consequence of a slip might be a turned ankle. Here spotting would be a more appropriate technique, although holding the actual waist loop might help. Confidence roping should only be attempted by walking leaders on ground where they personally feel at ease and do not need to use their hands for support. Normally both people move simultaneously, but boulder steps might be negotiated by ascending one at a time. If this necessitates paying out more than three or four metres a more formal belaying method will normally be required to safeguard against a slip.

FIGURE 12.07 WAITING UNDER A BUTTRESS FOR THE SAFE DESCENT OF THE REST OF THE GROUP

It is useful to experiment with holding slips on safe ground using various postures and different lengths of rope, in order to understand the forces involved more fully.

12.3.6 Belaying

If it is felt necessary to use a rope to tackle a step of rock[3] that cannot be adequately safeguarded by spotting, the party will be forced to move one at a time, with further loss of time changing the rope over to the next person. The whole process is very time-consuming, and thus alternative routes should always be sought.

Communication between the leader and other members of the party is vital when using ropes; otherwise, the feeling of protection may be entirely illusory. Because of this, the simple set of instructions developed by rock climbers is recommended, being clear and unambiguous. The party should

3 Often referred to as a *pitch*, hence the term *pitched climbing*.

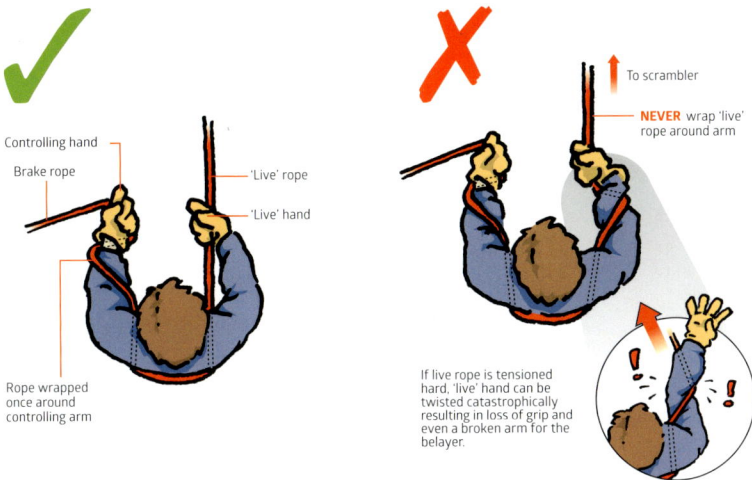

Controlling hand
Brake rope
'Live' rope
'Live' hand

Rope wrapped
once around
controlling arm

To scrambler
NEVER wrap 'live'
rope around arm

If live rope is tensioned
hard, 'live' hand can be
twisted catastrophically
resulting in loss of grip and
even a broken arm for the
belayer.

FIGURE 12.08 WAIST BELAY PLUS WRONG WRIST WRAP/EFFECT

be briefed about the system to be used before the leader starts scrambling. Explanation should be short and concise, otherwise attention will wander and the important points will be lost amongst a wealth of detail.

When a rock-step has to be negotiated as a roped pitch, the situation is serious but the danger may not be entirely apparent to the rest of the group, who may be tempted to play around while waiting their turns. It is vital that the leader takes control of the situation and carefully briefs the party about the procedure to be followed. A competent assistant can be of great assistance, adjusting knots to fit tightly and giving timely advice at the bottom of the rock step.

Whenever using a rope to safeguard people, the use of gloves is strongly recommended to protect the hands and reduce the likelihood of releasing the rope due to friction burns. Care should be taken to clear away any loose rocks, which might otherwise be dislodged from the top of the rock step onto anybody situated below.

It must be emphasised that a rope is far more likely to be used in descent than for continuing uphill. Visibility upwards is limited beyond an initial steepening, and it is highly likely that further difficulties will be met above. Visibility downwards is generally less restricted, but the belayer should check that the rope is long enough to reach safer ground before committing to the descent.

The leader needs to be positioned as directly as possible above the line of the descent or climb – ideally with an unrestricted view down the pitch – and secured effectively in order not to be pulled off in the event of a slip. Methods of achieving this are examined below, but in all cases, the leader must be able to maintain a good enough grip to hold any of the party falling heavily onto the rope. A simple hand grip is inadequate for heavy forces; sufficient friction is obtained by wrapping the rope around a suitable object; often the belayer's own body – known as a waist belay.

A *waist belay* is made by pulling up all the slack rope between the belayer and the party member (who is usually asked to yell, "That's me" when the rope draws tight). The rope joining the two people is referred to

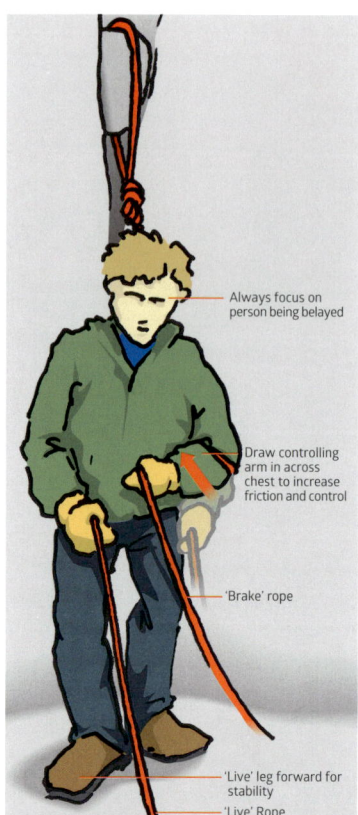

- Always focus on person being belayed
- Draw controlling arm in across chest to increase friction and control
- 'Brake' rope
- 'Live' leg forward for stability
- 'Live' Rope

FIGURE 12.09 ADJUSTING FRICTION

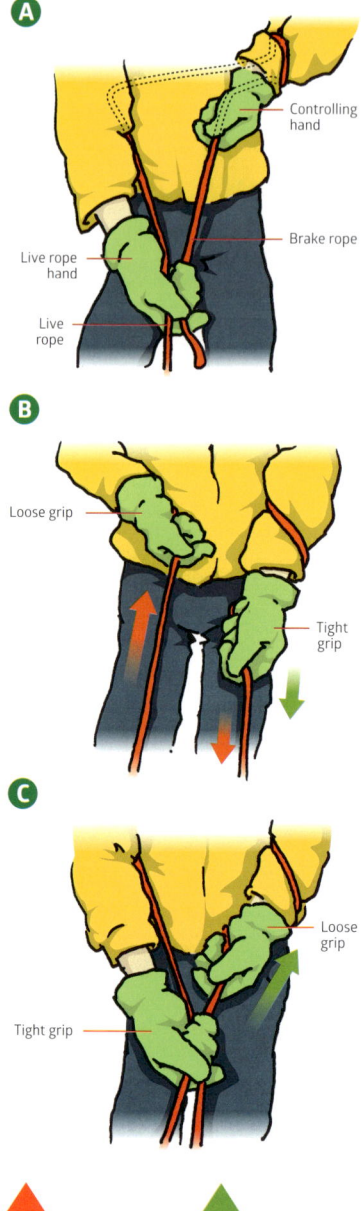

A

- Controlling hand
- Brake rope
- Live rope hand
- Live rope

B

- Loose grip
- Tight grip

C

- Loose grip
- Tight grip

Rope movement   Hand movement

FIGURE 12.10 TAKING IN THE ROPE

as the *live rope*. A loop is flicked over the head like a skipping rope in reverse direction – the rope attaching the waist to the anchor prevents the live rope potentially being pulled down with the result of whipping the legs out from under the belayer. The remaining rope is referred to as *dead* or *brake rope*.

The belayer manages the potential loading by using the body to create friction. The rope passes through one hand, then winds across the small of the back and is gripped in the other hand, referred to as the *brake hand*. The remainder of the rope lies in an orderly pile by the feet. It is usual to gain more friction by wrapping this brake rope once around the belayer's wrist – wrapping the live end, however, should be avoided at all costs because it would probably break the wrist by being jerked straight and forcing the arm to make a snap rotation in the event of a sudden heavy loading.

FIGURE 12.11 THE POTENTIAL CONSEQUENCES OF BELAYING OUT OF LINE

Once the belayer is satisfied that the rope is ready for safe use, the call "Climb when ready" invites the person on the bottom end of the rope to set off. As they begin moving, the shout "Climbing!" confirms to the belayer that they have understood and now need protecting with the rope. *Paying out* a rope to a descending scrambler is simply a matter of letting the rope ease through the hands as progress is made. Protecting a scrambler in ascent requires practice to achieve effectively.

As the protected scrambler starts to climb, the rope between the pair is taken up rather than allowing slack to build up. The hand holding the brake rope reaches across to allow the live rope hand to grip both ropes; the live rope fingers momentarily open as the brake rope is slapped into the open fingers and grasped by the live rope hand. The brake rope hand now loosely cups the rope, and is slid back close to the waist in order to re-grip the rope firmly. The brake rope is flicked out of the live rope hand as the next section of rope is pulled around the body by straightening the brake rope arm. This rhythm can easily be practiced in non-hazardous places until it becomes automatic. At all times both hands are kept on the rope so that if a slip occurred, the belayer could not be caught unawares with an inadequate hold on the rope. The tight grip simply alternates between hands as the slack is pulled through and the holding point adjusted.

Communication between the scrambler and belayer remains vital: an assertive approach is essential, with the belayer taking charge. If the scrambler is moving too quickly for the rope to be taken in at the same pace, he or she should be told to slow down. In the event of a slip, the belayer grips the rope, pulling the brake rope hand across the front of the body to increase friction.

The belayer should anticipate the direction of pull and brace the body in order to counteract this force. If allowed, the live rope will pull the shoulder around and rotate the body – with potentially disastrous consequences. Fortunately, a little forethought allows this force to be anticipated and successfully counteracted by extending the foot that is on the live rope side of the body. Thus for a *standing belay*, a sword-fencer's stance

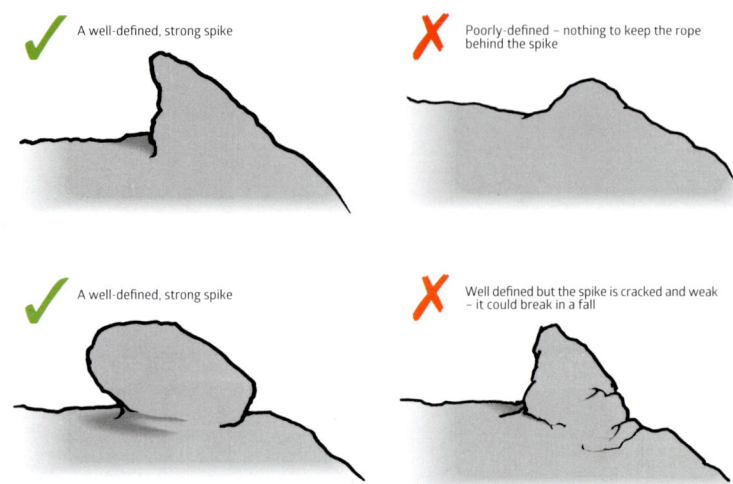

✔ A well-defined, strong spike

✘ Poorly-defined – nothing to keep the rope behind the spike

✔ A well-defined, strong spike

✘ Well defined but the spike is cracked and weak – it could break in a fall

FIGURE 12.12 GOOD AND BAD SPIKES

is taken, with the live leg and shoulder held forward. For a sitting belay, the live leg is braced, ideally against a firm boulder.

The belayer may choose to remove their rucksack in order to retain a better feel of the rope. On the other hand, if the rope passes around the middle of the rucksack, this reduces friction damage to the belayer's clothing. Passing the rope under the base of the rucksack is awkward and often tends to jam when trying to take the rope in quickly.

Security

The basic rhythm of taking in slack or paying out rope can be practiced anywhere, but in a real mountain situation the belayer must be *securely anchored* in order to prevent being pulled forward if the rope is heavily loaded. For short steps tackling relatively easy angled ground, it may be appropriate simply to brace the body without attaching oneself to fixed anchors. Sometimes this technique might be required when there are no suitable anchors within reach. Experienced leaders can often tell at a glance whether it is worth continuing for another few metres to check a potential anchor further on.

A reasonably level area is required, ideally with a solid boulder to tuck behind. The belayer sits down, leans back a little, and braces the feet. In order for this to work, the belayer should feel very stable and easily able to withstand the force of a slip. If secure rocks are not available to brace the feet against, it is often possible to kick the heels into the turf to create a hollow for the feet, increasing security. This method of belaying can be very efficient (particularly if further friction can be created by the rope running over a rounded rock shoulder) but to work safely within its limitations, practice gained in forgiving environments is required.

It is more usual to attach the belayer to a solid anchor in alignment with the pitch, so that *Anchor*, *Belayer* and *Scrambler* (remember: ABS!) are all in the same line. The rope joining the belayer to the anchor should be kept snug at all times once belaying begins. These basic principles prevent the belayer being pulled forwards or sideways under a heavy loading and possibly losing control of the rope in the natural reaction to protect themselves.

Later we will examine a compromise that is sometimes appropriate, called a direct belay. Here, the rope is passed around a solid anchor, which provides the friction. This technique can be very fast and effective, but requires even more judgement than the other ('indirect') belaying methods, as a failed anchor would be immediately catastrophic.

12.3.7 Anchors

Choice of anchors is a fundamental skill, requiring practice and judgement. A poor anchor giving merely the illusion of security is worse than no anchor at all.

Selecting anchors involves satisfying three criteria:
• Is the anchor in a suitable place?
• Is the anchor solid?
• Is the anchor the right shape?

Unfortunately, these qualities are more complex than is at first apparent to the uninitiated. Anchors come in many shapes and sizes, often requiring experience even to notice, and considerable practice to allow reliable judgements to be made. *Trees* and *rock spikes* or *boulders* are the main candidates, and sometimes a *constriction* in a crack may be utilised.

The *anchor* should be in line with the descent or ascent. The belayer should ideally be able to have an uninterrupted view down the pitch, but if there is enough rope available, the anchor could be some way back from the edge. On the other hand, an anchor too close to the edge may force the belayer to adopt an awkward position, making it difficult to safeguard people adequately in the risky transitional zone where the angle eases near the top.

Usually the anchor point should be located somewhat higher than the belayer's waist to minimise the tendency for the rope to be pulled up over the top of a spike anchor when loaded. In all cases a high anchor will help prevent the knees buckling under a heavy loading; an anchor at waist level can always be improved by adopting a sitting stance.

Testing anchors should be conducted with care, to avoid dislodging failed rocks onto people below.

Testing the solidity of an anchor is a combination of visual and physical checks. Rock anchors may be part of the bed rock, buried in the soil, or boulders simply lying on the surface. A boulder needs to be very large (at least a cubic metre) and well-seated, in order to resist potential dislodging. A rock spike needs to be firmly attached along its base, or very well buried, so any fault-lines should be treated with suspicion on the initial inspection. The anchor should also be tested by attempting to rock it backwards or forwards and also from side to side. This is quickly supplemented by kicking or thumping the rock, watching and feeling for movement – ideally with a hand resting on its surface. Loose rock is easier to spot in

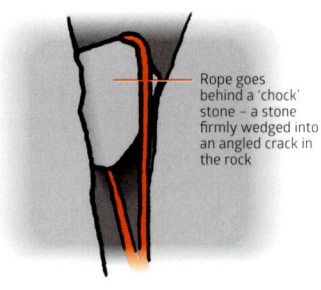

Rope goes behind a 'chock' stone – a stone firmly wedged into an angled crack in the rock

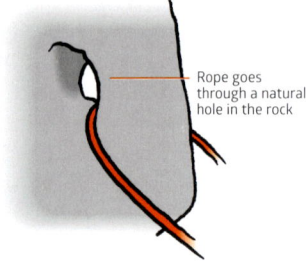

Rope goes through a natural hole in the rock

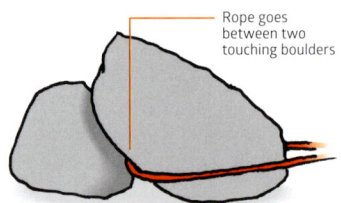

Rope goes between two touching boulders

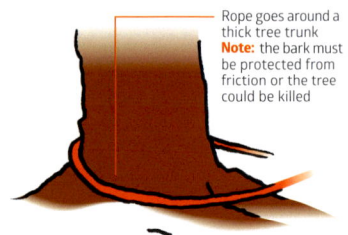

Rope goes around a thick tree trunk
Note: the bark must be protected from friction or the tree could be killed

FIGURE 12.13 THREAD ANCHORS

FIGURE 12.14 THREAD ANCHOR *PHOTO // STEVE LONG*

wet conditions as air escapes when cracks expand momentarily.

Any movement at all should be treated with caution and indeed rejected by leaders who do not possess considerable climbing experience to allow a more subjective assessment to be reliable. For the more experienced the crucial question remains: is the anchor sufficiently well keyed to serve for the anticipated direction of pull?

Thread anchors can be obtained where two boulders lie touching each other, or from a rock jammed in a crack or where the sides of a crack meet momentarily. The point of contact should be examined to check that it is rock rather than soil at this point – a rope under load can be pulled through a surprisingly small gap. All the rocks that contribute to the thread must be tested for stability. Chock-stones are acceptable if able to withstand the direction and force of the potential loading, but should also be checked to see that they will not rotate when loaded.

Tree anchors require healthy and strong root systems, with sufficient girth to withstand a heavy pull. Unless the tree is exceptionally strong, it is advisable to tie the rope around the base of the trunk to reduce leverage. Attempting to shake the tree will give plenty of information about its security. Sometimes tree roots emerge from the soil to form strong threads that may also provide sound anchors.

The shape of an anchor is equally critical; a perfectly strong anchor is useless if the rope cannot be tied around it. The ideal *spike anchor* would be a well-defined fang with an ample *saddle* at the back for the rope to sit on. The edges would be smooth, to prevent potential damage to the rope, and as a bonus the spike would be inclined slightly away from the direction of loading. At the other end of the scale is the rounded boulder that allows the rope to ride up and over its shoulders unless extreme care is taken by the belayer.

Sometimes a *rounded feature* can be utilised by scraping away at its base to reveal a slightly *undercut recession* into which the rope can be placed. Additionally the belayer may be able to coax security out of such an anchor by sitting much lower downhill, so that the force is transmitted through the heart of the rock rather than over its top. This type of *marginal anchor* demands great skill and judgement and is again best simply rejected by the inexperienced. A rough test can be executed by running the rope back and forth around the anchor from the belayer's intended position. If the rope still tends to ride upwards and over the top, the anchor should be rejected.

Attaching the rope to an anchor

Having chosen and tested an anchor, *attaching the rope* is a relatively simple task. A loop is tied around the anchor and the tension adjusted so that the rope linking the belayer and anchor is tight. This either requires adjusting the attachment at the anchor (simpler rope work but necessitating time-consuming adjustments) or at the belayer's end.

The simplest type of attachment is simply another loop tied in the spare rope using an overhand or figure-of-eight knot. This is dropped over a spike or block anchor and positioned carefully to minimise leverage. If the leader is already tied to the end of the rope, enough rope will be needed to reach to the anchor and back to the leader. If not, it is a simple matter to tie a loop in the end of the rope to place over the anchor, and for the leader to step into an additional loop tied at the appropriate point. Whilst the waist loop should be reasonably tight to stay around the waist, the loop attached to the spike is best made oversized to reduce forces on the knot and over rock edges. Getting the tension correct will often involve returning to the anchor to make adjustments, because alterations at the waist end also have to maintain the snug fit.

Trees, threads and large boulders usually require the rope to be tied around them rather than dropped into place ready-tied. A common method is to pre-tie an overhand knot using a single length of the rope a few metres from the end. (Larger anchors will require a longer distance from the rope end). The rope is threaded around the anchor and then threaded back through the knot, allowing a long tail to project (at least 30cm). A locking knot may be used additionally but is not essential.

There are other methods, which do not require a knot to be pre-tied. These include using a bowline (for which a locking knot may be regarded as essential), or threading the end of the rope around the object in order to tie a new loop in the doubled rope, at the desired point for the belayer to stand.

For leaders who are more confident of their rope-work, it is possible to attach the body to a spike belay and make the adjustments at the

FIGURE 12.15 TIED-OFF ANCHOR

FIGURE 12.16 TIED-OFF PERSON

Methods of attaching an anchor

A

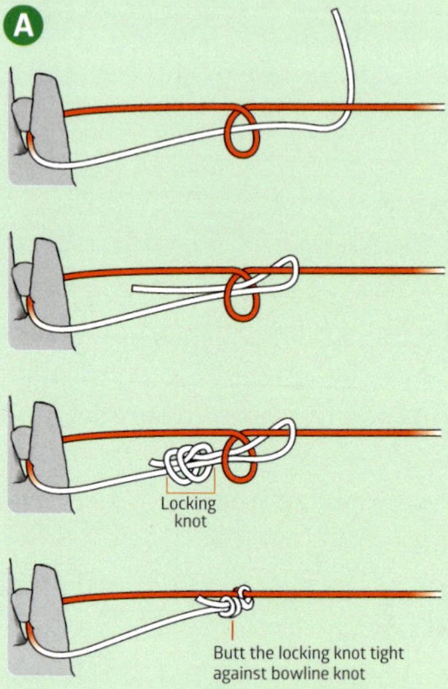

Locking knot

Butt the locking knot tight against bowline knot

FIGURE 12.17A BOWLINE WITH LOCKING KNOT

B

Tie an overhand knot in the main rope (red), thread the end (white) through the anchor and then feed the end back through the knot.

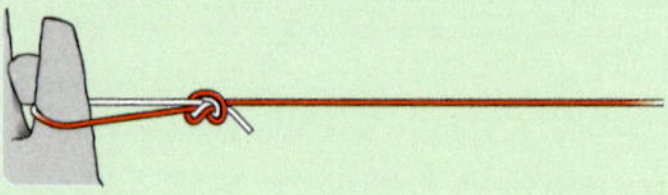

FIGURE 12.17B DOUBLE OVERHAND KNOT

More information about how to tie these and other knots can be found in *Some basic knots* on page 219.

C

1 Thread end through

2 Make a loop for a waist tie

3 Tie a large overhand knot to secure the waist loop

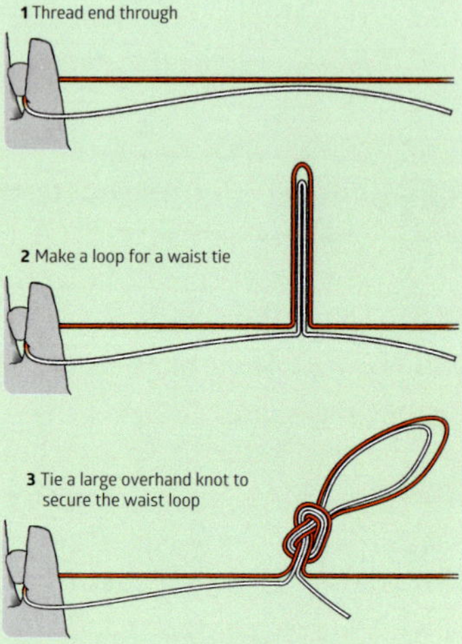

FIGURE 12.17C DOUBLE OVERHAND KNOT WITH WAIST LOOP

D

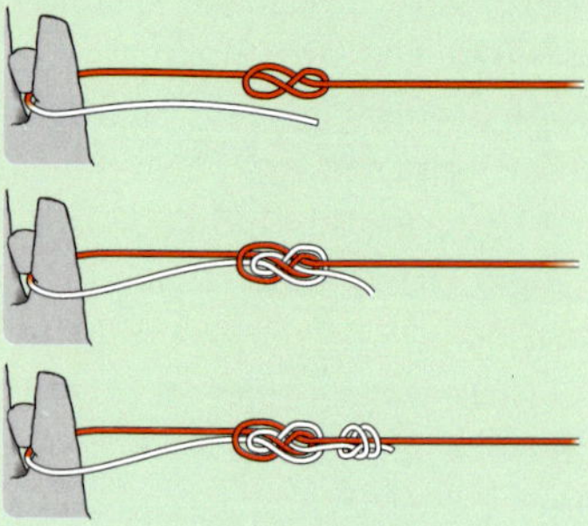

FIGURE 12.17D FIGURE-OF-EIGHT KNOT

belay point. One way is to initially leave plenty of slack rope between the belayer and anchor, and then shorten it to requirements by subsequently tying a big loop when standing or sitting in the desired belay position. This knot should be pulled tight to prevent it slipping undone if shock-loaded. Another method is to drop a loop over the anchor and tie it off by threading a bight through the waist tie to tie back around itself with a figure-of-eight or two half hitches. (Using an overhand in this instance is not recommended because it is frequently mistaken for a single half-hitch, which would unravel if loaded).

Using the above method it is also possible to use two anchors, each tensioned equally. If these are horizontally displaced by a metre or so, increased stability is achieved if the belayer cannot be braced directly above the scrambler, as the anchors and belayer are tensioned in a triangle, which gives some resistance to side-ways loading. However, this is time-consuming and complicated: if two anchors are felt to be necess-ary, the descent or ascent is probab-ly taking an inappropriate line.

12.3.8 Direct belays

 Sometimes it may be appro-priate to use the anchor itself to provide the friction rather than incorporating a body belay. This calls for consider-able judgement as a poor choice could result in sudden and cata-strophic failure.

The anchor must fulfil a number of criteria:
- Absolutely solid: bomb-proof
- Suitably shaped to allow free movement of the rope
- Situated directly above the climb or descent
- Situated in a position allowing the belayer to maintain a good grip.

In practice, this means that the anchor will be a solid spike or boulder, situated a short distance back from the edge. The edges should be reasonably smooth and there should be a distinct shoulder to prevent the rope riding up and

Pull tight

FIGURE 12.18 TYING A LOOP BACK INTO THE WAIST TIE WITH TWO HALF HITCHES

slipping off the anchor. The rope should be run backwards and forwards to ensure that it does not slip off; a tendency to ride up may be counteracted to a certain extent by bringing the brake rope over the top of the live rope to form a *half-hitch*. However, if any doubt remains, the anchor is unsuitable for a direct belay – and probably should not be used as a belay at all.

With practice, the degree of friction can be varied by pulling the rope further around the anchor or by 'unwrapping' slightly. It is also possible to incorporate a body belay into the system to increase friction. Care should be taken to avoid the rope *cleating* (jamming into the narrower part of a v-shaped crack) if there is a narrow gap behind the anchor. This could be potentially disastrous if somebody should end up hanging in space – without a harness the victim could quickly suffocate. As with all belaying, a more reliable grip can be obtained if the belayer wears leather gloves.

12.3.9 Diagonal progress

A risk assessment when negotiating a tricky step should take into account any sideways component. This will usually make it more difficult to safeguard because of the potential for a pendulum swing if the scrambler slips. Sometimes a belay stance over the centre of the diagonal line provides the best compromise. Occasionally it may be possible to flick the rope over a spike above the initial section to act as a running belay which can be flicked off when no longer providing a useful top-rope.

12.3.10 Using the rope to descend

It is more likely that the rope will be used in descent, as retreat is generally a more effective option than using the rope to continue ascending. Party management is perhaps even more critical in descent, as the waiting party need to be safeguarded from the drop, and also managed at the bottom of the pitch, where communication will be more difficult as they un-rope. Careful briefing is required to prevent people untying from the rope at an inappropriate point of the descent, or in an unsafe area.

When a rope is used to descend, the leader has to consider not only how to safeguard the rest of the party, but also how to make his, or her, own way down. Sometimes it is possible to climb down carefully once the rest of the party have safely negotiated the step. Alternatively, the rope may again be utilised.

For simple scrambles, the system is similar to the methods used for ascent. However, for ascents that are too difficult or time-consuming to climb down, the steepness of the crag becomes critical. For slabby descents where there is no possibility of the participant becoming detached from the rock, a tight waist loop with a secondary hand loop to hang on to may suffice to cope with a short vertical step en-route of at most a metre or two.

FIGURE 12.19 DESCENDING USING A DIRECT BELAY

(i) **23 Rope-work and party management**

If the rope is required to belay several people up or down a rock step, the leader may well need to safeguard against boredom leading to misbehaviour. A *safe place to stand* is required for people to step into the rope loop – rather than teetering on the brink of a drop. Transferring the belay loop to the next person can also be problematic, especially if communication is difficult; this is one of many good reasons to find a short route through the rock band.

Careful briefing is required while the leader and group are still together – but beware overloading with information, or key points will be missed. *Safe zones* should be delimited and a communication system discussed. The party need to understand that the belayer will set the pace.

Passing the rope on to the next person is eased if a competent assistant is available. The rope loop may well need to be adjusted to fit snugly on different members of the party; this should be achieved without having to re-tie the knot unless specifically under the leader's immediate supervision and clear view.

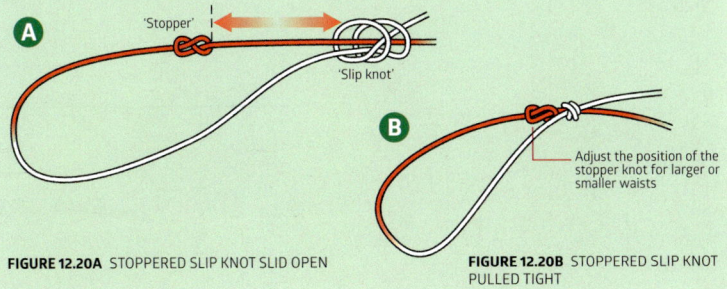

FIGURE 12.20A STOPPERED SLIP KNOT SLID OPEN

FIGURE 12.20B STOPPERED SLIP KNOT PULLED TIGHT

ⓘ 24 The leader's descent

It may be possible for the leader to climb unprotected down the pitch if it is comfortably within their abilities. However, it is more likely that roped assistance will be required; this will generally require a rope that is double the length of the step. One way to achieve this if a suitable anchor is available is by using a *direct belay*, and getting the rest of the party to hold on to the rope. A *high anchor* with little friction should be sought, otherwise the rope is very likely to get jammed, forcing the leader to re-ascend and making the exercise pointless. It is wise not to place too much trust in the party's belaying abilities.

With practice, the leader may be able to abseil down the step. A very simple step may be overcome by simply monkeying down the rope hand over hand. A variation of this is known as the *Angel's Wings* and gives more friction. A sideways stance is adopted, with both arms outstretched in a crucifix shape. The rope runs around the back to give friction and both hands grip the rope; friction can be increased by running a turn of rope around the lower arm. This method is only suitable for slabby descents as it affords little friction, requiring strong hands to keep a secure grip even at low angles. On a vertical crag it would be very easy to lose control.

There are much more secure abseil methods for a steeper descent, which should be practiced beforehand at a safe venue. The most widely used is the *Classic Abseil*, achieved by facing the anchor and straddling the rope, wrapping it around one thigh, across the front of the body, over the shoulder, and down the back to be held by the hand on the same side of the body as the wrapped thigh. It is advisable to wear gloves and exercise caution; this technique is painful and barely adequate on vertical or overhanging drops. A slightly less painful variation is to turn sideways so that the rope does not cut so directly into the groin. This abseil technique can be used with a single strand of rope if necessary.

The doubled rope is put to effective use with the *South African Abseil*. The abseiler steps between the two strands of rope, which are pulled up to near the armpits. The two strands are individually passed in opposing directions across the back and around the pelvis, then passed back between the legs. Each strand can be passed around a different leg to be held individually, or both passed around other same leg to be held in one hand, with the other hand kept free to protect the head from any projections.

FIGURE 12.21 ANGEL'S WINGS

FIGURE 12.22 CLASSIC ABSEIL

The leader's descent continued...

It is highly desirable that the rope is retrievable once all party members have descended. Before the leader finally abseils from a spike or block anchor, it is advisable to get the group to pull one end of the rope to check that it begins to run freely. Friction should be minimised by ensuring that the doubled rope is not wrapped around itself, and possibly by standing further away from the base of the step to pull. Great care should be taken to avoid falling over dangerous ground if the rope suddenly releases. If the rope cannot be moved, the leader should re-arrange the rope in such a way that retrieval is demonstrably possible before making the descent. It may be necessary to thread the rope through a sling, perhaps made by cutting a couple of metres from one end of the main rope.

Abandoning the rope is generally to be avoided on both safety and environmental grounds and it may well be required again lower down on the descent. However, a long steep abseil might necessitate tying one end of the rope to the anchor and using the whole length of the rope to descend. This is very committing, and should only be resorted to if the rest of the descent is known to require no rope. It may be possible to retrieve the rope at a later date if sacrificing it to achieve a descent is the safest option.

FIGURE 12.23 SOUTH AFRICAN ABSEIL

12.4 Caves, mines and quarries

 *Holes in the ground*, whether natural or man-made, often represent an extreme hazard and should be given a wide berth. Innocent explorations have ended in tragedy on several occasions. Mine and quarry workings are covered by the Mines and Quarry Act which effectively states that only a qualified inspector has the necessary experience to make a balanced risk assessment about the potential dangers.

Despite the dangers, many old workings have been left as gaping holes, with little or no fencing. Extreme care should be taken in any areas shown by the map to have quarry workings, and night navigation exercises should be planned to avoid straying close to old workings.

12.5 Weather hazards

The risk of being caught out by weather hazards is greatly reduced by obtaining and understanding an appropriate weather forecast (see *Chapter 9 The weather* on page 163). However sometimes weather conditions can become more dramatic than forecast or arrive earlier than anticipated, requiring defensive action.

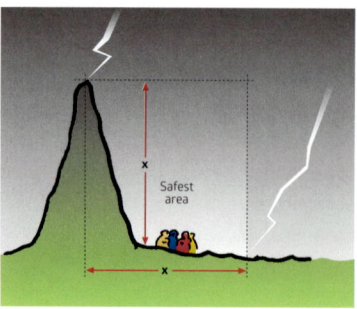

FIGURE 12.24 SAFETY IN LIGHTNING

12.5.1 Lightning

Lightning strikes rarely come as a 'bolt out of the blue'. Towering clouds build up as unstable air spirals upwards and condenses, giving a

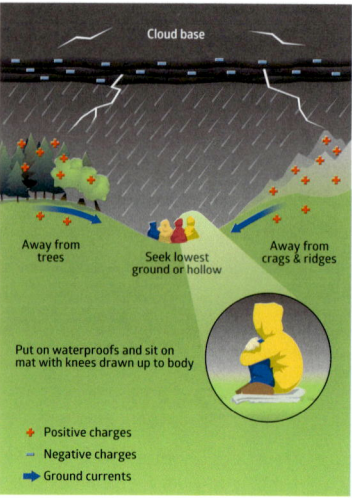

FIGURE 12.25 SAFETY IN LIGHTNING

good warning to the observant walker. As a storm approaches, its location can be estimated by noting the difference in time between lightning flashes and the rumble of thunder. The light will appear almost instantly, while sound travels at a speed of 1km per three seconds. A six-second delay therefore means that the storm is about two kilometres away.

Lightning strikes are quite frequent on summits and other projections such as pinnacles, because lightning takes the shortest route to earth. These are the areas of greatest risk, and at the first sign of an approaching lightning storm, the party should evacuate to a safer area. Scrambling terrain is particularly hazardous in lightning, and difficult to escape from quickly. A strike could easily knock somebody from his or her footing. Retreat should definitely not be by abseil, because the wet rope provides an excellent conductor. Steep or exposed ground should therefore be avoided if storms are forecast, or at least be pre-empted by a very early start and finish.

Direct lightning strikes on people are relatively rare, but can be extremely violent and often fatal. More common is a *partial strike*, either through induction from an adjacent or nearby conductor, or through the ground as the earth currents dissipate outwards. The actual power of the strike is a combination of the current and the contact time.

> A projection such as a pinnacle or post acts as a lightning conductor that services an area with a radius corresponding approximately to its own height. This means that the surrounding ground within this circumference is a relatively safe place to wait because the projection will deflect lightning strikes onto itself (and anything touching it).

Sheltering under an overhang or a tree is a hazardous course of action because a lightning strike will bridge the gap taking the most economical route, in this case through the people and into the ground. It is much safer to sit out in the open wearing waterproofs.

A walking party sitting out a lightning storm should ideally crouch or sit upright on top of insulating material such as rucksacks and sleeping mats. Hands should be kept on knees rather than touching the ground. Metal items of equipment do not significantly increase the risk of attracting a strike, but if they start to hum and spark, it would be wise to accept the hint and lay them to one side until the storm passes.

12.5.2 Gales

Strong winds at sea level almost invariably mean gales at greater altitude. Strong gusts in particular can be very hazardous as they can catch people unawares and knock them over. This can range in seriousness from a simple buffeting to a painful or dangerous fall. Exposed mountain ridges with sheer sides, such as Liathach or Striding Edge are very dangerous in windy conditions and should be avoided or evacuated if the weather is windier than anticipated.

FIGURE 12.26 DESCEND BEFORE THE STORM
PHOTO // STEVE LONG

If caught out by strong winds, *effective party management* is vital. A group will need to gather closely together in order to be able to communicate, and a plan of action should be outlined. The safest posture is a *low, defensive stance*. It may even be necessary to rope up some members of the party for safety. During very strong blasts it is safest for the whole party to lie down to avoid being knocked over. Sometimes prolonged gales mean that the only way to make progress is to *crawl*. It may be possible to link the leeward side of various land features to minimise the effect of the winds on the escape route.

Very strong winds can make progress into the wind impossible. In these conditions it may be necessary to revise the route and find a way off of the tops and into a leeward valley, even if this involves a long detour.

Since the party will be more tired towards the end of the walk, it is generally advisable to plan a route that utilises the forecast wind to assist rather than hinder progress. This may well mean heading into the wind at the start of a circular outing in order to benefit from a tail wind later.

Strong winds can bring severe *wind-chill*, and combined with the additional concentration required to make progress, this can be very tiring. To cope with these conditions, adequate clothing is required, and additional time should be allowed for coping with these difficulties. *Wind-blown hail* can be particularly unpleasant, making it impossible to look up, and it may be safer to stay put until the storm passes and visibility is restored.

12.6 Water hazards

12.6.1 Lakes

Extreme caution needs to be exercised when swimming in deep water, which is often colder than anticipated and normally much colder than the sea. Several people have drowned due to cramp seizing muscles in mountain lakes. Leaders should take great care to provide adequate briefing and supervision if party members might be tempted to swim in a mountain lake and a strong swimmer with experience in cold open water should be present.

12.6.2 Marshes and bogs

Caution should be exercised in wetlands, which can often be bypassed by spotting telltale signs such as marsh vegetation and given a wide berth. Generally the main hazard is water pouring into the top of people's boots, but sometimes the bog can be much deeper and can trap the unwary sufficiently to require some form of rescue. This is best made by the rescuer reaching out from firmer land, using a trekking pole or stick if available. It may be necessary to use rucksacks and their contents to spread the victim and rescuer's body weight out over a larger surface.

Subterranean streams also sometimes resurface in small holes, which can present an ankle-breaking hazard if care is not taken with foot placements.

12.6.3 Tidal areas

Some walks in the hills start or finish at the coast so a word on the hazards of tidal regions is not misplaced at this point. Any coastal strip, which is only exposed at low tides, can present a great hazard and should be treated with caution, especially by people with little experience of the ways of the sea. Several parties have been caught between rising tides and cliffs, sometimes with tragic consequences. Often strong currents sweep these areas, pulling a swimmer further away from safety. A careful examination of the map and its key will show the different tide levels allowing dangerous areas to be avoided.

12.6.4 Streams and rivers

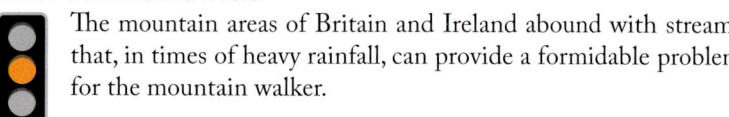

The mountain areas of Britain and Ireland abound with streams that, in times of heavy rainfall, can provide a formidable problem for the mountain walker.

Generally, streams are features that can be carefully crossed with one long step or by utilising a series of (ideally) flat boulders. One simply needs to choose the simplest and safest spot to do this; for a single step or jump, this will often be the narrowest point with firm banks on both sides. This may well require careful management – rather like managing a rocky step in steep terrain. Mutual support, spotting and a helping hand are all that are usually required. The group may require some coaching, to avoid stepping onto greasy slabs or loose boulders. Often the low point between two adjacent boulders offers the most secure footing.

Sometimes the risk of *boulder-hopping* may be too great, with the possibility of injury through a fall. The safer option is to get the feet wet and to wade across the stream. The consequences of a slip here should just involve getting very wet and then walking to the side. If a slip means that anyone might be washed away, then clearly the risk is very high and other strategies will need to be considered.

Weighing the risks of a river crossing is a classic leadership dilemma: a positive and considered approach is vital. Advice on where and how to place feet will be important. **Trekking poles** will prove useful for support and probing the stream bed. They can be made more effective by removing the baskets for ease of use. It is also worth considering tightening up the poles or even taping two together for additional strength.

For wheelchair users any watercourse or area of soft ground presents a potential hazard, as it is neither possible to step across to the other bank or between boulders. Some shallow slow-moving streams can be very easy to cross simply by raising the footbeds, whilst many streams will require either considerable assistance or be too hazardous to justify. Particular attention should be paid to both entry and exit points, and the condition of the stream bed. It is vital to prevent any risk of the wheelchair toppling over or getting stuck, so progress through the watercourse should be slow and measured. Other members of the party might flank the wheelchair during the crossing. An emergency evacuation plan should be practiced before entering the water: this is particularly important for motorised wheelchairs, which can be difficult to reverse and can also become immobilised by submersion of the electric components.

The hazards

Crossing a stream or river that requires wetting more than just feet presents many hazards. *Fast moving water* can be alarmingly powerful and difficult to exit from. The water will be cold – the body loses heat 25–30 times faster in water than in air. The river bed can be slippery and awkward. *Downstream obstacles* such as trees, waterfalls and boulder chokes may prove to be killers if anybody is swept away. Mountaineering equipment is not designed with swift water in mind and will generally hinder rather than help.

If things go wrong during a stream or river crossing there can be many potentially serious problems to deal with, such as a split party

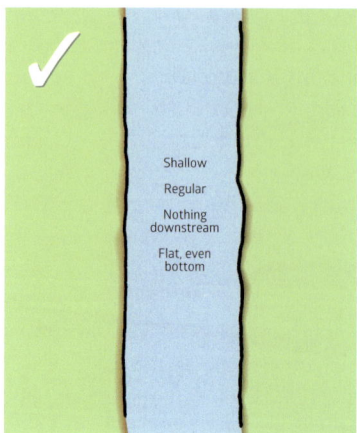
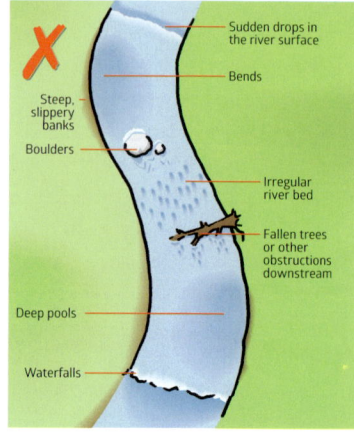

FIGURE 12.27 ASSESSING RIVER SAFETY: A SAFE CROSSING SITE CONTRASTED WITH WATER HAZARDS

with some members carried downstream, communication difficulties, immersion hypothermia, loss of equipment, injury and so on.

Clearly, a decision to cross where such hazards exist is a serious one. The risks will probably be too high.

The alternatives will always be safer:
- **A change of route?** Is the crossing really necessary? There is usually an alternative if the party walks far enough to avoid the hazard.
- **A bridge?** This is always worth considering – even if it is a long walk.
- **Wait!** Mountain streams rise very quickly but fortunately, they drop just as quickly. It may be worth waiting, particularly if camping equipment is available.

In order to weigh up alternative W, a good look at the map is required. The following possibilities may be identifiable:
- A bridge
- Braiding where the river divides into many shallow channels
- Tributaries that may be narrow
- Easier gradients mean slower water
- Lakes – the inflow and outflow will probably be slower

Avoidance is the key – careful planning of a trip and good observation as the journey progresses should almost eliminate the chances of a difficult crossing. However, local flooding in a catchment area is not always predictable from a map and occasionally a wet crossing is necessary, particularly in remote parts of the Highlands of Scotland.

Site assessment

Choice of a site requires careful consideration not only of the actual crossing point, but also the river downstream, where any swimmers will be swept. The ideal site will have slow flowing, shallow water.

A *narrow water course* reduces the time spent in the water and keeps communication more practicable, even if the noise level demands visual signalling. A *smooth, level streambed* allows ease of footing and holds no hidden surprises. *Low banks* allow ease of access and egress.

Unfortunately, the above criteria are often mutually exclusive – for example, water accelerates through a narrow passage. However, even from a distance, potentially suitable sites warranting further inspection may be identified while some unsuitable sites can be easily dismissed.

River bends should generally be avoided, as water is channelled around the outside of the bend, causing erosion. The cross-section of the river at this point is uneven, with shallow, slow water flowing through the inside of the bend, and fast deep water accelerating around the outside. The banks are often undercut, making egress difficult or dangerous where it is possible to become trapped under the overhang.

Knowledge of water features will allow more subtle water features to be identified and utilised. It may be possible to cross downstream of a small waterfall and use the eddy created in its wake. Water features downstream of the chosen site should also be identified – they may make an otherwise ideal site too dangerous to use. Trees, logs or man-made debris jammed across the river can be very dangerous, especially if branches and twigs act as a strainer, trapping a swimmer inextricably below the water surface. Even when there are no obstructions other hazards may exist such as an accelerating series of drops leading into a dangerous waterfall.

12.6.5 Preparation

 It is vital that all roles are clearly understood by the whole party. The co-ordinator needs to find a quiet place to brief the group and to check understanding – indeed, communication is so difficult against the roar of the river, that a dry run is a very good idea to confirm understanding before committing everyone to the water.

Clothing may need to be adjusted:
- Rucksack straps should be loosened, chest and hip belts undone. If someone does slip, the pack will protect the spine and if a swim results a well-packed rucksack with dry bags or poly bags inside will float and become a useful flotation aid.
- Boots should normally be worn with socks so that they fit well. Wet socks are inconvenient but not life threatening.
- Loose trousers will hinder movement, but gaiters will help to tuck everything away.

12.7 Crossing techniques

 All river crossings carry an element of risk and potential problems should be discussed in advance. Foot entrapment is one of the greatest dangers, because if somebody falls backwards with a foot jammed between two boulders, the water pressure can pull the head under and hold it down. The feet should generally point upstream and be placed carefully and firmly. If a party member is swept downstream, the safest swimming method is to keep the feet up and downstream in order to protect the body from any rocks.

FIGURE 12.28 SINGLE PERSON CROSSING   *PHOTO //*
JOHN COUSINS

FIGURE 12.29 LINE ASTERN

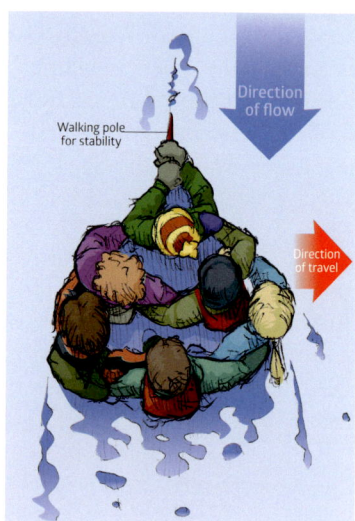

FIGURE 12.30 GROUP WEDGE

Other party members should go downstream to offer help. It may be possible to utilise the reverse flow of an eddy to assist in getting somebody. The aim is for the rescuer to avoid getting wet themselves. Ideally, a pole is offered for the swimmer to grab, as trying to catch the swimmer directly involves greater risk.

12.7.1 Single person

Sometimes it may be possible to cross one at a time; in a group situation this has the advantage that only one person is put at risk at any one time. The solo walker lacks any back-up and their only support is a stick or ski poles. The individual should face upstream, whilst leaning on the poles. The technique is to move one point at a time, maintaining one foot downstream of the other – a kind of shuffle step – and moving along sideways or diagonally like a crab. Presenting a low profile to the force of the water is important since a streamlined profile reduces the build up of pressure.

12.7.2 Group crossings

Most groups will use techniques involving mutual support. However, the more people in the water at one time, the greater the potential number to be swept away at once.

Line astern

The key to wading is to try and present as small a surface area to the current as possible. In this method, the leading person is supported by the people behind, who try to push downward on the shoulders or hips. This significantly reduces the likelihood of the leader's feet being washed from under them. The eddy created by the leading person protects other members.

The group wedge

This technique requires the biggest and strongest people at the *apex* of the wedge, where they make a very effective eddy behind them. The rest of the group are protected from the main force of the current and can cross in relative ease. At least three people are needed.

Any group method requires an appointed leader to co-ordinate movement. In a formal leadership situation, it may be appropriate for the leader to accompany each group. However, if the leader is unhappy about making a solo return this method is inappropriate. A dry run is again a good precaution, ensuring that everyone understands the procedure.

12.7.3 Crossing with the aid of a rope

As a general principle ropes and moving water do not mix. If a stream or river in the UK cannot be crossed safely by means of the methods described above the group should either re-route to avoid the obstacle, or in an extreme flooding situation where retreat is not possible, arrange for specialist assistance for evacuation.

Dealing with incidents

Incidents in the great outdoors will rapidly escalate
if prompt action is not taken. Assertive leadership
is required in order to maintain party morale and
prevent further difficulties.

FIGURE 13.01 GROUP SHELTER IN USE *PHOTOS // STEVE LONG*

Safety is the first consideration in dealing with any incident. Any course of action must take into account the safety of all concerned and seek to minimise danger. If dealing with an injury suffered by another group, a party leader should remember that their first concern is for the safety of their own charges – this includes both their physical and mental well-being. It is possible that the difficult decision to alert the rescue services rather than lending a hand might have to be made if conditions are too dangerous to approach; for example choosing not to cross a swollen river to reach a casualty.

13.1 Shelter

One of the first considerations when dealing with any incident is *protection from the environment*. If the party is reasonably mobile, shelter from the elements may be available by moving, for example, to the lee of a wall or away from a windy saddle, and this can be further improved using equipment carried within the party. However, if moving is not practical it may well be necessary to improvise shelter and insulation.

A portable shelter is the most versatile solution to providing instant protection in all but the windiest conditions. This can range from a tent to a simple sheet of nylon, but should be large enough to house the whole party. A *group shelter* (like a large floorless tent without poles) represents excellent value in terms of effectiveness for its weight. For further information, see *4.5.6 Shelter* on page 115.

Tests show that the temperature within a group shelter full of people rises very rapidly and in addition, the effect of wind-chill is significantly reduced. By keeping the whole party together, it is easier to monitor their condition while dealing with any incident. The party should also be insulated from the ground, especially if there are any casualties.

13.2 Energy

Decision-making is easier on a full stomach. The brain requires energy to function properly; this is why the signs of both heat and cold exhaustion include irrational behaviour. When dealing with an incident the whole party will benefit from eating some high-energy food if it is feasible – a combination of sugar and starch is best. A casualty will benefit from food as well, unless they feel nauseous or their injuries preclude it; an injured person is particularly vulnerable to heat loss.

FIGURE 13.02 ARM AROUND A NECK SUPPORT
PHOTO // STEVE LONG

13.3 Evacuation

Self-reliance is a strong tradition in mountaineering and a fundamental principle of the voluntary mountain rescue structure in the UK. There is an underlying assumption that parties will make reasonable efforts to manage their own way down from the hills if injuries allow, enabling the mountain rescue teams to concentrate their resources on the genuinely needy.

FIGURE 13.03 SEAT FORMED FROM LOCKED ARMS

It may become necessary to assist somebody back to a road. This might simply be a matter of stopping for some food and drink, swapping loads and using an escape route; but on the other hand, a casualty may need physical assistance in order to achieve this.

Before attempting to *evacuate* a casualty, it is vital to consider the effect that this will have on them. Improvised transport, even on a makeshift stretcher, may well exacerbate the condition of a casualty suffering from shock or severe hypothermia. In extreme cases it could endanger their life. Somebody with suspected fractures of the spinal column should not be moved unless their survival depends on it. On the other hand, waiting for a rescue team to deal with a minor injury might result in unnecessary hypothermia for the whole party.

13.4 Assisted movement and carries

At times all that is required for the casualty to make effective progress is a steadying hand. The casualty may find that wrapping an arm loosely over the shoulders of a supporting group member provides sufficient support – a helper on both sides may prove to be even more effective, especially for a leg injury. This is a strenuous technique, and the casualty's state of health should be continually monitored in order to change tactics if it begins to deteriorate. Walking poles may be of considerable assistance in this type of evacuation.

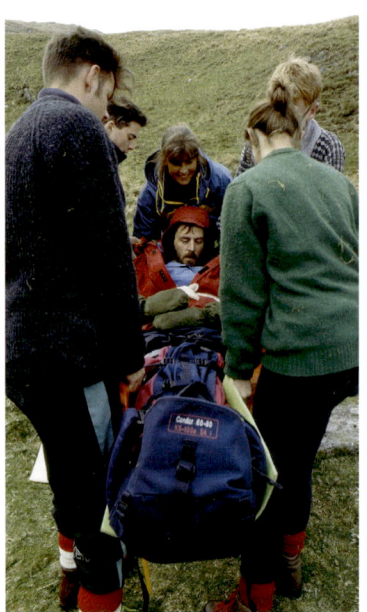

FIGURE 13.04 RUCKSACK AND POLE COMBINATIONS FOR IMPROVISED STRETCHERS   *PHOTO // JOHN COUSINS*

Casualties who are unable to walk or limp even with assistance might still be capable of holding themselves sufficiently upright for some sort of assisted carry. All carries are strenuous and are only feasible for relatively short distances, typically to move someone to a place of shelter.

Two people can lock arms to form a seat, which the casualty utilises by placing an arm around each carrier's shoulder. Forming a lattice of wrists can more effectively lock the arms; each carrier grasps one of their own wrists and one of their partners. A light person may be carried by one pair of arms forming the seat and the other pair forming the backrest.

Walking equipment can be utilised to improvise chairs and stretchers. A rucksack's shoulder straps may be used as carry slings with the main sack forming a back rest; it may even be possible for a larger person to carry a small casualty sitting within the extended shoulder straps. Walking poles are very adaptable and can be incorporated into an improvised seat or stretcher if several poles are strapped together for strength. Modern tent poles are of limited use for carries as they are very thin and are designed to flex.

Stretchers can be improvised from strong poles or sticks threaded through clothing or bivy bags. A bivy bag, or even better, a group shelter, can make an effective stretcher even if no poles are available. A pebble inserted at each grab point can make it easier to grip. Improvised stretchers offer limited support however, and *should never be used for somebody with a suspected back injury*, serious limb fracture, damaged pelvis or indeed anybody suffering from shock (unless their survival depends on immediate transportation by any means available).

A coiled rope may be used for one or two person carries or uncoiled and tied off in a series of parallel loops at approximately 20cm intervals to form a stretcher.

The *coiled rope carry* is relatively comfortable for the load bearers, as no twisting of the torso is required. Adjusting the relative length of the loops can compensate for differences in height. To carry somebody in this way, the rope needs to be tied securely into coils. These should be long enough to hang at about waist level when hung over the rescuer's head and across one shoulder. Traditional climber's coils can be used, as illustrated in *Figure 13.02*, or body-length coils can be gathered and tied in half with an overhand knot. Additional padding over the knot will be required for comfort.

Front   Back   With two people

Use a strap or cord to
secure the rope at the front

FIGURE 13.05 ROPE COIL CARRY

Practising improvised carries under careful supervision can be an excellent group activity for trainee leaders, and reinforces the difficulties of transporting casualties for more than a few metres, particularly over broken ground. It is important that sensible lifting protocols are followed; keeping the back straight and upright, while using the leg muscles to lift. People should assist each other in the initial stages of a lift; heavy individuals can be considerably heavier than loads that are normally recommended by the Health and Safety Executive for safe lifting.

With any evacuation, **assertive leadership** is required in order to make best use of the available resources and to manage the whole party effectively; it is all too easy to lose track of other members of a party while dealing with a casualty.

 Correct posture
Back straight, eyes looking straight ahead, resting on one knee for support and on one foot to assist moving into a standing position

 Poor posture
Bent back is liable to sprain and full kneel means moving into a standing position will be difficult

FIGURE 13.06 PROTECTING THE BACK WITH SAFE LIFTING METHODS

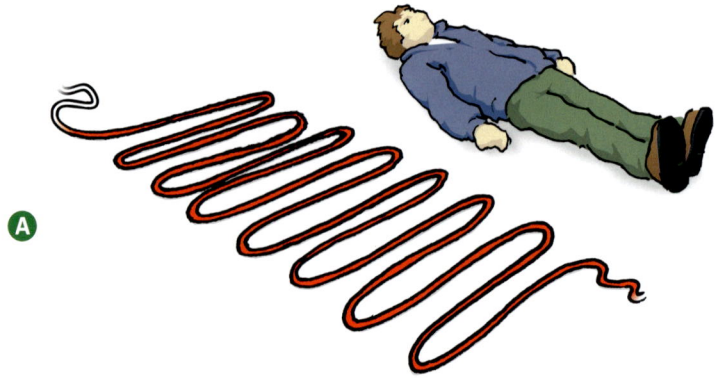

A Measure off 8 lengths of rope from the middle of the rope. If possible do this against the casualty as a guide to the size. This will form the stretcher bed, so it should be slightly longer than the casualty and about 30cm wider.

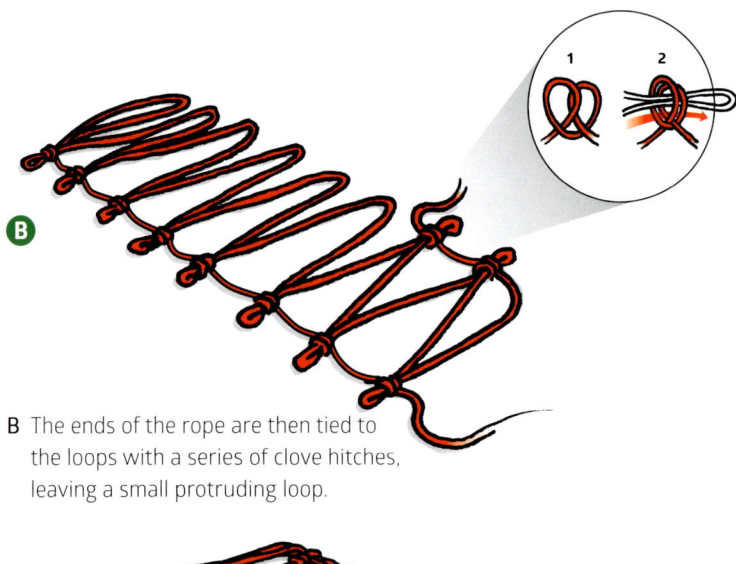

B The ends of the rope are then tied to the loops with a series of clove hitches, leaving a small protruding loop.

C All the rope is used up by threading through the small end loops. The ends of the rope are tied together and the clove hitches are then slid outwards and tightened.

FIGURE 13.07 ROPE STRETCHER AND HOW TO MAKE IT

13.5 Asking for help

 A serious incident will usually require outside assistance, probably the emergency services. The decision to *call for help* needs to be made as soon as the situation demands it; but in addition the first aider will need to plan a course of action. It is essential that appropriate information is relayed when sending for help. It is therefore an excellent idea to carry some sort of *aide mémoir* in the party's first aid kit – ideally, this will be printed on waterproof paper that can allow writing in any conditions. *Figure 13.09* provides a sample template that can be used for noting details about the incident and also for monitoring a casualty.

Making a **999** (or **112**)[1] call from a mobile phone

 Firstly, make a note of all relevant details. Written notes will assist in making an effective phone request for help: the *aide mémoire* in *Figure 13.09* provides a useful template that could be copied and kept in the first aid kit.

In brief, the vital information includes:
* Location, including a 6 figure grid reference
* Name, sex and age of casualty
* Nature of injuries
* Number of people in party
* The number of the mobile phone

Dial **999** (or **112**) and ask specifically for **Police – Mountain Rescue**, in order to speak to a suitably trained operator.

Be sure to tell the operator where you are so they can put you through to the appropriate area police, and once connected to a police control room, check that it is the right one: assertive action at this point minimises the danger of misunderstanding. Explain the nature of your call, giving the details previously prepared. Do NOT change your position until contacted by the rescue team, who will agree future protocol for use of phone. If you have to make a further 999 (or 112) call, follow the exact procedure again.

As an emergency tool, the mobile phone requires some care. It should be kept in a waterproof protective container and is best stored switched off: battery life will be further increased by switching off the back light and other apps and/or warming the battery before use – a compatible spare battery pack is worth considering as an expedient back-up policy. When seeking a signal it should be remembered that peaks, ridges and open slopes tend to have better signals than valleys and hollows. Stop moving immediately when a signal has been established. If a voice call fails send a text to a point of contact to relay the message, and request a return text to confirm receipt.

1 Throughout most of Europe, including the UK, dialling 112 forces a mobile phone to try the call with any available network, regardless of the SIM card contract, but remember that the emergency services will not be able to track the phone number.

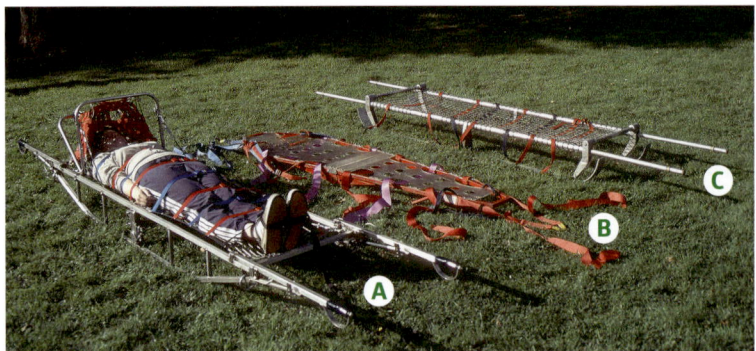

FIGURE 13.08 TYPES OF STRETCHER: ABOVE **A** BELL STRETCHER, **B** TROLL STRETCHER AND **C** THOMAS STRETCHER
PHOTO // STEVE LONG

Sending a text message for help

Technological solutions to remote communication issues are developing rapidly. Several types of emergency distress beacons[2] allow a message to be sent by radio. GPS-enabled models are carried quite frequently in genuinely remote wilderness regions of the world; some models are becoming quite commonplace in the UK and are now legal for terrestrial use. However, the advantage of coverage regardless of telephone signal is outweighed at the time of writing by the fact that even devices that allow a customisable message to be sent cannot currently receive messages, meaning that the caller cannot be certain that a message got through, nor can the receiver request further details.

At the time of writing a text service for mobile phones is being developed in the UK to assist those needing emergency assistance in the hills when mobile reception is poor and there is not enough signal to make a voice call.[3] The benefit is that a text message can be composed and sent in a single operation. It is important to specify 'Police-Mountain Rescue' when sending the text, and include the same information as above. To use this service it is necessary to have pre-registered with emergency SMS: *www.emergencysms. org.uk*. Various smartphone apps have also been developed integrating this system and the GPS location information built into most phones.

Attracting attention

However, if the above options are not available or fail, the process of calling for help will need to be started immediately. The simplest and generally most effective solution is for the whole group to yell very loudly for help. If this brings no response, it may be possible to signal for help, ideally by using the international distress signal. Depending on conditions and equipment available the signal can be given using light or sound – or a combination of both. Walking leaders should be familiar with these signals in order to both send and respond to requests; however the most important factor is simply to make plenty of

---

2 Originally developed for the hearing impaired but soon adopted for mountain rescue situations.

3 Distress radio beacons, also known as emergency beacons, PLB (Personal Locator Beacon), ELT (Emergency Locator Transmitter) or EPIRB (Emergency Position-Indicating Radio Beacon), are tracking transmitters which aid in the detection and location of boats, aircraft, and people in distress.

noise in order to attract attention. A whistle and torch should be included in any party's equipment. It may also be possible to use a camera flash bulb to signal help, although the battery will not last for long. Also, given good visibility, the back light of a mobile phone can be seen by a helicopter crew or mountain rescue team from a distance of several miles.

The *Alpine distress signal* is six blasts or flashes made in quick succession, then repeated after a one-minute interval. Alternatively the *SOS Morse signal* may be used. This consists of three short, three long and three short blasts or flashes made in quick succession, (··· — ···) with the same combination repeated after a one minute interval. The standard *signal for replying* to the distress signal is three blasts in succession, repeated after a minute's silence.[4]

It is a good idea to take a compass bearing immediately towards the location of any response (visual or auditory) to assist locating the signaller. Both parties should continue to signal in order to assist 'homing in' on the incident site.

The location of the nearest *telephone* can be identified from local knowledge or the map. It may be possible to flag down a car on the nearest road, otherwise telephone boxes are marked on maps and most clusters of buildings will have at least one working telephone line. Making a 999 (or 112) call from a landline is less prone to misunderstandings as the rescue authorities will automatically be notified of the location. The caller will probably be asked to wait at the phone for the police to arrive.

Deciding whom to send for help will depend on the nature of the party. A group of competent adults will be able to send a self-contained party, armed with written notes, to navigate safely to the nearest telephone and request help. Other parties will not be able to achieve this ideal and may well have to make compromises – however, sending a single person off for help is less satisfactory as there is no assistance in the event of injury or other unforeseen problems, and leaving a casualty alone while arranging assistance is also to be avoided if possible. Leaders working with very young groups should seriously consider recruiting an assistant to facilitate dealing with unexpected incidents.

Ideally, a *trained first aider* will be left with the casualty, with a realistic expectation of how long they will have to wait for help. The site should be marked to assist the rescue team to locate it; perhaps using bright bivy bags or clothing (pinned down with rocks if a helicopter evacuation is anticipated). *Leaving a casualty* or an inexperienced young party alone is to be avoided if possible. Their judgement may be irrational and they might well move into a dangerous situation or become difficult to locate. Briefing of the casualty or indeed anybody left behind should include a warning to stay put, and they should be left with warm clothes and signalling equipment.

An *unconscious casualty* is unable to safeguard their airway and should be kept in the *safe airway position* if their breathing cannot be monitored at all times. If circumstances dictate that the unconscious casualty must

4 However, there is potential for confusion as this is used as the distress signal outside of Europe (due partly to its similarity to the SOS), so a single blast may be more appropriate after the initial response.

First Aid Report Form

Rescue Request

Approach! Airway, Breathing, Circulation

What time did it happen? ....

Ask: What happened? ....
Where does it hurt? ....
Felt this before? ....
Allergies? ....
Medication/drugs? ....
Last meal? ....

State of consciousness: ....

Respiration: ....

Pulse: ....

Head: Scalp – wounds ....
Ear – fluid ....
Eyes – pupils ....
Jaw – stability ....
Mouth – wounds ....

Neck: Wounds, deformity

Chest: Movement, symmetry

Abdomen: Wounds, rigidity

Pelvis: Stability

Extremities: Wounds, deformity. Sensation and movement. Pulse below injury

Back: Wounds, deformity

Skin: Colour   Temperature   Moistness

Spinal check
for evaluation:
☐ Alert/no intoxication   ☐ No distracting injury
☐ No neck pain/tenderness   ☐ No numbness, tingling, weakness
☐ Normal motor/sensory   ☐ Painless range of motion

First Aid Given
....
....
....
....
....
....
....

Casualty's name: ....

Age: ....

Time			
Conscious level			
Breathing			
Pulse			

Date: Time:

Completed by:

Time of incident: ....am/pm

Date: ....

Description: Details: ....
Impact ☐   ....
Illness ☐   ....

Excessive: ☐ Heat   ☐ Cold

Location: ....
....
....

Grid ref: ....

Others in party:

Central contact:

Name: ....

Phone number: ....

Injuries: ....
....

First Aid Given
....
....
....
....
....

Time			
Conscious level			
Breathing			
Pulse			

FIGURE 13.09 EMERGENCY INFORMATION FOR CALL OUT: *AIDE MÉMOIRE*

be left unattended, a note should be left explaining what actions have been taken, and care should be exercised to protect the casualty from any dangerous surroundings. Perhaps rucksacks and rocks may be used to prevent the casualty rolling towards danger.

13.5.1 Mountain rescue

Rescue teams

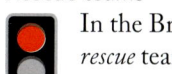

In the British Isles, there is a long-standing tradition of *mountain rescue* teams operating on a voluntary basis. Teams have developed in clearly defined areas, working in cooperation through co-coordinating agencies in home nations: Mountain Rescue England and Wales, Mountain Rescue Ireland, and Scottish Mountain Rescue.

Mountain rescue call outs are managed by the local police, who are also responsible for the insurance of team members. The RAF, navy, coastguard and the Aeronautical Rescue Coordination Centre (ARCC) also form part of the structure; civilian rescues are a central aspect of their work and mountaineering incidents also provide important training opportunities for technical assess in emergency situations. However, military incidents have to be given priority by these teams, so they are not always available. In addition, the *Search and Rescue Dog Association* (SARDA) has a long pedigree of assisting with searches for missing persons and avalanche victims since its formation in 1965.

Mountain rescue teams undertake all training and rescue operations on a voluntary basis. The costs of maintaining equipment, training, vehicles, insurance and buildings are met by a complex network of fund-raising activities as well as some central government support and donations from rescued parties or their families and friends. It should be remembered that an unnecessary call-out channels these limited resources away from genuine requirements, so it important that arrangements to notify a central contact at the end of an expedition are adhered to. On the other hand the central contact should not hesitate to contact the rescue services if a concern about the safety of the party arises, such as an unexplained significant failure or delay in communications.

13.5.2 Helicopters

Military provision of helicopters is gradually being phased out by the government, to be replaced progressively by Search and Rescue services by Bristow Helicopters limited. Helicopters can dramatically accelerate rescue response and the recovery of casualties. However, the contribution of helicopters is very much a supplement to the ground rescue team, as aircraft are not always available, either due to simultaneous operations, or poor visibility – in particular heavy rain, thick cloud or snow at night, which severely limits the effectiveness of night vision goggles.

If awaiting a helicopter for rescue, the party can assist by making sure that nothing is left lying where the powerful draft from rotors will sweep it into the air. Any clothing or bags used as site markers should be very

FIGURE 13.10 A MACINNES STRETCHER IN USE DURING A MOUNTAIN RESCUE OPERATION *PHOTO //* ELFYN JONES

well pegged down, or removed once the helicopter has arrived near the site. If an obvious flat site is available the party should ideally be situated to the windward side so that the helicopter can approach by flying into the wind. At night, the use of torches should be minimised and never shone directly at the helicopter, as night vision goggles accentuate the light and can dazzle the navigator. Under no circumstances should laser pens be aimed at approaching helicopters.

Helicopter teams are highly trained and will find their own safe working places, so any signalling beyond attracting attention is redundant. The universal signal for help is to stand facing the approaching helicopter with both arms raised to make a 'Y' shape. A crew member (usually the winchman) will normally be lowered and released from the winch, to give advice and to help the group on the ground. It is important to follow their directions of how to approach so that the pilot can maintain visual contact whilst keeping the helicopter upright. The winchman will normally accompany the casualty to the waiting helicopter. If required to approach a helicopter, keep the head low to minimise the danger from the rotors, and stay away from the hot exhaust. At all times, obey the explicit instructions given by the aircrew.

13.5.3 Rescue posts

The service provided by the rescue teams has in the past been supplemented by rescue posts where a supply of equipment such as splinting materials and one or more stretchers was stored. Some of these were located in more remote areas where a considerable delay can be expected before the arrival of a rescue team. Due partly to the difficulties presented in managing these resources none remain accessible to the public and they are no longer marked on current maps. Valley rescue posts are typically only manned during rescues, so can be discounted when planning where to send volunteers to seek assistance.

14

Dealing with injuries

Leaders of walking parties will want to undertake adequate first aid training to deal with accidents that might befall themselves or their charges – indeed, a current certificate in first aid training is a pre-requisite for the validity of all Mountain Leader Training Qualifications. This should be at least equivalent to the Health and Safety Executive recommendations for Emergency First Aid: for which the Voluntary Services' First Aid Manual is the appropriate literature.

14.1 Basic life support

The standard first aid protocol becomes even more crucial in remote environments. The first aider should work through the mnemonic ABCDE in order:

A	Awareness Assessment	
B	Breathing	Airway, presence and quality of breathing
C	Circulation	Heart working, check for cuts and bleeding
D	Deformities	Feel for abnormalities
E	Evaluate	Give emotional support

The significant delay which potentially spans between an accident and handing a casualty over to a medic means that the first aider in a remote setting requires a significantly higher skill level than in the home or most urban work places. A complete discussion of first aid techniques is outside the scope of this book. However, in an emergency the first three stages of casualty care are urgent and involve special considerations in remote locations. These are discussed below.

A Awareness/assessment

The first aider's first responsibility is to *avoid personal injury* and to *protect the uninjured*. An appraisal of the situation must be weighed up before rushing in to help; an injured first aider becomes part of the problem. Unfortunately, it may not even be possible to reach the casualty without taking unjustifiable risks; in these circumstances the party would have to accept that the situation is beyond self-help and make arrangements for fetching assistance.

If it is possible to administer first aid, the task of *constructing shelter* should ideally be delegated as soon as convenient. Most casualties in remote environments have reduced defences against the environment and will need shelter to protect them from *hypothermia*. Other members of the party may also become chilled while waiting, a potential problem that is best pre-empted.

Casualties on a hillside should ideally be approached from below to avoid knocking rocks on them. Stepping over casualties is also to be avoided (if possible) because of the potential for accidentally losing balance and causing further injury by falling on the casualty.

As in all first aid the initial stage of *assessing* a casualty is to talk to them. If necessary, squeeze their shoulders and shout to try gaining their attention. The casualty may well be able to pass on vital clues about the accident, which may not be discovered if they sink into unconsciousness. A good starting point is to ask about sources of pain, ask what happened, and ascertain whether the casualty has any pre-existing medical conditions.

B Breathing

A talking casualty is clearly breathing, but it is vital to check the *airway* and *breathing* of a casualty who does not make any attempt to communicate. This can be extremely difficult in outdoor environments, but it is the single most important task.

FIGURE 14.01 SAFE AIRWAY POSITION
PHOTO // STEVE LONG

It may be necessary to turn a casualty over in order to see the mouth and nose. Even if there are worries about the stability of the backbone, the casualty's survival depends on ability to breathe. *Look, listen, feel* and *smell* for any signs of breathing. Tight clothing around the neck should be loosened, and if no signs of breathing can be felt, the throat should be checked for obstructions and if necessary the head carefully tilted back to counteract gravity pulling the tongue back to block the airway.

An unconscious casualty should ideally be rolled carefully into the *safe airway* (or '*recovery*') *position* if found lying in a pose that would not allow blood or vomit to drain freely out of the mouth. If a *neck fracture* is suspected, movement should be minimised – however, maintaining breathing must take precedence so a position approximating the safe airway position will probably become necessary. In any case, every couple of minutes, breathing and the level of consciousness should be checked and monitored. If possible, when turning the casualty into the safe airway position, they should be rolled onto a layer of insulating material to reduce heat loss into the ground.

The recommended protocol for dealing with casualties who are not breathing (despite an opened airway) is modified every few years in the light of continued research by international resuscitation councils. Advice in this book therefore cannot be a substitute for regular revalidation in basic life support. The priorities in this case would be to keep the lungs oxygenated through rescue breathing, and to obtain help from the emergency services as quickly as possible. Balancing these two requirements can, however, be very difficult.

C Circulation

With a conscious, breathing casualty the priority is to check for *major bleeding*. This can be very difficult as outdoor clothing – particularly waterproofs – can very effectively hide blood. The first aider should check under natural hollows where blood is likely to pool and investigate further if suspicious signs are found, by feeling under clothing and looking at the skin. Any serious wounds should be *immediately treated* by applying *direct pressure* and *elevating* unless other injuries make this impractical (an elbow fracture, for example).

If a casualty is breathing and no signs of serious bleeding are found, it is good practice to begin *monitoring the pulse* as soon as possible in order to evaluate a trend developing over time in the vital signs. For example, continued rising of the pulse rate for no apparent reason would lead the first aider to suspect undiscovered injuries or illness.

In simple terms the first priority is to look for *signs of life*. Blue or grey tones to the skin, particularly the lips, suggest that the *heart has stopped*. In a remote location lacking access to a defibrillator within half an hour, the chances of recovery from heart failure are very slim, apart from notable exceptions such as when caused by drowning or lightning strike. The decision whether to start *Cardio Pulmonary Resuscitation* will have to be made according to individual circumstances.

14.2 Other considerations for first aid on mountains and hills

Beyond the practicalities of basic life support, most first aid treatment is outside the scope of this book. However, a few specific injuries and conditions will be highlighted, as they are particularly pertinent for walking parties.

14.2.1 Leg and ankle injuries

Soft tissue injuries are relatively common and should be treated with care, as it is possible that a fracture is also involved. The injury should therefore be treated as a *suspected fracture*, requiring immobilisation and elevation. Splint the leg to the other leg and check that circulation is not impaired, otherwise it will be necessary to move the limb to a position that does not restrict blood flow. The casualty should be evacuated with care and checked by a casualty department.

14.2.2 Friction blisters

These *superficial heat burns* are frequently caused by ill-fitting footwear. Education and prevention are far better than cures. Protective tape is best applied as soon as a hotspot is felt, or even before beginning the walk. Time spent on foot-care early will be repaid later in the trip both through quality of experience and efficiency of progress, so a wise leader will encourage the group members to speak up if any friction is felt.

Left untreated a blister will probably burst with attendant risk of infection. Applications of proprietary protection such as *Compeed* or *Second Skin* are generally the most effective solutions. Sometimes a *ring pad* applied around the edges of the blister can provide considerable relief. On multi-day expeditions it may be necessary to pre-empt the blister bursting with a *sterilised needle* and then allowing the blister to dry out overnight. However, this kind of treatment carries significant risk of infection and is therefore to be regarded as a last resort.

14.2.3 Other burns

In outdoor environments *burns and scalds* are disturbingly frequent injuries. The most common examples are sunburn and cooking mishaps, both of which can often be avoided by appropriate training in safe practice for group members.

Heat burns and scalds require thorough cooling; this may be very difficult to achieve in remote environments if cold water is not available. If possible, the damaged skin should be plunged into cool water while protecting the rest of the body from hypothermia. Cling-film is an ideal protective dressing for burns, as it does not stick to the wound and allows further inspection.

Casualties with anything beyond very minor burns and scalds should be taken to a doctor in case further treatment is required.

14.2.4 Exhaustion

Exhaustion leads to a reduction in sugar and oxygen supplies to the brain: many of the signs and symptoms of diabetes, hypothermia and hyperthermia are thus very similar, and include withdrawal, irrational behaviour, mood swings and bad language. An exhausted walker will gradually lose the ability to spot these signs and to take appropriate action.

Cold exhaustion

The British Isles have a relatively mild climate, but because of the combination of wind and wet weather that frequently prevail in wild places, *cold exhaustion* or *hypothermia* is a significant hazard – particularly for casualties, who suffer reduced resilience to the environment. An awareness of early signs of hypothermia is essential for party leaders and first aiders, as prompt action is essential in order to prevent deterioration.

In cold wet conditions, the body loses heat through the combined forces of *conduction*, *convection* and *radiation*. Blood flow to the extremities is reduced and the blood vessels constrict in order to maximise efficient delivery of oxygen with minimal heat loss. Body hairs trap air which acts as insulation – this is severely reduced by wind. Shivering produces heat as a by-product and is a remarkably effective mechanism; however, it is very costly in terms of energy input, so an unfit, hungry or injured walker will become exhausted trying to maintain core warmth – declining into unconsciousness and ultimately death.

Damp clothing caused by perspiration whilst active is a contributing factor which can be significantly reduced by wearing wicking underwear that transports moisture away from the body's surface before evaporation occurs. Walking leaders can reduce the likelihood of over-perspiration by educating the party about strategic layering: wearing the amount of clothing that balances the outside temperature with the amount of energy expenditure. Setting an appropriate pace allows a group to minimise perspiration, especially when walking uphill.

Action for the early stages of hypothermia is straightforward for parties carrying the required resources. *Protection from the environment* is required, and *replacement of energy levels* by eating high energy food. Waterproofs, spare clothing, hats and gloves, will all make a significant difference. Wet clothing should be replaced with dry materials if sufficient protection from the environment can be provided for this process. If adequate *shelter* is not available, it is safer to place insulating clothing over the wet clothing instead of removing the wet clothes.

A *warm drink* can be a great morale booster, and any calorie content will be useful in helping fight hypothermia. Drink should never be poured into an unconscious casualty's mouth, as this would cause drowning.

If hypothermia is not dealt with in its early stages the victim will decline into profound hypothermia; a life-threatening condition which can develop particularly rapidly during immersion in cold water.

It may become virtually impossible to detect signs of life, but one should never assume death. In such cases, little is possible other than plenty of insulation and an urgent request for rescue assistance, because breathing and circulation may be sufficiently reduced to be imperceptible, though still present. A profoundly hypothermic casualty must be evacuated with great care on a stretcher; improvised carries may well be fatally inappropriate because adequate support cannot be given.

For all serious cases of hypothermia, hospital treatment is recommended because of the need for appropriate re-warming in order to avoid 'after-drop' – where the recommencing of blood flow to the extremities leads to a critical cooling of the blood supply to the heart, which has been known to cause heart failure.

Heat exhaustion

Though less publicised, heat exhaustion can be just as serious as hypothermia. In the British Isles, hot conditions are relatively uncommon, but can catch people unawares because of inexperience in dealing with them. As secreted beads of water evaporate from our skin, the heat demanded by this process cools the body.

Regular and sufficient water intake is particularly important in hot conditions in order to provide the raw material for perspiration. Otherwise, the blood gradually becomes more viscous as liquid is lost leading to reduced ability to transport oxygen to the organs. Dabbing the head and neck with cold water can help reduce the temperature by taking over the function of perspiration.

Heat exhaustion leads to deterioration into *heat stroke* if left untreated. This potentially fatal condition develops as the body ceases to maintain its working core temperature. Characteristic signs are dry skin due to the impossibility of sustaining sweat production, and a full, bounding pulse. *Urgent hospitalisation* is essential, again requiring a proper stretcher.

14.2.5 Sheep ticks

These small parasites deserve special mention because they frequent uplands and regularly make a meal of human blood. Their bite can transmit *Lyme's Disease*, a debilitating illness that can develop later, with potentially serious long-term effects. The bite may also

become infected if not kept clean. As the tick gorges on blood it swells to about the size of a pea. Vigilance is the best solution, but if a

FIGURE 14.02 SHEEP TICK

feeding tick is found, the best solution is to lever it out gradually with pincer tweezers applied to the head. This method is least likely to result in infection.

14.2.6 Common conditions

Conditions such as *asthma*, *diabetes* and *epilepsy* need not preclude people from taking part in walking activities: their personal risk assessment must take into account the individual's condition, motivation, skills and the history of the fit pattern, or lack of fits, over several years. It must also consider the ability of other party members to cope if complications arise due to the condition; so awareness and education are important. Although there is no legal requirement, it is desirable that leaders are informed if party members suffer these conditions. Such declarations must be solicited sympathetically, otherwise people tend to keep this information to themselves.

14.2.7 Medication

Only medical practitioners are qualified to prescribe medication, much of which can have serious or fatal consequences if misused. In general terms an adult might choose to take medicine such as paracetamol for headaches, but should not dispense it to other members of the party. There are a few common-sense exceptions to this observation, however. If a member of the group has been prescribed medicine but is unable to find it, the first aider should assist if possible. A good example of this is lending out a replacement *Salbutamol* inhaler to somebody experiencing an asthma attack.

First aiders should refer to the current edition of the *Voluntary Aid Societies' First Aid Manual* for further advice on the use of other medication, such as the use of *aspirin* as emergency relief for a heart attack. Group members with known serious allergies should carry an *EpiPen* and inform the leader of its location.

> **Key Points for hill walkers with medical conditions**
>
> **1** Inform your companions of your condition. Ensure that they understand the risk to you and to themselves in relation to the planned activity. If they are not willing to accept your illness do you really value them as companions?
>
> **2** Every mountain trip involves a complex series of continually changing risk assessments. Epilepsy, diabetes, or any other condition simply adds one more variable to the equation.
>
> **3** Carry spare and emergency medication and ensure companions understand basic first aid and how to use emergency medication.

appendices

PHOTO // KARL MIDLANE

A1 Bibliography

A1.1 General

Expedition Guide,
CD (Duke of Edinburgh Award
– available from DofE website)
Mountain Walking and Trekking
(Rucksack Guides), A. Richardson
(A & C Black Publishers Ltd)
ISBN: 0-713686-87-1
*National Guidelines for Climbing
and Walking Leaders*
4th (internet) edition, (Mountain
Training, 2010 – available from
Mountain Training website)
Mountaincraft and Leadership,
E. Langmuir (sportscotland 2005)
ISBN: 1-85060-295-6
Safety on Mountains,
J. Garside (British Mountaineering
Council, 2010)
ISBN: 0-90390-819-0

A1.2 Part I

Navigation in the Mountains,
C. Forte (Mountain Training UK)
ISBN: 978-0-9541511-5-7
Navigation for Walkers,
J. Tippett (Cordee)
ISBN: 1-871890-54-3
Mountain Navigation, P. Cliff
ISBN: 0-871890-55-1
The Backpacker's Handbook,
Townsend (Cordee)
ISBN: 0-87742-357-1

A1.3 Part II

Tread Lightly, (British Mountaineering
Council, 2000)
How to Shit in the Woods, K. Mayer
(Ten Speed Press 1994)
ISBN: 0-89815-627-0

*Hostile Habitats – Scotland's Mountain
Environment: A Hillwalkers' Guide
to Wildlife and the Landscape,*
(Scottish Mountaineering Trust 2006)
ISBN: 0-907521-93-2
Weather for Hillwakers and Climbers,
M. Thomas (Alan Sutton)
ISBN: 0-7509-1080-1
Mountain Weather,
Pedgley (Cicerone 1997)
ISBN: 1-85284-256-3
Rock Trails series, e.g. Lakeland
P. Gannon (Pesda Press 2009)
ISBN: 978-1-906095-04-08
*Snowdonia: A Beginner's Guide
to the Upland Environment,*
M. Raine (Pesda Press 2009)
ISBN: 1-90609-510-8

A1.4 Part III

Outdoor Leadership, J. Graham.
(The Mountaineers)
ISBN: 0-89886-502-6
*Leading and managing groups
in the Outdoors,* K. Ogilvie
(N.A.O.E. 1993)
ISBN: 1-89855-00-1
*Safety, Risk and Adventure in
Outdoor Activities,*
B. Barton (Sage Publications 2006)
ISBN: 1-41292-078-7
*5 Steps to risk Assessment:
HSE Care and Maintenance:
Equipment Standards,* (British
Mountaineering Council, 2001)
*Medical Handbook for Walkers &
Climbers,* P. Steele (Constable)
ISBN: 0-09-478210-5

A2 Mountain Training

Mountain Training's awards and skills courses are nationally recognised and have been developed to educate and train people in walking, climbing and mountaineering.

Our awards and skills courses are run by approved Providers who are scattered all around the UK and Ireland. When you book onto a course, they're the ones who will train and assess you, teach you how to climb, navigate, lead etc.

On a day to day basis, Mountain Training is run by a small staff team in the UK and Ireland. There are also quite a few volunteers who represent the interests of outdoor and educational organisations and help to steer Mountain Training at a strategic level.

When we're not busy creating and refining our awards and ensuring the quality of our courses, Mountain Training also provide:
• Advice on safety in the outdoor industry
• A range of publications to support the awards
• Opportunities for Continued Personal Development through the Mountain Training Association

A2.1 Mountain Training's walking awards pathway

The walking awards pathway is made up of five leadership awards, an optional module and two skills courses, covering terrain from lowland countryside in the UK and Ireland to international trekking at altitude. It is possible to progress from Hill Skills to International Mountain Leader and information about each award and skills course can be found on our website: *www.mountain-training.org*.

A2.2 Who uses the awards?

The users of our awards come from a variety of places including organisations within the public sector, such as local authority education establishments, and voluntary youth organisations. In recent years there has been a rapid increase in the provision of mountain-related activities by the private and voluntary sector. Specific users include teachers, *Duke of Edinburgh's Award* assessors, Scout leaders and a wide range of independent operators.

A2.3 What is involved?

Although the details of each scheme vary there are a number of common elements.

Registration

Before attending any course candidates must create an account on our Candidate Management System (CMS), or log in if they already have one, and register for the appropriate scheme. *https://cms.mountain-training.org/Login.aspx*

Training courses

All the awards and skills courses involve practical training delivered by specially approved training staff. The relevant awarding body monitors the standards of training.

Some schemes have the facility to recognise relevant prior experience and training by granting exemptions from training.

Consolidation period

In pursuit of a leadership award, training courses alone cannot turn people into effective leaders and it is important that candidates use the time between training and assessment to practice your skills, paying particular attention to any weaknesses identified during the training course.

Assessment

All of our walking leadership awards have mandatory practical assessments conducted by specially approved assessors. There is no assessment element to the Hill & Mountain Skills scheme.

Continuing personal and professional development

Having gained an award candidates are expected to maintain and record their involvement in the activities as both an individual and as a leader. Opportunities for development are available through the Mountain Training Association which candidates can choose to join at any point after they have registered for a leadership award.

A2.4 The Mountaineering Councils

The British Mountaineering Council, Mountaineering Council of Scotland and Mountaineering Ireland are the representative bodies for hill walkers, climbers and mountaineers in the UK and Ireland. They lobby and advise government on a range of important issues such as access, risk and responsibility and changes in legislation.

Mountain Training and the Mountaineering Councils work closely together in a number of areas concerned with mountaineering good practice for individuals, leaders and groups. On a broad level, Mountain Training administers formal training schemes and the Mountaineering Councils dispense advice and expertise in more informal areas of activity such as student clubs, mountaineering clubs and youth participation.

A3 Planning

A3.1 Sample pro-forma for expedition planning

Proposed visit to: ....

Dates: From: ....

         To: ....

Party Leader: ....

Contact telephone no. at destination: ....

Participant details: ....

Total number of participants on visit: ....

Name	Age	Sex	Address	Parent/guardian consent	Medical consent
		☐ M ☐ F		☐ Yes ☐ No	☐ Yes ☐ No
		☐ M ☐ F		☐ Yes ☐ No	☐ Yes ☐ No
(Add lines as needed)		☐ M ☐ F		☐ Yes ☐ No	☐ Yes ☐ No

Staff names and contact details			
Name	Address	Contact number	Alternative contact number

Central contact name and contact details during trip			
Name	Address	Contact number	Alternative contact number

1   Supervision: is the leader/pupil ratio appropriate for the planned activity?
The following factors must be considered here:
- The nature of the activity
- Overnight supervision: Mixed staff if appropriate
- The degree of danger likely to be encountered
- The experience and expertise of the staff involved
- The ages and competence of the participants

2   Assembly and departure
- Where?
- When?
- Parents/guardians informed?   ☐ Yes   ☐ No

3   The journey
- Vehicle arranged?   ☐ Yes   ☐ No
- Road atlas/route map?   ☐ Yes   ☐ No
- Sufficient drivers?   ☐ Yes   ☐ No
- Insurance   ☐ Yes   ☐ No

4   Arrival at the destination
Have all emergency procedures been thoroughly considered:
- Fire arrangements   ☐ Yes   ☐ No
- Accident drill   ☐ Yes   ☐ No

Residential accommodation or camp

5   Accommodation booked? ☐ Yes ☐ No   **Sleeping bags/linen arranged?** ☐ Yes ☐ No

6   Food arrangements
Special diet needs?   ☐ Yes ☐ No   Menu and shopping?   ☐ Yes ☐ No

7   Sleeping arrangements
Adequate rooms   ☐ Yes ☐ No   Adequate wash/toilet   ☐ Yes ☐ No

8   DECLARATION
I confirm that the above visit has been authorised by [Supervising authority]

Signed: .... [Supervisor]

A3.2 Suggested expedition information for parents

When organisers initially inform parents about residential visits and invite bookings, certain information (such as location, dates, purpose and cost) will be given, but it is important that further details are given in writing to parents indicating a wish for their children to take part in the visit.

The following should be regarded as the minimum:
* Purpose of visit
* Dates, places and times of departure and return
* Transport arrangements
* Name and address of travel company/agency (if appropriate)
* Financial costs and arrangements for payment
* Pocket money (suggested amounts and arrangements for care)
* Insurance arrangements
* Proposed programme and itinerary (including activities to be undertaken, places to be visited and bad weather alternatives)
* List of recommended clothing and equipment, including any special requirements, along with a request that all items should be named. Details of any clothing, equipment or other items not allowed, such as radios, jewellery and so on.
* Details of recommended type and size of luggage and labelling
* Information regarding the training and experience of accompanying staff, voluntary helpers and activity centre staff
* Group membership, including numbers of staff and participants, and name of party leader
* Supervision arrangements during activities
* Supervision arrangements at times other than during activities. Ratios of participants to accompany school staff should be given
* Code of conduct. Parents should be made aware of the standards of conduct expected of children and the possible sanctions that could be applied (in extreme cases, parents could be asked to collect their children from an activity centre, for example)
* Name and telephone number of responsible person who can be contacted in case of emergency
* Accommodation (if appropriate):
  * Address and telephone number.
  * Details of accommodation provided.

A.3.3 Suggested information request form for parents/guardians

Please complete and return this form to ....

no later than ....

Participant's name ....

Section A

Address and telephone number where parent/guardian or other person with parental responsibility can be contacted in case of emergency.

- **Daytime**
  Name: ....
  Address:..
  ....
  ....

- **Evening**
  Name: ....
  Address: ....
  ....
  ....

- Does your child suffer from any allergies? .... ☐ Yes ☐ No
  If yes, please give details: ....

- Is your child taking any medication? .... ☐ Yes ☐ No
  If yes, please give details of dosage etc: ....

- Has your child suffered any infectious, contagious or other conditions
  in the last 3 months?... ☐ Yes ☐ No
  If yes, please give details: ....

- Has your child received a tetanus injection in the last 5 years? ...... ☐ Yes ☐ No

- Please give name, telephone number and address of your family doctor.
  Name: ....
  Surgery address:...
  ....
  ....
  Telephone number: ....

- Does your child have any specialist dietary requirements? .... ☐ Yes   ☐ No
  If yes, please give details:
  Vegetarian: ....
  ....
  Diabetic: ....
  ....
  Other (please specify): ....
  ....

- Does your child suffer from travel sickness? .... ☐ Yes   ☐ No
  If yes, what arrangements need to be made? ....
  ....

- Is there anything else (medical or otherwise) you think we should know about your child,
  such as bedwetting? ....
  ....

Section B: If other activities are also proposed

- Is your child confident in water? .... ☐ Yes   ☐ No
  If yes, how far can he/she swim? ....

- Are there any activities in which your child is unable to participate? .... ☐ Yes   ☐ No
  If yes, please give details: ....

Section C
Additional residential section for parents of primary-school-aged children or children
with special needs.

- Has your child been away from home without you before? .... ☐ Yes   ☐ No
- Does your child sleep with the light on? .... ☐ Yes   ☐ No
- Please give details of any significant bedtime routine? ....
  ....
  ....

Signed: ....
Date: ....

This form should be signed and returned completed in all sections, together with the signed
Consent Form for the visit.

A3.4 Sample consent form

I agree that my son/daughter: ....

may take part in: ....

from (date): ....

to (date): ....

I agree that medical and dental treatment may be given to my son or daughter if necessary, including the administration of a general anaesthetic and to surgical operations in the case of an emergency, in accordance with the recommendation of a qualified medical practitioner.

Participants are not insured by .... against personal accidents. Personal Accidents Insurance can be arranged for pupils taking part in off-site visits and staff can give advice about a policy specifically designed for such parties. The policy covers personal accident, loss of personal possessions, medical expenses and the cost to parents of visiting their children if they are detained in hospital away from home.

.... accepts no responsibility for accidents or injury to pupils or for loss of or damage to personal effects, unless caused by the negligence of the .... or any member of its staff.

Parents must provide staff with telephone numbers (day and night) at which they can be contacted in case of emergency, in particular should urgent medical treatment be necessary.

I have received full information and agree to my child's participation in all outlined activities.

Signed (Parent/guardian): ....

Date: ....

Address: ....

Telephone numbers (including dialling codes):

Home: ....

Work: ....

Mobile: ....

Other: ....

This form should be completed and returned together with the form:
Information Required From Parents Prior To Expeditions

A4 Useful contacts

A4.1 Mountain Training

Mountain Training
Siabod Cottage
Capel Curig
Conwy   LL24 0ES
T 01690 720 272
info@mountain-training.org

A4.2 Mountaineering Councils

British Mountaineering Council
BMC
The Old Church
177–179 Burton Road
Manchester   M20 2BB
T 0161 445 6111
office@thebmc.co.uk

Mountaineering Council of Scotland
MCofS
The Old Granary
West Mill Street
Perth   PH1 5QP
T 01738 493 942
www.mcofs.org.uk

Mountaineering Ireland
Irish Sport HQ
National Sports Campus
Blanchardstown
Dublin 15
T 00 353 (0)1 625 1115
info@mountaineering.ie

A4.3 National Mountaineering Centres

Glenmore Lodge
Aviemore
Inverness-shire   PH22 1QU
T 01479 861 256
enquiries@glenmorelodge.org.uk

Plas y Brenin
Capel Curig
Conwy   LL24 0ET
T 01690 720 214
info@pyb.co.uk

Tollymore Mountain Centre
Bryansford
Newcastle
Co Down   BT33 0PT
T 0284 372 2158
admin@tollymore.com

A5 Index

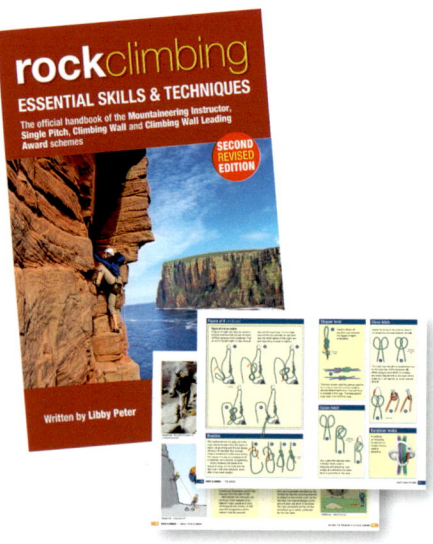
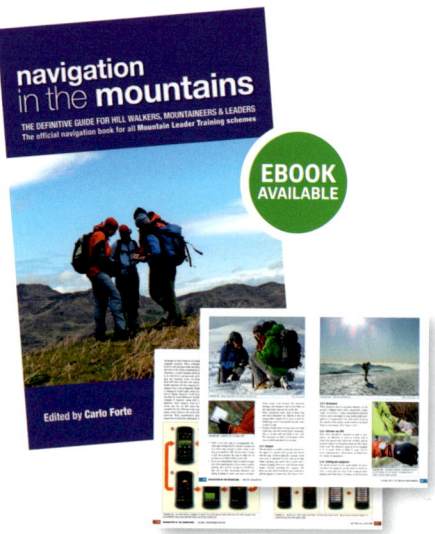

You will find the other essential Mountain Training publications helpful too

INTERNATIONAL MOUNTAIN TREKKING
PLAS Y BRENIN INSTRUCTIONAL TEAM
ISBN 978 0954 151171
A practical manual for trekkers and leaders covering all elements of international trekking.

WINTER SKILLS
ANDY CUNNINGHAM & ALLEN FYFFE
ISBN 978 0954 151133
An essential reference tool for every mountaineer venturing onto non-glaciated snow and ice.

www.mountain-training.org